Studies in Regional and Local History

General Editor Jane Whittle

David and Mary Dymond

Shaping the Past

Theme, Time and Place in Local History
Essays in honour of David Dymond

Edited by
Evelyn Lord and Nicholas R. Amor

University of Hertfordshire Press
Studies in Regional and Local History

Volume 18

First published in Great Britain in 2020 by
University of Hertfordshire Press
College Lane
Hatfield
Hertfordshire
AL10 9AB
UK

British Library Cataloguing in Publication Data
A catalogue record for this book is available from the British Library

ISBN 978 1 912260 22 5 hardback
ISBN 978 1 912260 23 2 paperback

Design by Arthouse Publishing Solutions
Printed in Great Britain

Contents

Illustrations

Tables

Contributors

Dr Nicholas R. Amor (solicitor) is an honorary fellow of the University of East Anglia and the University of Suffolk, and chairman of the Suffolk Institute of Archaeology and History (SIAH). He is author of *Late medieval Ipswich: trade and industry* (Woodbridge, 2011) and *From wool to cloth: the triumph of the Suffolk clothier* (Bungay, 2016) as well as various papers in the *Proceedings* of the SIAH. In the early 1990s he studied under the tuition of David Dymond and Mark Bailey for a certificate in local history and has been a friend of both ever since.

Professor Mark Bailey is professor of late medieval history at the University of East Anglia, High Master of St Paul's School, London, and president of the SIAH. In 2019 he was the James Ford Lecturer in British History at the University of Oxford and a visiting fellow of All Souls College, Oxford. He is the author of *Medieval Suffolk: an economic and social history* (Woodbridge, 2007) and numerous other books and articles. He worked closely with David Dymond at Madingley Hall in the early 1990s and has been a friend ever since.

Dr Lyn Boothman has been investigating the local and demographic history of Long Melford for many years, her early interest stimulated by evening classes with David Dymond. After her retirement she completed a University of Cambridge PhD entitled 'Immobility and the immobile: a case study of Long Melford, Suffolk 1661–1861'. She is an affiliated researcher with the Cambridge Group for the History of Population and Social Structure (CAMPOP) and is continuing her study of Melford.

Dr Alan Crosby has been a professional local and regional historian for over thirty years and has taught for many universities, including Oxford, Cambridge, Liverpool and Central Lancashire. Since 2001 he has been the editor of *The Local Historian*. He has published many books and articles on local, landscape and social history, including *A history of Thetford* (Bognor Regis, 1986). He is a council member of a number of record societies. He is a long-standing friend and colleague of David Dymond.

Professor Claire Cross is emeritus professor of history at the University of York, where she taught from 1965 to 2000. After she retired she served five years as chair of the British Association for Local History, of which she is now a vice president. She has published articles on Yorkshire clergy before and after the Dissolution. She worked alongside David Dymond on the council of the British Association for Local History. Since then they have engaged in historical discussions, particularly on the English church in the late Middle Ages.

Dr Heather Falvey is a tutor in local and social history for the Institute of Continuing Education at the University of Cambridge and for the Department of Continuing Education at the University of Oxford. She is the editorial assistant of the *Economic*

History Review and honorary secretary of the Hertfordshire Record Society. She is a long-standing friend and colleague of David Dymond.

Dr Jacqueline Harmon completed a Master of Studies in Local History at the University of Cambridge, where she was tutored by Evelyn Lord and David Dymond. In 2005 she submitted her Master's dissertation, 'The relationships between Barnwell Priory and its neighbours, *c*.1380–*c*.1540', and in 2017 completed a PhD at the University of East Anglia entitled 'Some aspects of the history of Barnwell Priory'.

Dr Andrew Jackson is head of research at Bishop Grosseteste University, Lincoln. He has been engaged in local history and adult education for some decades, through the universities of Exeter and Oxford and the WEA, U3A and other organisations and societies. His current research interests relate to early twentieth-century urban and rural change. He is a great admirer of the work of W.G. Hoskins and David Dymond.

Dr Evelyn Lord was, prior to her retirement, the course director for the University of Cambridge's Master of Studies in Local History and tutor for local history at the University of Cambridge, Institute for Continuing Education. In that role she worked closely with David Dymond. She has published books and articles on local history and is involved in promoting research into Cambridgeshire history.

Dr Sean O'Dell studied local history at the University of Cambridge under the tuition of David Dymond, where he successfully gained his Master's degree, and subsequently completed his PhD at the University of Essex. In conjunction with lecturing at the University Centre, Colchester, he has worked as an historical consultant for Essex County Council, has published two local history books and contributed to the latest *VCH* Essex volume.

Dr Harvey Osborne is associate professor and course leader for history at the University of Suffolk. He is a historian of modern Britain with a particular interest in the history of the countryside and rural society. His PhD was entitled 'The preservation and poaching of salmon in Victorian England: fresh perspectives on nineteenth-century poaching crime'. He is a council member of the Suffolk Record Society (SRS), of which David Dymond is president.

Professor Carole Rawcliffe is professor emerita of medieval history at the University of East Anglia. She has published widely on the history of medical practice, hospitals, disease (notably leprosy and plague) and urban health in the pre-modern period. David Dymond has contributed to two festschrifts that she has edited. She co-edited a two-volume history of Norwich in 2004 and has recently completed an edition of *The Norwich Chamberlains' Accounts 1539–1545* (Norwich, 2017).

Professor Alan Rogers has been teaching and writing local community history in adult education for more than thirty years, specialising in the East Midlands and late medieval urban history (especially Stamford, Lincolnshire). He is on the executive committee of the Rutland Local History and Record Society and is a fellow of the Royal Historical Society and of the Society of Antiquaries. He is a long-standing friend and colleague of David Dymond.

Dr Joanne Sear teaches local history for the Institute of Continuing Education at the University of Cambridge. Her research focuses on the social and economic history of the late Middle Ages with a particular emphasis on the trade and commercial development of East Anglian market towns during this period. She is currently the editor of the *Proceedings* of the SIAH. She studied local history at the University of Cambridge under the tuition of David Dymond.

David Sherlock was brought up in east Suffolk and read ancient history at UCL. He was an inspector of ancient monuments in the Ministry of Works and its successors and worked mainly in East Anglia and northern England. He was editor of the *Proceedings* of the SIAH and is now co-ordinating editor for the SRS. He is a long-standing friend and colleague of David Dymond.

Dr Kenneth Sneath, following early retirement, took the Master's course in local history under the tution of David Dymond and then completed a PhD, both at the University of Cambridge. His publications include *Godmanchester: a celebration of 800 years* (Cambridge, 2011). He and Joanne Sear are joint authors of a forthcoming volume entitled *The origins of the consumer revolution*. He lectures in seventeenth- and eighteenth-century history at the University of Cambridge, Institute of Continuing Education.

Dr David Woodward, after a career as a teacher, enrolled on the University of Cambridge Master's course in local history under the tuition of David Dymond. In order to look in more detail at the development of suburban Surrey he was accepted for research leading to a PhD at Kingston University London. In 2012, although terminally ill, he managed to complete his thesis, and Dr Chris French, his supervisor, was able to tell him three days before he died that he had been awarded a PhD.

Acknowledgements

Many people, family members, friends and archivists have helped the editors and authors in the production of this book, not least Jane Housham, Sarah Elvins and the staff of University of Hertfordshire Press and Jane Whittle, the general editor of the *Studies in Regional and Local History* series.

Papers
Thanks to Dr Christopher French, formerly director of the Centre for Local History Studies at Kingston University, for his help in compiling the paper of the late David Woodward.

Illustrations
Thanks to J.A. Frost for photographs of York stained glass images (Plates 3.1–3.5); to Mike Durrant for the photograph of the niche at All Saints' Icklingham, Suffolk (Plate 5.1); to the Rijksmuseum, Amsterdam, for permission to publish the devotional image of Henry VI (Plate 5.2); to Bob Carr for the photograph of Southwold church porch (Plate 6.1); to N. Hill for the photograph of North Luffenham Bede Farm (Plate 9.1); to Suffolk Record Office Ipswich for the photograph of the Woodbridge Union workhouse at Nacton (Figure 13.1); and to Ray Whitehand for the photograph of the Plomesgate Union workhouse at Wickham Market (Plate 13.1).

Maps
Thanks go to Catherine D'Alton (Map 4.1), Max Satchell of CAMPOP (Maps 7.1, 7.2, 7.3 and 12.1) and David Addy (Map 9.1).

The editors and authors would also like to thank the staff of Bedfordshire Record Office; Cambridge University Library; Edinburgh Central Library; Essex Record Office; Morningside Library, Edinburgh; Susan Maddock and colleagues at the Norfolk Record Office; the Scottish National Archives; the Scottish Fisheries Museum; Suffolk Record Offices at Bury St Edmunds and Ipswich; The National Archives, Kew; and Thetford Town Council.

Finally, our sincere thanks go to the Suffolk Institute of Archaeology and History, without whose generous contribution this book would not have been possible.

Evelyn Lord and Nicholas R. Amor

Publication grant

The publication of this volume has been supported by a generous subvention from the Suffolk Institute of Archaeology and History, of which David Dymond is a Vice-President.

Previous titles in this series
Founding Editor Nigel Goose

Abbreviations

BFHS	Bedfordshire Family History Society
BHRS	Bedfordshire Historical Record Society
BIA	Borthwick Institute of Archives
BL	British Library, London
BPM	*Brightlingsea Parish Magazine*
BPP	British Parliamentary Papers
CAMPOP	Cambridge Group for the History of Population and Social Structure
CChR	*Calendar of charter rolls, 1226–1517*, 6 vols (London, 1903–27)
CCR	*Calendar of close rolls, 1272–1509*, 47 vols (London, 1892–1963)
CPR	*Calendar of patent rolls, 1232–1509*, 52 vols (London, 1891–1916)
CRR	*Curia regis rolls, 1196–1272*, 21 vols (London, 1922–2008)
CSPD	*Calendar of state papers domestic, 1547–1649*, 35 vols (London, 1856–72)
ERO	Essex Record Office
LPFD	J.S. Brewer and others (eds), *Calendar of letters and papers foreign and domestic, Henry VIII*, 21 vols and Addenda, 2 vols (London, 1862–1932)
NA	Norfolk Archives
NAS	National Archives of Scotland
NCC	Norwich Consistory Court
NNAS	Norfolk and Norwich Archaeological Society
NRO	Norfolk Record Office
NRS	Norfolk Record Society
ODNB	*Oxford dictionary of national biography* (Oxford, 2004)
OS	Ordnance Survey
PCC	Prerogative Court of Canterbury
PSIA	*Proceedings of the Suffolk Institute of Archaeology and History*
RCHM	Royal Commission on the Historical Monuments of England
RLC	*Rotuli litterarum clausarum*, 1204–27, 2 vols (London, 1833 and 1844)
Rot. Parl.	J. Strachey and others (eds), *Rotuli Parliamentorum ut et petiones et placita in Parliamento*, 6 vols (London, 1767–77)
SIAH	Suffolk Institute of Archaeology and History
SROB	Suffolk Record Office Bury St Edmunds
SROI	Suffolk Record Office Ipswich

SRS	Suffolk Record Society
Statutes	A. Luders and others (eds) *The statutes of the realm (1101–1713)*, 11 vols (London, 1810–28)
TNA	The National Archives, Kew
VCH	*The Victoria History of the Counties of England*

Studies in Regional and Local History

General Editor's preface

Approaches to English local history have been shaped not only by research but also by teaching. As well as publishing numerous academic books and articles, David Dymond taught local history for nearly half a century, largely at the Continuing Education department at Cambridge University. He also published the classic guide to 'doing' local history: *Researching and Writing History: A Practical Guide for Local Historians* (most recent edition, 2016), which began in 1981 as *Writing Local History: A Practical Guide*. This extended his teaching advice to thousands of people beyond those who could afford the time and money to attend a University course. His sound advice and vision of what local history should be chimes strongly with the aims of this book series, making this collection of essays in his honour an entirely fitting addition to the series.

David Dymond's own research centred on Suffolk, as do many of the essays in this volume. Those wanting to find out more about the history of Suffolk will find much of interest. But both this volume and the work of David Dymond aimed to promote the wider relevance of local history. Good local history is not just about the place that is in focus, but raises larger issues. Thus, as he noted, local and national history depend on each other. The trends identified in national histories cannot be explored or explained adequately without using local examples; themes identified in local studies cannot be explained without looking beyond the borders of the locality. Comparison is vital in identifying what is unique to a particular community or region, and what is part of a wider trend. While grander forms of history suffer from increased specialisation, fragmentation and abstraction, local history unifies a range of themes. Local history brings together the history of society, economy, politics and religion; its small scale allows the history of actual, often ordinary, people to be placed in a rounded historic context.

The definition of local history offered in *Researching and Writing History* is profoundly social: 'the study of local people, as individuals but particularly as groups, in the places where they lived, worked and died' (p.1). David Dymond's vision of how local history should be practiced was social too. It involved not only the wise but commonplace exhortation to approach historical evidence critically, and to define carefully the theme, place and time that are the focus of a particular study, but also observations about the impact of undertaking historical research on the historian. For him local history was not just an intellectual pursuit, but a social activity that helps to bind together modern society: 'local knowledge undoubtedly helps to make grass roots democracy more informed, sensitive and effective' (p.3). Researching the history of the place where you live helps everyone, whatever their background, feel more rooted in that place. Unlike other forms of history, many historians who write local history do so not as a researchers with academic posts and salaries, but as enthusiasts whose work is motivated by a passion for history. While some work alone, many research as part of local history groups which bring together a range of interests and make research a sociable activity. David Dymond has led and inspired many such groups. It is in whole-hearted support, therefore, that we publish this collection of essays: both as a tribute to David Dymond's life's work, but also as a tribute to a field of history that brings together so many different types of researcher united in curiosity about people's lived experiences in the past.

Jane Whittle
January 2020

Chapter 1

Introduction

Mark Bailey

The breadth and depth of David Dymond's scholarship is manifest from the bibliography of his writings at the back of this volume. The man who has written with such care and knowledge about various social and ecclesiastical institutions is himself something of an institution within the field of local history. For five decades he has taught this subject to hundreds of adult education classes (for most of that time working as a tutor for the Institute of Continuing Education at the University of Cambridge), pitching the material adroitly to his audience and steering a clear and uncluttered pathway through both narratives and explanations. Above all, he conveyed a passion, excitement and infectious enthusiasm about each subject. A characteristic of his teaching was the careful selection and meticulous preparation of a documentary source relevant to the topic, which then formed the basis of class discussion, dissection and debate. The range of knowledge – of subject, events, timeframes and sources – and the technical ability required to teach such eclectic courses and sources should not be underestimated, and the requisite knowledge and skills far exceed the capabilities of most academic historians.

David has produced works of eclectic, but high, scholarship. He has edited volumes of medieval documents with model precision and rigour. He has drawn our attention to the camping close (an early form of contact sport) and elucidated the workings of the glebe. Only a local historian of the highest calibre could have written on the latter subject, because the evidence had to be collected over decades of research, from many thousands of sources and across several centuries. These articles are masterpieces of the local historian's craft. Yet David has also reflected upon the discipline of local history, emphasising the importance of avoiding the pitfalls of parochialism and of remaining sensitive to the wider influences upon communities, such as the importance of kinship, networks and regional variations. He has also written about changes to the delivery of local history nationally, charting its expansion through the adult liberal education movement of the 1960s to the introduction in the 1990s of certificated university courses. Yet David has never been nostalgic, instead reflecting critically upon the quality of the early adult education courses and in 1995 jointly introducing the first part-time Master's course degree at the University of Cambridge: in Local History, of course. He has done perhaps more than anyone since W.G. Hoskins to promote local history as an academic discipline, while never losing his instinctive empathy for those individuals who made that history.

This breadth and depth of his scholarship is reflected in the varied contributions to this festschrift, many of them written by former students. The volume begins with five papers that explore the multi-facets of medieval religion, a subject close to his own research interests. Jacqueline Harmon studies the *Liber memorandorum ecclesie* of the Augustinian priory at Barnwell in Cambridge. This manuscript combines official history, documents and records with contemporary comment. It does not always present the priory in the best light, recounting two cases of thirteenth-century litigation between the canons and members of the local community that illustrate the lengths they were prepared to go to protect their interests. The dispute with Luke de Abington, appointed by them as vicar of Guilden Morden, led to almost twenty years of acrimonious conflict over the terms of his employment and the meagreness of his stipend.

Claire Cross identifies the donors of the glass in some of the parish churches of later medieval York. The Hessle family paid for a window in the church of All Saints, North Street, that portrays the unrelenting horror of the destruction of the universe as a prelude to the Last Judgement. The Blackburn family were rather more upbeat. Their window in the same church shows a merchant feeding the hungry, providing drink to the thirsty, welcoming the stranger, clothing the naked, relieving prisoners and visiting the sick (Plate 3.2). A century later, just as the Reformation hit England, a host of donors, both clerical and lay, funded new windows in the church of St Michael-le-Belfrey. The break with Rome meant that some of these were destroyed almost immediately after completion.

Carole Rawcliffe discusses the lives of ten hermits in fifteenth-century Norwich. They performed pastoral ministry and were regarded as a communal asset whose very presence brought spiritual benefit. However, they do not appear to have lived solitary lives of poverty and, indeed, shunned the less affluent northern parishes. Robert Goddard may have exemplified the illiterate working man drawn to the eremetic life as he laboured on the city's gates and ditches, but Richard Walsham, once a busy obedientiary at Norwich cathedral priory, and the well-connected Richard Furness certainly did not. Furness enjoyed the patronage and confidence of one of the city's most influential families, who paid for him or his proxy to go on pilgrimage to Rome and Jerusalem.

Heather Falvey explores the cult of the murdered King Henry VI, which peaked in the final twenty years of the fifteenth century. Although a Tudor bid to have him canonised failed, a spate of miracles was attributed to his intercession and his tomb at Windsor became an important destination for pilgrims. An alabaster image of the king, now held by the Rijksmuseum, Amsterdam (Plate 5.2), serves as an introduction to the importance of devotional images and pictures in late medieval churches and of the candles that illuminated them. Testamentary bequests reveal the presence of images and pictures of Henry in Walberswick (Suffolk), St Albans (Herts.) and Houghton Regis and Eversholt (both Beds.).

David Sherlock takes a detailed look at the will of Robert Scolys, vicar of Southwold 1444–70. Scolys was a Cambridge man and, as well as being a professor of theology, he fostered a keen interest in physics and astronomy. In addition to the religious tracts that one might expect to be mentioned in the will of a vicar, and the astronomy books and astrolabe that he left to his college, there was a surprising bequest to his adopted town of a formidable armoury. This included bows, arrows, helmets, hauberks, jacks, sallets, lances and battle axes. They are a salutary reminder that medieval clergymen were expected to serve in the defence of the realm.

Three papers follow on medieval trade and industry. Jo Sear looks at the smaller provincial fairs, which have not received the academic attention they deserve. She examines six fairs in the vicinity of Thetford (Norfolk) and close to both the river Little

Ouse and the main London–Norwich road, which played a vital role in the transport of goods and people to and from those fairs. Thetford Priory accounts and fair rolls list the names of traders who paid tolls and customs, allowing tentative but important conclusions to be drawn about the fortunes of these fairs in the late thirteenth and early fourteenth centuries. The number of traders, where they came from and the nature of their occupations reveal the wide range of goods and services available.

Nick Amor compares the production of early fourteenth-century Norfolk worsted and late fifteenth-century Suffolk woollens to try to establish why medieval industries succeeded. Both were versatile fabrics, were manufactured in a range of qualities and, particularly in the case of worsted, could be put to a variety of uses. As rural-based industries, they could operate free of urban constraint and call on a ready labour force who subsisted on small holdings and needed additional income to supplement meagre agricultural earnings. Cloth-makers were well organised, took opportunities presented by the commercialisation of the English economy, such as growth in the number of markets, and built long-distance trading networks that enabled them to distribute and sell their wares.

Alan Rogers has already produced much valuable scholarship on the town of Stamford, and develops Amor's industrial theme. He returns to Stamford to study the account book of successive wardens of Browne's Hospital for the period 1495–1518, and what it tells us about ordinary domestic builders working on small-scale construction projects and repairs to houses, barns and walls. Most of those whose names appear in the accounts came not from Stamford itself, but from neighbouring villages around the town. They were masons, carpenters/wrights, slaters and thatchers. Rogers offers new insights to explain the location of building industries in rural areas and draws attention to long-standing natural diversification of peasant economies. His paper also provides valuable data for those interested in the debate over the importance and relevance of 'real wages' for establishing levels of welfare in pre-industrial England.

Alan Crosby and Lyn Boothman are both interested in local elites. Alan Crosby turns his attention to members of the Thetford Corporation. Following the restoration of Charles II an Anglican Tory faction led by Burrage Martin staged a *coup d'etat* to remove dissenting members and take over control of town government. In a series of remarkable events Martin sought to surrender and then renew the borough charter in a way that would entrench his cabal in power. They were opposed by the town clerk and mayor. Baron Townshend's attempts to mediate were unsuccessful and, on account of their obduracy, Martin and his supporters were imprisoned. They lost this battle, yet dominated the corporation for the next twenty years. Later Martin's political heir John Mendham tried again to surrender and renew the charter, but despite initial success he too suffered imprisonment and ultimate failure.

Boothman studies several generations of parish office holders in the well-documented Suffolk town of Long Melford. She applies principles of population reconstruction to analyse the continuity of office holding within families over time, particularly churchwardens, overseers of the poor, constables or ale-tasters, foremen (or deputies) of the manorial court baron jury and members of the court leet jury. She identifies six nineteenth-century office holders who had ancestral links to office holders in both the seventeenth and eighteenth centuries, but also finds in each period members of the local office-holding elite who were newcomers to the parish.

Evelyn Lord explores the provision of Suffolk cheeses to whaling ships setting forth from mid-eighteenth-century Anstruther in Fife. The production and marketing of Suffolk cheese, so unpalatable the Royal Navy stopped using it for ship's victuals, and the development of the whaling industry in Anstruther are discussed in parallel. In earlier periods customs accounts provide clear evidence of links between Anstruther and East Anglia, and in later periods newspapers report the Anstruther fishing fleet sailing south to Lowestoft, but for the intervening period these links are speculative and based on indirect evidence. Lord's paper suggests a continued but unrecorded link perhaps through Anstruther ships on the home leg of Baltic voyages stopping off in Suffolk.

The final five papers bring us forward into the nineteenth and twentieth centuries, reflecting Dymond's eclectic enduring interest in modern history and the diversity of local history. Harvey Osborne reminds us that, on the eve of the 1834 poor law reform, Suffolk was more deeply pauperised than any other county in England and over half its population was receiving some form of relief. The new workhouses, founded on a harsh regime of deterrence and discipline, were not well received. Paupers routinely refused to work, assaulted workhouse staff, damaged property, absconded and occasionally rioted. Able-bodied temporary residents, brought low by seasonal troughs in demand for labour, were frequently the worst offenders. Women enthusiastically broke panes of glass. Staff numbers were often insufficient to maintain order and, during wintertime, some were reinforced by policemen to deter trouble. For twenty years Suffolk accounted for a disproportionately high percentage of all those sent to prison for offences in workhouses in England.

The late David Woodward devoted the final years of his life to completing a doctorate on the growth of suburbia and his paper is a tribute to his fine scholarship. He charts the transformation of Sutton (Surrey) from a rustic one-street village in 1800 to a suburb of greater London by 1900. The driving forces behind this change were population growth, improved transport, the availability of building land and capital and, perhaps above all, the aspirations of the 'middle classes' for a better life. Suburban Sutton was not, however, an idyll. It was divided into separate neighbourhoods for labourers, artisans and the 'middle-class', and also into the separate worlds of working men and their dependants. There was little social inter-mixing between these different strata, despite the formation of local cultural societies and clubs.

Ken Sneath's analysis of the Godmanchester (Huntingdonshire) censuses of 1851 and 1891 (with occasional references to that of 2011) reveals a starkly contrasting experience to Sutton, because its population fell rather than expanded. His assessment of Anglican parish registers confirm that baptisms far outnumbered burials, but sustained outward migration meant that the town contracted. The push of agricultural depression and the pull of more attractive employment possibilities elsewhere meant that younger people moved away and the average age of the remaining residents rose. Greater mobility meant that the proportion of Godmanchester residents born in the county and the village fell over time, while the proportion of marriage partners found from further afield rose.

Sean O'Dell recounts the extraordinary life of Canon Arthur Pertwee, who was Anglican vicar of the parish of Brightlingsea, Essex, from 1872 to 1912. He was highly active and involved in the lives of all his parishioners. Many went to sea, dredging for oysters as far away as the Terschelling Banks, off the Dutch coast. Their working lives were extremely difficult and often very dangerous, and, as a result, casualty rates were high. Pertwee went to sea with the oyster crews to experience for himself the hardships they endured and, on stormy nights, climbed the tower of All Saints', Brightlingsea, with a lantern to guide them home. His most tangible legacy is a frieze of commemorative tiles inside the parish church providing a poignant monument to each lost mariner (Plates 16.1 and 16.2).

Andrew Jackson begins by tracing Dymond's evolving concept of place in the study of local history. An author must reassure the reader that he or she has visited the place, and also strike a balance between making 'broader judgements and generalisations' about places and appreciating and recognising 'particularism' wherever it is found. Through engagement with their home environments local historians can 'inform and influence the future' of places. Jackson moves on to consider the construction of place in regional fiction through the creative writings of Lincolnshire-born Bernard Samuel Gilbert and his literary district of 'Bly' – a village set in an East Midlands or East Anglian landscape and community in the years leading up to and through the First World War.

David Dymond has served in a variety of offices, locally and nationally, in support of local history. He is a vice president of the British Association for Local History and of the Suffolk Institute of Archaeology and History, president of the Suffolk Records Society and an honorary fellow of the University of East Anglia. Supported by Mary, his wife, his contribution to the study of local history generally, and in his adopted county of Suffolk in particular, has been immensely influential. The essays in this *festschrift* are offered as a token of esteem, respect and affection.

Part I: Medieval religion

Chapter 2

Barnwell Priory:
tensions in the local community

Jacqueline Harmon

It is now more than a century since John Willis Clark published his research into the Augustinian priory at Barnwell, Cambridge. His work, on both the history and archaeology of the site, renewed interest in the house, which, until that point, had received very little scholarly attention. The antiquarian histories of Nichols (1786), Prickett (1837) and White (1889) are all deeply indebted to the only surviving Barnwell manuscript, the *Liber memorandorum ecclesie de Bernewelle*, and offer no new insights.[1] Given this dearth, Barnwell provides many opportunities for new, and more focused, research. A more wide-ranging history, taking advantage of up-to-date methods and techniques, would go a long way toward redressing the historic neglect not only of Barnwell but of the Augustinian order in England in general.[2] This paper focuses on two examples of litigation and grew out of the desire to discover how the canons of Barnwell interacted with the local populace through the medium of the court system. The roots of the piece can be found in books including David Dymond's *The register of Thetford Priory: Part 1, 1482–1517* and *Part 2, 1518–1540*, and his invaluable *Researching and writing history: a guide for local historians*.[3] His teaching, alongside that of Dr Evelyn Lord, also provided much of the inspiration.

Barnwell Priory was founded in 1092 by Picot, the Norman sheriff of Cambridgeshire, on a piece of flat ground between Cambridge Castle and the river Cam. The sheriff, not otherwise known for his piety, vowed to build a religious house

---

1   BL, Harley MSS 3601. J.W. Clark (ed.), *The observances in use at the Augustinian Priory of S. Giles and S. Andrew at Barnwell, Cambridgeshire* (Cambridge, 1897); J.W. Clark (ed.), *Liber memorandorum ecclesie de Bernewelle* (Cambridge, 1907); M. Prickett, *Some account of Barnwell Priory in the parish of St Andrew the Less, Cambridge* (Cambridge, 1837); W.M. White, *A jubilee memorial of the consecration of Christ Church, Cambridge, which took place June 27th, 1839, to which is prefixed; A short history of Barnwell Priory, from its foundation to its present time* (Cambridge, 1889); J. Nichols, 'The history and antiquities of Barnwell Abbey' (sic) in *Bibliotheca topographica Britannica: antiquities in Cambridgeshire, Suffolk, Scotland and Wales*, Vol. V, no. 38 (London, 1786). For ease, all references in this paper to *Liber* will refer to Clark's transcription and not to the original manuscript Harley MSS 3601.

2   D.M. Robinson, 'The Augustinian canons in England and Wales: architecture, archaeology and liturgy 1100–1540', *Monastic Research Bulletin*, 18 (2012), pp. 2–26.

3   D. Dymond, *The register of Thetford Priory, Part 1 1482–1517*, Records of Social and Economic History (Oxford, 1996), *Part 2 1518–40*, Records of Social and Economic History (London, 1996); *Researching and writing history: a guide for local historians* (Bognor Regis, 1999).

in exchange for his wife Hugolina's recovery from a serious illness.[4] When Picot's prayers were answered, the couple dedicated the new community of six canons, under the priorship of Geoffrey of Huntingdon, to Hugolina's patron saint St Giles. After Picot's death and the disgrace of his son Robert, exiled for his involvement in a plot against Henry I, the priory suffered a long period of neglect before it was gifted by Henry I to Pain Peverel. Peverel had grandiose plans and his first action was to move the canons to a site in the fields to the east of the town, close to the Barnwell spring.[5] Here, as befitting the second founder's status – Peverel had acted as standard bearer to Henry's elder brother Robert Curthose in the Holy Land – a new and much larger monastic community could be established. From Picot's original six canons, Peverel envisaged an increase to thirty.[6]

Its early foundation date placed the priory near the top of the hierarchy of Augustinian foundations in England, and it grew to become one of its richest houses and a venue for meetings of the order's English chapters. In 1388 it was honoured by Richard II when he held a meeting of his parliament in the town and lodged himself at Barnwell. After its dissolution in November 1538 the buildings were dismantled and their contents dispersed, and the priory drifted into obscurity, appearing only as a footnote to other works or in antiquarian accounts.

One early appearance is in William Camden's entry for Cambridge in the second edition of his *Brittania*:

> I let passe here little Monasteries and Religious houses because they were of small note, unlesse it were Barnwell Abbey, which Sir Paine Peverell a worthy and valiant warriour, Standard-bearer to Robert Duke of Normandy in the holy warre against Infidels, translated, in the reigne of Henry the First, from S, Giles Church, were Picot the Shiriffe had ordained secular Priests, unto this place, and brought into it thirty Monkes, for that himselfe at that time was thirty yeeres of age.[7]

It was not until the late nineteenth century, when the Cambridge antiquary and Fellow of Trinity College John Willis Clark published his transcription of the Harley manuscript, that new research began to be conducted.[8] While this did not lead to an

---

4   *Liber*, pp. 38–9. The church of St Giles and Magdalene College now stand on the site at the junction of Castle Street and Chesterton Lane.

5   *Liber*, p. 46. The canons moved to the new site in 1112.

6   *Liber*, p. 47.

7   William Camden, *Brittania sive Florentissimorum Regnorum, Angliae, Scotiae, Hiberniae et Insularum* (London, 1610), here from the online resource by Dana F. Sutton: <http://www.visionofbritain.org.uk/text/chap_page.jsp?t_id=Camden&c_id=17> accessed 20 April 2012. This quote does not appear in an earlier edition, *Brittania sive Florentissimorum Regnorum, Angliae, Scotiae, Hiberniae et Insularum* (London, 1586). In this Picot appears only in the entry for Bourn, 'a BRUNE castro, quod olim Picotti vicecomitis huius agri, & peuerellorum qui ex eius filia oriundi baronia', and the priory is not mentioned, p. 272.

8   This was mostly Clark's own work and concentrated on the archaeology that remained. See, for example, J.W. Clark, 'An attempt to trace the architectural history and plan of the church and conventual buildings of Barnwell Priory, Cambridge', *Cambridge Antiquarian Society*, 7 (1890–1), pp. 222–51.

immediate resurgence of studies it did make the text of the *Liber* more available to scholars.[9] More recently, with the work of Dr David Robinson and others, interest in the Augustinian order in England has re-emerged and this has led to the hope that more focused studies will begin to appear.[10]

While it has much in common with other contemporary religious manuscripts, what makes the Barnwell *Liber* of special interest is the unique manner in which it combines the priory's official history, documents and records with contemporary comment. It was this structure that led to its title: *The church of Barnwell book of things worth remembering.* When asked to write a second introduction to Clark's transcription, the historian and lawyer F.W. Maitland chose to explain what in his opinion the *Liber* was *not*:

> On the one hand we have not here the work of a man who year by year sets down those events, those donations, those oppressions, those law-suits, which affected the fortunes of his house; and on the other hand we have not a systematic collection of documents of title, of enfeoffments, releases and bonds, arranged according to a chronological or geographical scheme.

In his view the selection of documents was governed not by the past but by the future, and was created to be used as 'an armoury of offensive and defensive weapons'.[11] This didactic purpose is also set out plainly by the author in his preamble:

> Wherefore, in order that the servants of God may the more readily, by the help of God Almighty, escape out of the hands of wicked men, having regard to the fact that human memory is defective, it is worthwhile to reduce to writing certain things which may be useful to our church, and by inspection of this little book, may help our brethren, both present and to come, when difficulties arise, and they are persecuted by a cruel world.[12]

The use of the possessive 'our' when writing of the priory and its brethren is the first indication in the text that the authorial voice will at times be in evidence. As Maitland pointed out, alongside the formal language of charters and copies of official documents 'we have anecdotes which are told in an unusually colloquial type of Latin', making the records of these events 'spirited and humorous'.[13] One example of this contemporary voice can be found in the case of Phillip le Champion. Le Champion, whom the author describes as a *uir stature magne*, a man of great stature, was the leader of a band

---

9   Its print run totalled around 300 copies.

10 The recent resurgence of interest has led to three significant conferences devoted to the Augustinian canons over the last ten years and the publication of new volumes of essays including J. Cannon and B. Williamson (eds), *The medieval art, architecture and history of Bristol Cathedral: an enigma explored*, Bristol Studies in Medieval Cultures 2 (Woodbridge, 2011).

11 *Liber*, pp. xliii–xliv.

12 *Liber*, Prologus, p. 37.

13 *Liber*, p. xliv. In Maitland's view Book 3 (*De placitis, infortunijs, itineracione justiciariorum et alijs uexacionibus diuersis*) contains an especially 'rich mixture of records and anecdotes', *Liber*, p. li.

of soldiers who threatened the priory with violence during the Barons' War. What is of particular interest is that it reports a conversation using speech tags as well as offering personal comment.[14] Such entries, while retaining the overall didactic nature of the writing are, as might be expected, also those carrying the heaviest bias. In another dispute, this time over access to a piece of land, the author calls the townsfolk 'malicious' and 'envious' men who acted badly and made great threats.[15]

This paper will consider two cases of thirteenth-century litigation between the canons and members of the local community. One of these involves the right of presentation to the church of All Saints, Croydon (1199–1212) and is not recorded in the *Liber* but can be found in the Curia Regis Rolls. The other, that of the installation of a vicar to the church at Guilden Morden (1269), is one of the *Liber*'s most comprehensive examples.[16] It is entirely possible that the author experienced the latter conflict at first hand, and therefore felt he had the right to reflect in personal terms the anger that the new vicar's behaviour had aroused in the community.[17] Whatever the reason, it fulfils its stated didactic role and is an example of how future cases of a similar nature should be handled.

John of Croydon's writ of *mort d'ancestor*

Domesday Book records the village of Croydon as having *c.*1,605 acres and around twenty-eight inhabitants. It was held by five men, among whom was Picot the sherrif. Picot's total of three hides and virgates, worth £5 10s, was held of him by two men: Anschil (two hides less half a virgate) and Alfred (one hide and one virgate). There was sufficient land for four ploughs and meadow for a further two, all of which was worked by one villein, seven bordars and two cottars. Those on Alfred's holding also had access to an area of woodland, but only for the purpose of repairing fences.[18] In his foundation charter Picot had granted two parts, or 2 per cent, of the 10 per cent tithe tax (the VCH says two-thirds) from Croydon to his new priory.[19]

By the early twelfth century the manor was held by Hugh of Croydon, probably as part of a knight's fee. Hugh the elder was succeeded by his son, William, and his grandson, another Hugh. This younger Hugh is recorded as being a tenant in 1166 and having died by 1199.[20] After the death of Hugh the younger, his son John (d.

---

14   *Liber*, p. 122.

15   *Liber*, p. 134.

16   *Liber*, entries 103 to 107, pp. 171–6. Entries 103–06 are copies of original documents, 107 is the author's account.

17   *Liber*, p. 173. *Iste Lucas vicarius multa gravamina fecit prioris et canonicus de Bernewelle dominius suis.*

18   A. Fairley (ed.), *Domesday Book seu liber censualis Willemi Primi*, 4 vols (London, 1783–1816), f. 193r.

19   The *VCH* states two-thirds but I have assumed the charter to be correct, as it is the stated source. *VCH Cambs*, vol. VIII, p. 39.

20   *CRR of the reigns of Richard I, John and Henry III*, 17 vols (London, 1922–), VI, pp. 347–8. *VCH Cambs*, vol. VIII, p. 31. *The Red Book of the Exchequer* (Rolls Series), 3 vols, ed. H. Hall (London, 1896), I, p. 366. For convenience the former Hugh will be termed 'the elder'.

1229), wishing to establish himself as the rightful heir to the property and sue for the advowson of the village church, entered into litigation with Prior William of Devonshire (*c.*1208–d. 25 May 1213) by raising a writ of *mort d'ancestor*.[21] The prior responded by claiming that, sometime before 1135, Hugh the elder had gifted the advowson to Barnwell on the occasion of his entering the convent, and that there was a charter confirming this. John claimed that the charter in question had been made *after* Hugh the elder's entry and that he, John, should not be disadvantaged by it.[22] Whatever the circumstances, neither William nor Hugh the younger appear to have had any issues with the gift.[23]

As a minor at the time of the original writ, John's legal standing was limited, but these limitations were part of English custom and, while they could not be called as warrantors, minors were able to raise doubts in cases that involved disputes over land or property, especially where the land in question was held in *socage*.[24] *Socage* was a feudal duty whereby the land-holder paid rent, or performed a non-military service, to the landowner. Generally a claimant or defendant being deemed under age led to a postponement until majority was reached. However, it was permitted for a minor to bring an assize of *mort d'ancestor,* and John took advantage of this.

The Croydon case was first presented to the court in Hilary Term 1200, when it was recognised by all parties, who were ordered to return at Easter, in a month's time.[25] There is no record of this hearing taking place and the case does not re-emerge until Trinity Term 1203, when two entries appear. The first records the names of the parties and the details of the dispute; the second requests a postponement of fifteen days.[26] There is then another gap in the proceedings, with the next record appearing in Michaelmas 1204. At this point a judgement was made by the Justices Itinerant in Canterbury, Archdeacon Richard Barre, Osbert son of Harvey and William Warenne. It was only at this time that John's status as a minor was marked by the court.[27]

Another much longer gap of eight years follows until Easter Term 1212, when the prior paid an oblation of two marks to have the case revived as John was now of age. The court ordered the sheriff to seize John's pledges and hold them.[28] Finally, in Trinity Term 1212, a final ruling was made and John had to recognise the priory's right to the advowson as stated in his grandfather's charter, and accept that Hugh the

---

21 Clark, *Liber*, pp. xv–xvi. The writ of *mort d'ancestor* provided an heir with a summary action against any who tried to dispossess him of the inheritable estate held by his father or other close relative at the time of their death. Originally only covering children, siblings, nephews and nieces it was extended in the thirteenth century to grandsons, great-grandsons and other kinsman. J.H. Baker, *An introduction to legal history* (Oxford, 2002), p. 234.

22 *CRR*, VI, 348. *Idem Hugo reddidit se religioni apud Bernewell(e) et canonius fuit.* It is possible that Hugh became a canon on entry, as this suggests, but supporting evidence is not extant.

23 William's charter confirming the gift was also later produced.

24 C.T. Flower (ed.), *Introduction to the Curia Regis Rolls* (London, 1944), p. 256; *CRR*, IV, p. 254.

25 *CRR*, I, p. 142.

26 *CRR*, II, pp. 251, 257.

27 *CRR*, III, p. 210. *Johanni filio Hugonis de Crauden', qui est infra etatem.*

28 *CRR*, VI, p. 269.

elder's entry into religion before the gift was no obstacle.[29] The court also recorded that William's charter upheld this right. The case was concluded on the Sunday of the third week after the Feast of St Peter and St Paul.[30]

A troublesome priest: Luke de Abington and the living of St Mary's, Guilden Morden

The widespread practice of appropriation enabled religious houses to divert directly to themselves the income of a church for which they held the advowson. To do this a vicar was recruited, and paid a fixed stipend for his services. The most common reason given for this redirection of funds was poverty as a result of some past catastrophe, which had left the house unable to fulfil its obligations of hospitality and poor relief.

The Lateran Council of 1215 attempted to regulate the practice by recommending that any priest appointed to the position of vicar should have security of tenure and be adequately trained and paid. The standard stipend was set at 5 marks (£3 6s 8d), about one-third of the value of the average living. Following this, in 1222 the Council of Oxford decreed that vicars must hold, at the very least, the position of deacon to ensure against spiritual neglect. The system remained open to abuse, however, and it was not unknown for religious houses to appoint sub-deacons, clerks or even acolytes if they thought it advantageous.[31] Moorman states that, 'The tendency was to secure the cheapest man available, with obvious disadvantages both to the parish and the employee who had no security and often a totally inadequate wage.'[32]

In 1269 the appointment of Luke de Abington, as vicar of Guilden Morden by prior Simon de Ascellis (1265 or 1266–resigned 1297), led to almost twenty years of acrimonious conflict over the harsh terms of employment and the meagreness of the stipend.[33] On 16 November 1269 a formal request was made to the bishop of Ely for Luke, *nostrum capellanum*, our chaplain, to be instituted into the vicarage. Following this the bishop of Ely tasked one of his archdeacons, Alan de Rokelund, to investigate the requested presentation and produce a report.[34] De Rokelund's report, which Clark dated as 4 December 1269, listed the income from the church that the vicar was

---

29 *Ibid.*, pp. 347–8. The decision was also recorded in the Cambridgeshire feet of fines: J. Hunter (ed.), *Fines sive pedes finium: sive finales concordiæ in curia domini regis 1195–1214*, Vol. I (London, 1895), p. 337.

30 22 July 1212. According to Farrer in 1217 John returned 'to allegiance' and recovered lands in both Cambridgeshire and Northumberland: W. Farrer, *Feudal Cambridgeshire* (Cambridge, 1920), p. 15. T. Duffus Hardy (ed.), *Rotuli litterarum clausarum in turri Londinensi asservati*, 2 vols (London, 1833–44), p. 326.

31 J.R.H. Moorman, *The history of the church in England*, 2nd edn (Edinburgh, 1967), p. 97.

32 *Ibid.*, p. 97.

33 *Liber*, p. 172. The *Liber* uses copies of the documentation to show the official version of events.

34 *Liber*, pp. 171–2. Neither of the documents are dated but Clark gives a date of 2 November for the bishop's letter (entry 104) and 16 November for the prior's request (entry 103). The fact that these documents are not recorded chronologically is not unusual in the *Liber*.

not entitled to collect and which would go directly to the priory:[35] 'The said vicarage receives the altarage, with certain exceptions namely, the hay tithe and that of the mills, and excepting the first legacy and the tithes of the court of the said prior in the same vill and excepting land belonging to the legate.'[36] On this limited amount the vicar was expected to cover his living costs and the wages of any assistant priest or clerk that he might need to employ, and to pay for the upkeep of the fabric of the church.[37] He was also responsible for parish poor relief, which meant that his poverty also directly affected the most vulnerable members of the community.[38]

It did not take long for the vicar to discover that he could not adequately perform his duties on such a limited income and his first action was to withhold payment of the pension and rent. Although this gave the prior an opportunity to rethink the exemptions and to resolve the issue he chose instead to petition the pope for an order to compel payment.[39] The pope referred the case to the prior of Ipswich, who upheld the request and ordered Luke to pay. Luke, however, was not about to submit to the judgement and, when the archbishop of Canterbury Robert de Kilwardby visited the diocese he made a personal appeal. Kilwardby's assessors investigated the case and ruled that Luke should receive the tithes from all the crofts in Morden to supplement his income. Once again, the prior appealed to the pope and, once again, the prior of Ipswich judged in Barnwell's favour. This time Luke accepted defeat and the prior, satisfied in his victory, released the vicar from costs of forty marks.

Luke, however, proved tenacious and seven years later, when Kilwardby's successor John Peckham visited the diocese, he took the opportunity to make a fresh appeal. This time the case was referred to the archdeacon of Ely, who was immediately restrained by the prior of Ipswich at Ascellis's request. Peckham did not take kindly to the interference and summoned Ascellis to appear before him. Instead the prior sent a delegation of his canons and advocates to represent him.[40] Peckham, not unknown for acting in a high-handed manner, lost patience at what appeared a blatant disregard for his authority and promptly excommunicated the prior.[41]

While this was happening Luke, assisted by some friends, collected the tithes. Having obtained letters of protection from the king he had considered himself safe,

---

35   Clark's note gives the date of the report as 4 December, *Liber*, p. 172. For his part the vicar was required to pay the prior a pension of one mark p.a. and a rent of 4s for his dwelling.

36   *Liber*, p. 172, *et quod dicta vicaria consistit in altaragijs, exceptis quisbusdam, scilicet decima feni, et molendinorum, et excepto primo legato, et preter decimas de curia dicti Prioris in eadem villa provenientes, et excepta terra legata is qua fuerit.*

37   The *Liber* gives no indication as to whether any other ancillary costs that might arise were the vicar's responsibility, nor is it made clear whether the fabric included that of the whole church, or just the chancel. In its entry for Guilden Morden the VCH states that 'The vicarage was worth only £5 a year c. 1270, although the church yielded £46 13s 4d', *VCH Cambs*, vol. III, p. 107.

38   *Liber*, pp. 196–7.

39   *Liber*, p. 173. *Propter quod idem Prior dominum papem ap[pellauit].*

40   *Liber*, p. 174. *Tunc quidam canonicus cum aduocato suo sequebatur curiam archiespiscopi apud Mortelak et in parties Gloucestrie.*

41   *ODNB*, Vol. 43, Patel–Phelips, ed. H.C.G. Matthew and B. Harrison, pp. 362–8.

but the sheriff, who should have maintained his neutrality, confiscated what had been gathered.[42] The prior of Ipswich was again summoned and this resulted in Luke also being excommunicated. In an effort to reach some sort of compromise both parties were called to appear before the prior of St Albans, who, perhaps recognising the difficult personalities involved, referred the case to the Roman curia. A canon was immediately dispatched to Rome, not returning for three years.

While the prior of St Albans' representative was abroad the matter resolved itself with the sudden death of the vicar.[43] As might be expected, the *Liber* proclaimed this an act of God and the prior, on the grounds that the vicar's excommunication had not been revoked, forbade Luke's body from entering the church or being buried in the cemetery. It was left to the vicar's executors to negotiate a settlement and, in exchange for a posthumous absolution they offered the prior one hundred sheep, a palfrey worth five marks and a further five marks in silver.[44] The prior accepted and a funeral mass was finally held. Even in death, it seemed, the vicar was required to pay. While it is tempting to imagine that Luke might have eventually won himself a fairer portion it is also worth noting that his successor, Guy of Croydon, settled into the position without incident.[45] At the very least he does not appear to have been so troublesome as to have warranted a mention in the *Liber*.

As a historical source the *Liber* can be described as a polemic statement intended to lend credence to one particular version of a far more complicated history, and the cases discussed above are only two examples of a much wider practice. Arguments over property and liberties were a constant feature of daily life and the available primary sources show that the passage of time did nothing to soften the priory's attitude toward either its tenants or the wider community.

A complete review of all the litigation in which Barnwell Priory was involved during its lifetime, 1092 to 1548, would fill a large volume, but a small first step toward this would be to compile a database of surviving records. The lawsuits listed by Maitland in the *Liber* cover only the first 200 years of the house's history, and even this list is incomplete.[46] To it must be added the cases that the prior deemed not sufficiently important to include, and those contained in the various court and private papers. Finally, one would have to add all the legal activity that took place during the years 1296 to 1548. Such a database would serve as an interesting starting point for any future research into Barnwell's relationships with others, from royal patrons to burgesses, tenants and other religious houses. It is an area in which there is still much to be discovered.

---

42 *Liber*, p. 175. *Quapropter vicecomes Cantebrigie decimas ipsas collegit, et reponi fecit quasi in equali manu etc. Sed Prior dolens quod iam sublata erat ei possession decimarum.*

43 *Liber*, p. 176. *Infirmitate incurabili, id est ydropisi, de qua mortuus est.* It is likely that the vicar died from congestive heart failure as a complication of this condition.

44 The identities of the executors are not given, but they were evidently wealthy men.

45 Previously vicar of Tadlow, another Barnwell church.

46 *Liber*, pp. lii–lxi.

Chapter 3

The donors of the glass in some parish churches of later medieval York

Claire Cross

One of the benefactors who had his name emblazoned on the external wall of the Lady chapel of the newly rebuilt Suffolk church of Long Melford in 1496 maintained that he had done this not 'that I may win praise but that the spirit be remembered'.[1] What he and his fellow contributors to the building fund in fact hoped to achieve were prayers for the salvation of their souls, their families' souls and all the souls for whom they were bound to pray.[2] York citizens were also constantly embellishing and extending their forty or so parish churches in the later Middle Ages, though not on remotely the same scale as in East Anglia, and they, too, expected exactly the same reward when they included representations of themselves and their wives and children in the windows they gave to their churches. The donors of the glass in five of these churches and their pious concerns form the subject of this paper.

St Denys, Walmgate

Some of the earliest representations of York donors occur in the now truncated church of St Denys in Walmgate, where in the first quarter of the fourteenth century, fifty years before the Percys, earls of Northumberland, built their mansion in the parish and turned the church into an aristocratic preserve, the laity were installing commemorative glass in the windows in the north wall of the north aisle.[3] The name of the bearded merchant praying for mercy to the risen Christ flanked by St Thomas and St John the Evangelist in the easternmost window had already been lost before antiquarians visited the church in the early modern period. A little more, however, is known about the merchant in a red robe who kneels, holding up his window, alongside his wife and adult son below St Margaret with the dragon and the Virgin and child in the second window in the aisle of around the same date (Plate 3.1). In this case the original inscription has been preserved, although in a much mutilated state, and

1   D. Dymond and C. Paine, *Five centuries of an English parish church: 'The state of Melford church', Suffolk* (Cambridge, 2012), p. 179.

2   S. Badham, *Seeking salvation: commemorating the dead in the late medieval English parish* (Donington, 2015), pp. 80–8.

3   RCHM, *An inventory of the historical monuments in the city of York, vol. V The central area* (London, 1981), pp. 17–18; F. Drake, *Eboracum* (printed by William Bowyer for the author, 1736), p. 361; P. Gibson, 'The stained and painted glass of York', in A. Stacpoole *et al.* (eds), *The noble city of York* (York, 1972), pp. 179–81.

it identifies the family group as Robert de [Ske]ltun, Joan (or Joanna) his wife and John his son. In all likelihood Robert derived his toponymic from Skelton, a village some four miles north of York, and he may well be the Robert de Skelton who was witnessing vicars' choral charters between 1337 and 1362, who possibly acted as one of the three city bailiffs, the forerunners of the sheriffs, in 1339, and who certainly held that office in 1355.[4]

All Saints, North Street

Wills that survive for the diocese of York from the end of the reign of Richard II provide considerably more detailed information on the parishioners who donated glass to the church of All Saints, North Street in the early fifteenth century. In around 1400 this small riverside community was coming to the end of a major church reconstruction that had resulted in the building of a tower with a 120-foot spire and the total renovation of the north and south aisles. To complete the project the windows had then to be glazed, and sponsors were not slow in coming forward. In his will of November 1429 the merchant Reginald Bawtre, who had obtained his freedom in 1413 and been elected as one of the city chamberlains in 1428, bequeathed 100s for the window third from the east end of the north aisle containing images of Christ, Thomas the Apostle and St Thomas Becket. Around the same time another parishioner, Robert Chapman, free in 1422, joined with James Baguley, rector between 1413 and 1440, in presenting the window in the south aisle, which commemorated St Michael and St John the Divine, while a now lost window in the same aisle was given by Richard Killingholme, tanner, who died in 1450.[5]

Rather than celebrating individual saints in two of their windows, the influential Hessle and Blackburn families opted for a narrative theme. The Hessles had risen to prominence in York in the early fourteenth century, with Abel Hessle elected chamberlain in 1330 and bailiff in 1336, and Henry Hessle, probably his brother, gaining his freedom in 1341: both appear with their wives in the first window in the north aisle given by their sons-in-law, Roger Henryson of Ulleskelf, free in 1400/1, and another incomer and possibly a yeoman with the surname of Wiloghby.[6] The subject matter of the window was taken directly from the fifth book of the middle English poem *The Pricke of Conscience*, which sets out in minute detail the signs foretelling the end of the world. Beneath a Last Judgement in the top lights, the fifteen main panels, each originally with an explanatory couplet in English, portray the sea rising, receding and returning to its accustomed level, fish spewing from the waters, the ocean burning,

---

4   N.J. Tringham (ed.), *Charters of the vicars choral of York Minster: city of York and its suburbs to 1546*, Yorkshire Archaeological Society, Record series, 148 (Leeds, 1993), nos 30, 182, 196, 432, 529.

5   E.A. Gee, 'The painted glass of All Saints, North Street, York', *Archaeologia*, 102 (1969), pp. 164–5, 168, 188, 190, 199; F. Collins (ed.), *Register of the freemen of the city of York, vol. 1 1272–1558*, Surtees Society, 96 (Durham, 1897), p. 134. Drake, *Eboracum*, pp. 275–6.

6   Gee, 'Painted glass', pp. 161–2, 187, 198; R.H. Skaife (ed.), *The register of the guild of Corpus Christi in the city of York*, Surtees Society, 57 (Durham, 1872), p. 251; Collins, *Freemen's register*, pp. 25, 36, 181; RCHM, *City of York, vol. III: south-west of the Ouse* (London, 1972), p. 8.

fruit hurled from trees, buildings wrecked by an earthquake, rocks and stones colliding, the populace fleeing to caves, the earth made featureless, desperate men and women emerging from hiding, graves giving up their dead, stars falling from the heavens, the death of all living things and, in a final consummation, the whole universe destroyed by fire.[7]

Compared with these scenes of unrelenting horror, the adjacent two Blackburn family windows in the north aisle of All Saints, North Street offered a much gentler route to salvation. One of the richest men in early fifteenth-century York, Nicholas Blackburn senior had initially crossed the Pennines from his native Blackburn to trade primarily in wool and cloth in Richmond in the North Riding. Already a merchant of the Staple in Calais, he was made a freeman of York in 1396–7 and readmitted to the freedom two years later on the understanding that he would reside in the city until Martinmas 1402. In fact, from this date, having married Margaret, the sister of William Ormeshede, a merchant and fellow immigrant, he lived permanently in the parish of All Saints, North Street. He owned a considerable amount of property in Skeldergate, Petergate and Walmgate as well as in North Street, and his great wealth seems to have been the reason for his election as lord mayor of York in 1412 without having held any of the preliminary civic offices.[8]

Nicholas Blackburn senior had at least three sons and two daughters. The two elder sons, John and William, apparently either died early or moved elsewhere, as it was Nicholas, his third son, with whom he collaborated in providing the windows. As he disclosed in his will, he cherished a special devotion to St Anne, and the glass in the first window, now transferred to the east window of the chancel, features St John the Baptist, St Anne teaching the Virgin to read and St Christopher above the donor panels of Nicholas Blackburn senior and his wife Margaret, on the right, and of his son Nicholas and his wife, also called Margaret, on the left.[9]

In successive panels in the second window – known as the Corporal Acts of Mercy window, after Jesus's teaching in verses 34 to 41 of chapter 25 of St Matthew's gospel – a venerable merchant, popularly thought to be Blackburn himself, is shown feeding the hungry, giving drink to the thirsty, welcoming the stranger, clothing the naked, relieving prisoners and visiting the sick (Plate 3.2). Clearly much influenced by the parable, at his death in 1432 Nicholas Blackburn senior set aside the huge sum of £260 for his executors to spend on food, drink, fuel, clothes, boots and shoes for the sick, the bed ridden, the poor, the blind, the lame, the lepers and those in prison for debt. Despite his and his family's investment in All Saints, however, he chose to be buried in the much grander surroundings of the south part of the minster under a marble stone before the image of Our Lady.[10]

---

7   S. Powell, 'All Saints, North Street, York: text and image in the *Pricke of Conscience* window', in N. Morgan (ed.), *Prophesy, apocalypse and the day of doom*, Harlaxton Medieval Studies 12 (Donington, 2004), pp. 292–316.

8   The Latin project (ed.), *The Blakburns in York; testaments of a merchant family in the later Middle Ages* (York, 2006), pp. 1–3.

9   RCHM, *City of York, vol. III*, p. 7; The Latin project, *The Blakburns in York*, pp. 14–15, 22.

10   RCHM, *City of York, vol. III*, p. 8; The Latin project, *The Blakburns in York*, pp. 14–15, 18–19, 54–5.

St Martin's, Coney Street

In contrast to All Saints, North Street, where the affluent laity seem to have taken the initiative, the church of St Martin, Coney Street, owed its reconstruction and refashioning entirely to its vicar, Robert Semer.[11] Having been admitted a vicar choral in York Minster soon after the turn of the fifteenth century, by 1420 Semer had risen to become the bursar, or receiver of rents, of the vicars' college in the Bedern. Like many, if not all, of his colleagues he combined his role as a vicar choral with that of a chantry priest in the minster, at one time serving the chantry of Archbishop Walter de Gray at St Michael's altar and subsequently that of Thomas Dalby in the chapel of St Mary and the Holy Angels. In 1425 he acquired the dean and chapter living of St Martin, Coney Street, which he held together with his other offices for the rest of his life.[12]

Finding his church in great decay, soon after his institution Semer embarked upon a wholesale restoration, starting with the tower and the west end before progressing to the south aisle and the nave. On the completion of the first stage of the work he turned his attention to the commemoration of the church's patron saint in the west window beneath the tower. (After the Second World War, in which the church was almost entirely destroyed in the bombing of 29 April 1942, this glass, which had been removed for safe keeping at the onset of hostilities, was reset in a new window in a north projection in the rebuilt south aisle.)[13] A full-length figure of St Martin of Tours has pride of place in the window's central light, while thirteen panels in the surrounding lights, each originally with an explanatory Latin text, narrate the key events in his life: his birth, schooling, service in the army, encounter with the beggar, ordination, elevation to the episcopate, miracles and holy death. Kneeling in supplication below St Martin, Semer himself, in a blue clerical gown, dominates the lower part of the scene, with his monogram 'RS' repeated in each panel of the two rows of quarry-panels to his left and his right (Plate 3.3). A Latin inscription that stretches the whole width of the window records that he presented the glass to the church in his old age on 7 October 1437.[14]

Semer in fact lived for another five years, not dying until 1443, when, in his will, drawn up on 1 January and proved six months later on 7 June, he asked to be buried under a marble stone in his parish church near the St Martin window. After making provision for an elaborate funeral he considered appropriate for a cleric of his status, he left plate and other valuables to his two executors, John Appilton, the sub-treasurer of the minster, and his servant Robert Butler; his copy of Giles' *De regimine principum* to the minster library; his *Polichronica* to Whitby Abbey; and another book called *Breton* to Dom Robert Steresakre. Then, apart from some further token bequests to vicars choral and other clergy, he gave all the rest of his goods, which after payment of debts amounted to the considerable sum of £80, to St Martin, Coney Street, on

---

11   P. M. Tillott (ed.), *VCH City of York*, p. 308; RCHM, *City of York, vol. V*, pp. 25–6.

12   F. Harrison, *Life in a medieval college: The story of the vicars-choral of York Minster* (London, 1952), pp. 100, 159, 160; Tringham, *Charters of the vicars choral*, nos 454–5; J. W. Kirby (ed.), *York sede vacante register 1423–1426: a calendar* (York, 2009), p. 61.

13   *VCH City of York*, p. 308.

14   RCHM, *City of York, vol. V*, pp. 28–9.

condition 'that the said parishioners build anew the said church and its chancel within seven years from henceforth following, just as I proposed to and agreed with the said parishioners I would do'. If they failed to fulfil this provision his executors were to use half of the money to augment the salary of the chantry chaplain at St Mary's altar and dispose of the rest at their discretion.[15] Semer's strategy seems to have worked. Soon after his appointment his successor, Thomas Ellerbek, entered into a contract to buy stone from Sir John Langton's quarry at Huddleston, and made a final payment to the masons just before the deadline in 1449.[16]

Holy Trinity, Goodramgate

By having exploited to the full the opportunities open to him as a vicar choral in the minster Semer possessed the means to carry out the refurbishment of his parish church. Later in the century another city priest with a similar aim but with far fewer pecuniary advantages had to adopt a rather different tack. In 1471, on the death of the previous incumbent, John Walker, a local man with relatives in Yorkswold – the region between Malton and Bridlington in the north of the East Riding – and family connections to the cloth trade, acquired the rectory of Holy Trinity, Goodramgate, valued at a mere £4 7s 4d in the *Valor Ecclesiasticus* of 1535.[17] Before he secured a benefice he seems to have lived the precarious life of a stipendiary priest in the village of Bolton Percy, some eight miles from York, where the impressive church of All Saints had been totally rebuilt at the expense of its rector, a York Minster prebendary, Thomas Parker, in 1423. The glass, which consisted of life-size figures of St Peter, St Anne teaching the Virgin to read, the Virgin and Child, St Elizabeth and St John the Evangelist, together with a series of northern saints, may have been inserted in All Saints at a later date.[18] Perhaps inspired by the example of Bolton Percy, almost immediately on his arrival in York Walker set about replacing the east window in Holy Trinity, Goodramgate.

Before the introduction of the reredos in the early eighteenth century the east window was composed of five lights with four panels in each light. The Holy Trinity still occupies the centre panel in the top tier, which also includes a tiny figure of the priest himself in a crimson robe kneeling at the foot of the cross (Plate 3.4). Walker's name saints, St John the Baptist and St John the Evangelist, fill the panels on either side of the Trinity, with St George and St Christopher, the patron saints of the York fraternity

---

15   The Latin project (ed.), *The testamentary circle of Thomas de Dalby, archdeacon of Richmond, d. 1400* (York, 2001), pp. 189–90; J.A. Hoeppner Moran, *The growth of English schooling: learning, literacy and laicization in pre-Reformation York diocese* (Princeton, 1985), p. 203.

16   RCHM, *City of York, vol. V*, p. 25.

17   P.E. Sheppard Routh, 'A gift and its giver: John Walker and the east window of Holy Trinity, Goodramgate, York', *Yorkshire Archaeological Journal*, 58 (1986), pp. 110–12; RCHM, *City of York, vol. V*, p. 5; *VCH City of York*, pp. 372–3.

18   N. Pevsner, *Yorkshire, The West Riding*, 2nd rev. edn (Harmondsworth, 1967), pp. 116–17; J. Allen, 'A canonised archbishop from Bolton Percy', *Vidimus*, 32 (2009), <https://vidimus.org/issues/issue-32/panel-of-the-month/>.

to which he belonged, in the two far panels. The coronation of the Virgin is the subject of the centre panel in the next tier down, while the surrounding panels are devoted to the new cult of St Anne, her three daughters and their offspring, known collectively as the Holy Kin. The first panel from the left is given over to St Mary Cleophas with her husband Alphaeus and their children, the second to St Anne, the Virgin Mary and the Christ child, the fourth to St Mary Salome, Zebedee and their family, and the fifth – as Jesus had no more near relatives – to St Ursula with some of her 11,000 virgins. The now lost third tier celebrated the attributes of the Virgin Mary, as Domina Mundi, Regina Celi, Mater Christi, Mater Ecclesie and Imperatrix Inferni, while the bottom tier concentrated on northern saints: St Paulinus, St William of York and possibly St Aiden, St John of Beverley and St Wilfrid.[19]

A stained glass window in the late fifteenth century cost in the region of £10, an outlay Thomas Parker, a residentiary canon of the minster and the incumbent of one of the richest rectories in the West Riding, could easily have afforded.[20] Matters were far less easy for Walker, despite the fact that in his later years he was supplementing his meagre income from Holy Trinity, Goodramgate by acting as a stipendiary priest in the altogether more prosperous London parish of All Hallows by the Tower.[21] Pluralism undoubtedly enabled him to live above the breadline. It is also just possible, as he disposed of an unusually large number of small parcels of unmade up woollen and linen cloth in his will, that he had some financial involvement in the cloth trade, but to pay for his window he needed some help from his friends.[22]

The bottom tier of the Holy Trinity east window once had at least three and perhaps as many as five donor panels. William Egremond, an Augustinian friar consecrated a suffragan bishop in the diocese of York in 1463, appeared in the central panel, while two other panels depicted John Biller and his wife and William Thorpe and his wife, the one couple possibly parishioners, the other certainly so. John Biller, baker, died in 1472; William Thorpe, a merchant and a member of the city council, six years later.[23] Unlike Semer's window in St Martin, Coney Street, the east window of Holy Trinity, Goodramgate, therefore, seems to have been a joint venture in which the richer members of the parish were acting in tandem with their parish priest. Walker died in London in the early summer of 1481. In his will he made arrangements for his funeral in All Hallows by the Tower, his burial in the churchyard and the offering of requiem masses for his soul and the soul of Thomas Broune daily for half a year in the London church, and for a whole year in Holy Trinity, Goodramgate in York.[24]

---

19   Sheppard Routh, 'A gift and its giver', pp. 109, 117–19.

20   R. Marks, *Stained glass in England during the Middle Ages* (London, 1993), p. 6.

21   J. Caley and J. Hunter (eds), *Valor Ecclesiasticus, vol. V* (London, 1810–34), p. 22; Walker seems never to have held the living of All Hallows, L.J. Redstone, *Survey of London, vol. 12, the parish of All Hallows, Barking, part 1: the church of All Hallows* (London, 1929), pp. 52–3.

22   BIA, York Prob. Reg. 4 f. 32 (John Walker); a full translation of the will appears in Sheppard Routh, 'A gift and its giver', pp. 110–11.

23   Sheppard Routh, 'A gift and its giver', pp. 117–19; E.B. Fryde, D.E. Greenway, S. Porter and I. Roy (eds), *Handbook of British chronology*, 3rd edn (Cambridge, 1986), p. 350.

24   BIA, York Prob. Reg. 4 f. 32 (John Walker).

St Michael-le-Belfrey

Fifty years after Walker's death, when Protestant ideas had been filtering into the country from the continent for at least a decade, a protracted building campaign was nearing completion in the adjoining parish of St Michael-le-Belfrey. A stone's throw from the west end of the minster to which it belonged, the church was served only by a stipendiary priest. Because they never instituted a vicarage, throughout the Middle Ages the dean and chapter remained responsible for the maintenance of not only the chancel but also the nave.[25] At successive visitations over the course of the fifteenth century the parishioners had complained about the poor state of the fabric and by 1510 matters had deteriorated to such an extent that they were claiming that they could 'not sit in their stalls to hear divine service when any rain is'.[26] Forced at last into taking action, the cathedral authorities decided to demolish the old building and began the construction of an entirely new church in 1525.

In the early 1530s, with the work all but finished, attention switched to the windows, and the parish succeeded in attracting a host of donors, both clerical and lay. The most eminent but also the most puzzling of the clerical sponsors was Hugh Ashton, whose window once had a Latin inscription requesting prayers for his soul and still contains representations of his namesake St Hugh of Lincoln, together with St Paul, St Peter and St William of York.[27] Having begun his career as receiver general of Lady Margaret Beaufort, the mother of Henry VII, Ashton had spent the greater part of his life overseeing her two university foundations of Christ's College and St John's College in Cambridge, and had added the 'golden' prebend of Strensall in York Minster to his numerous other benefices only in 1515. As archdeacon of York, an office he obtained in 1516, and as a residentiary canon he may well have known of the plans for St Michael-le-Belfrey, but the rebuilding had not even begun when he died in the city in December 1522.[28] There is no record of his having any particular connection with the church and he made no mention of it in his will. Indeed, if Thomas Baker, the learned early eighteenth-century historian of St John's College, was correct in stating that the window had originally been in St Leonard's Hospital in York, it is conceivable that Ashton never intended it for St Michael-le-Belfrey, and that it was only transferred there after the dissolution.[29]

All the other clerical donors enjoyed a far closer relationship to St Michael-le-Belfrey. Two, Christopher Seele (or Ceele) and Thomas Marsar, were admitted as vicars choral in the minster in 1507 and 1510 respectively, and subsequently supplemented

25 RCHM, *City of York, vol. V*, pp. 36, 38–9; O.M. Saunders, 'Minster and parish: the sixteenth-century reconstruction of the church of St Michael-le-Belfrey', MA thesis (University of York, Centre for Medieval Studies, 1996), p. 8.

26 J. Raine (ed.), *Fabric rolls of York Minster*, Surtees Society, 35 (Durham, 1858), pp. 248, 253, 261–3.

27 Saunders, 'Minster and parish', p. 94, quoting Bodleian Library, Dodsworth MS 161, f. 39r.

28 C. Cross, 'Ashton, Hugh (d. 1522), Catholic ecclesiastic and university benefactor', *ODNB*, vol. 2, pp. 675–6; Saunders, 'Minster and parish', p. 97.

29 J.E.B. Major (ed.), *History of the college of St John the Evangelist, Cambridge, by Thomas Baker*, vol. 1 (Cambridge, 1869), p. 4.

their incomes with parochial livings in the city or one of the Ridings. Having previously been vicar of Withernsea and then rector of East Retford, John Coltman joined the minster community somewhat later, becoming a chantry priest in St Sepulchre's chapel in 1518. Very significantly, all three held the post of clerk of the works to the dean and chapter, Seele from at least 1515 to 1519, Coltman from 1521 to 1525 and Marsar from 1525 to 1536, and so oversaw the planning and rebuilding of the church.[30]

Although described as 'chanter of the church of York and sometimes clerk of St Peter's works' in the glass he gave to St Michael-le-Belfrey three years before his death in 1540, Christopher Seele had in fact left York in 1520 for Ripon, where he went on to play an active part in the worship and the upkeep of the minster, and in 1534 gained the prebend of Stanwick, worth a substantial £50 a year.[31] The inscription in John Coltman's window records that 'the first stone' of the new church had been laid in 1525 during his term of office, while that in the window presented by Thomas Marsar in 1535 reveals that the church had been 'newly erected and builded' when he was clerk of the works.[32] Having at some earlier stage secured the degree of Bachelor of Decretals, Marsar acquired the rectory of Escrick in 1529, the mastership of St Mary Magdalen's Hospital in Bootham in 1536 and the prebend of Langtoft in York Minster in 1541, and from relatively humble beginnings amassed a sizeable fortune. His canonry alone brought him an annual income of almost £44, and towards the end of his life he was supporting two households, one in the Close, the other at Escrick. When he died in January 1547 his estate was valued at £161 8s 11d.[33] Coltman also passed his last years as a member of the chapter, though his prebend of Apesthorpe, one of the poorest, produced a mere £8 a year: his goods amounted to a relatively modest £43 13s at his death in 1552.[34] Because of subsequent rearrangements of the contents of the windows it is no longer possible to assign the existing panels of saints to any of these three clerical donors, though it is highly likely that Seele's window originally contained one of the two surviving St Christopher panels, Marsar's window the panel of St Thomas the Apostle and Coltman's window that of St John the Baptist.

Three of the leading lay donors came from families with close connections with York and were among some of the wealthiest and most influential men in the city. Robert Elwald, a mercer, the son of a former lord mayor and lord mayor himself in 1539, was serving as sheriff when he gave his window to the church.[35] Also a 'sometime

---

30   Saunders, 'Minster and parish', pp. 96, 105–6; L. Reilly, 'Three sixteenth-century windows in the church of St Michael le Belfrey', MA thesis (University of York, Centre for Medieval Studies, 1979), pp. 15, 17, 18.

31   Saunders, 'Minster and parish', p. 96; Reilly, 'Three sixteenth-century windows', p. 50; S. Werronen, *Religion, time and memorial culture in late medieval Ripon* (Woodbridge, 2017), pp. 43, 48; J. Stevens, *The history of the antient abbeys, monasteries, hospitals, cathedrals and collegiate churches*, vol. 1 (printed for Thomas Taylor and others, 1722), p. 67.

32   Saunders, 'Minster and parish', p. 95; Reilly, 'Three sixteenth-century windows', pp. 51, 66.

33   Saunders, 'Minster and parish', pp. 105–06; C. Cross (ed.), *York clergy wills 1520–1600: I Minster clergy*, Borthwick Institute Texts and Calendars 10 (York, 1984), pp. 69–76.

34   Cross, *York clergy wills*, pp. 90–2.

35   RCHM, *City of York, vol. V*, p. 38; Saunders, 'Minster and parish', pp. 95, 101–03.

sheriff', the three-times-married John Lister, draper, though never lord mayor, left a considerable amount of property when he died in 1541.[36] While apparently not of sufficient age to have stood for civic office, Ralph Beckwith, goldsmith, and a member of a minor gentry family from Stillingfleet, had accumulated a sizeable estate that included leases of the site of the former Carmelite friary and a large house in Petergate at the time of his premature death in the same year.[37]

The past history of a fourth lay donor and another goldsmith, Martin Soza, was altogether more exotic. A native of Spain and – to judge from his surname – probably a member of the Sephardic Jewish community expelled in 1492, in the early decades of the sixteenth century he married an English wife and settled in York, where he had a family of three daughters and seven sons. Having obtained his freedom in 1530, he served first as a city chamberlain in 1535 and then as sheriff in 1545, and when he died in 1560 was accorded a prestigious burial in the minster choir.[38] At his death in 1539 William Tomson, a glazier and a fifth lay donor, had to content himself with a grave in St Michael-le-Belfrey.[39] It is not now possible to establish which saints these donors chose to honour, as the antiquaries who recorded the inscriptions in the seventeenth century did not go on to describe the contents of the windows. Modern versions of the original inscriptions were randomly placed under surviving panels of saints after the Second World War.

All of these donors, whether clerical or lay, seem to have had free choice in the content of their windows, and the panels of saints, although stylistically similar and produced within a single decade, follow no discernible iconographic programme. The sole exception was the glass in the north wall of St Thomas's choir, which related in immense detail the life of Thomas Becket as set out in the *Golden Legend*, beginning with the saint's parentage and ending with his martyrdom and miracles, although only the panels dealing with his father's adventures in the east and his courtship of and marriage to the Saracen princess now remain in situ.[40] As a fragmentary inscription refers to a registrar, one of the patrons of the project may have been the wealthy public notary Thomas Water, who had served the dean and chapter in this capacity between 1527 and 1539, but, unlike the rest of the windows in the church, the sponsorship for this series does not seem to have been exclusively confined to an ecclesiastical or urban elite.[41] On a visit to Tickhill, near Doncaster, in 1620 Roger Dodsworth transcribed inscriptions stating that two of the windows in that church had been commissioned by guilds.[42] While there are no such inscriptions extant in St Michael-le-Belfrey, there is some visual evidence that suggests that a guild may also

---

36   RCHM, *City of York, vol. V*, p. 38; Saunders, 'Minster and parish', pp. 48, 96, 103–04.

37   RCHM, *City of York, vol. V*, p. 38; Saunders, 'Minster and parish', pp. 95, 106–08.

38   Saunders, 'Minster and parish', pp. 94, 98–9.

39   Saunders, 'Minster and parish', pp. 94, 99–100.

40   R. Koopmans, 'Early sixteenth-century stained glass at St Michael-le-Belfrey and the commemoration of Thomas Becket in late medieval York', *Speculum*, 89/4 (2014), p. 1059.

41   Saunders, 'Minster and parish', pp. 29, 109–10.

42   J.W. Clay (ed.), *Yorkshire church notes 1619–1631*, Yorkshire Archaeological Society Record Series, 34 (Leeds, 1904), pp. 108, 110.

have been involved. The church had previously had a fraternity of St Thomas, and a donor panel in the Becket cycle showing two separate groups of seventeen men and seventeen women each headed by a priest could well represent a guild (Plate 3.5).[43] Perhaps some of the middling sort in St Michael-le-Belfrey had a greater hand in the renovation of their parish church than it might at first appear.

Because he had had the audacity to defy his royal predecessor, Henry VIII entertained a particular animus against Thomas Becket and, in November 1538, scarcely more than a year after the installation of the last of the windows in St Michael-le-Belfrey, ordered the destruction of images and pictures of the saint in all churches and chapels throughout the realm. The removal of the martyrdom scenes from the St Michael-le-Belfrey Becket sequence almost certainly dates from this time.[44] A far more widescale purge of monuments of superstition associated with the old religion took place in the reign of Edward VI, when reforming churchmen denied the existence of purgatory and the validity of the intercessory powers of the saints, and no longer permitted prayers to be offered for the souls of the dead. Widespread iconoclasm began again throughout England on the re-establishment of Protestantism on Elizabeth's accession and continued with various degrees of ferocity until at least the end of the Stuart period. It was only in the nineteenth century, when the nation was swept with a passion for all things medieval, that York donors once more began installing memorial stained glass windows in their parish churches.

---

43   Koopmans, 'Early sixteenth-century stained glass', pp. 1080–1; Saunders, 'Minster and parish', pp. 22, 56–7.
44   Koopmans, 'Early sixteenth-century stained glass', p. 1057; RCHM, *City of York, vol. III*, p. 24.

Chapter 4

The hermits of late medieval Norwich[1]

Carole Rawcliffe

In an essay published in 2004 the ecclesiastical historian Norman Tanner advanced the bold, but not implausible, claim that Norwich might well be considered the most religious city in late medieval Europe. As evidence of the 'almost Baroque high-church Christianity' of its people, he cited its profusion of richly decorated and lavishly equipped parish churches (there were no fewer than forty-six in 1528), its four spectacular friaries, its numerous religious guilds and, of course, its massed ranks of over fifty anchorites and hermits. He opened and closed his case by invoking the most famous of the city's recluses, Dame Julian, the trump card in a winning hand, whose celebrated exhortation that 'all will be well' furnished a persuasive introduction.[2]

It is understandable, if nonetheless unfortunate, that Dame Julian should so often overshadow the rest of her fellow anchorites, whose contribution to the spiritual life of England's second city has only recently attracted the scholarly attention that it deserves.[3] These men and women were enclosed in cells (anchorholds) attached to parish churches, chapels and friaries throughout Norwich, whereas the hermits, who came from a variety of social backgrounds, remained at large and are harder to categorise. Perhaps for this reason, they have collectively excited far less interest during the thirty-five years since Tanner produced a list of names and locations in his study of *The church in late medieval Norwich*, and they are still a curiously neglected group.[4] Before then a brief, unreferenced survey of the city's hermits and recluses compiled by Ian Dunn in 1973 constituted the only attempt to build on Rotha M. Clay's pioneering *Hermits and anchorites of England*, which drew upon a considerable amount of local evidence.[5] Significantly, neither Dunn nor Tanner felt that the hermits (who were invariably male) merited separate study, pigeonholing them, rather, along

---

1   This chapter is based upon a keynote lecture given at the International Anchoritic Conference held at the University of East Anglia in 2018. I am grateful to members of the audience for their valuable comments and especially to Dr Carole Hill for sharing with me her expertise on the religious life of late medieval Norwich.

2   N. Tanner, 'Religious practice', in C. Rawcliffe and R. Wilson (eds), *Medieval Norwich* (London and New York, 2004), pp. 137–55.

3   C. Hill, 'Julian and her sisters: female piety in late medieval Norwich', *The Fifteenth Century*, 6 (2006), pp. 165–87.

4   N.P. Tanner, *The church in late medieval Norwich 1370–1532* (Toronto, 1984), Appendix 7, pp. 198–203.

5   F.I. Dunn, 'Hermits, anchorites and recluses: a study with reference to medieval Norwich', in F.D. Sayer (ed.), *Julian and her Norwich* (Norwich, 1973), pp. 18–27; Rotha M. Clay, *Hermits and anchorites of England* (London, 1914).

with the anchorites as members of a single community dedicated to 'unusual forms of religious life'.[6] Yet, although some hermits maintained close links with the city's recluses, they differed from them in many crucial respects, not least regarding the wide range of activities open to them and the freedom of movement that they enjoyed to 'wander about alone'.[7]

In theory, but not always in practice, late medieval English hermits followed some rudimentary form of rule, most commonly that dedicated to St Paul the hermit. Its simple provisions made few specific demands beyond a commitment to chastity and poverty, the assumption of a coarse, hardwearing habit, and the readiness to undertake a daily round of prayer appropriate to the educational attainments of the individual, who might well be illiterate. Profession would be made before a bishop or his representative in the simplest of ceremonies, notable for the blessing of the brown robe and white scapular that hermits customarily wore to denote their quasi-religious status. Such flexibility appealed to ordinary working men with a strong sense of religious vocation, who were encouraged to place their skills at the service of God and the community through a combination of devotion, charity and hard manual labour.[8] Idleness, the 'enmy of Crystyne mene saule' ('enemy of the Christian soul') was to be avoided at all costs, for, in the words of one version of the rule attributed to Pope Celestine V, a former hermit: 'he that wyrkes nott ys not worthy'.[9] Members of the clergy who chafed under the institutional constraints of parochial or monastic life or who sought to lead a more austere, ascetic existence 'while remaining attached to the outside world' were also drawn to this type of rule.[10] As the Norwich evidence so clearly demonstrates, the eremitical calling, which had originally been associated with

---

6   Tanner, 'Religious practice', p. 140. It is highly unlikely that the Alice Hermyte who gave a chalice to the parish church of St Giles in Norwich at some point before 1368 lived as an actual hermit, or, as Aelred Watkin assumes, that she survived as late as 1415, having been the servant of a recluse: A. Watkin (ed.), *Inventory of church goods temp. Edward III*, NRS 19, 2 parts (Norwich, 1948), i, p. 18; ii, p. 161.

7   See E.A. Jones (ed.), *Hermits and anchorites in England, 1200–1550* (Manchester, 2019), p. 5, for concise definitions of the 'two distinct vocations'. Confusion between them is, nevertheless, common. D.M. Owen (ed.), *The making of King's Lynn*, Records of Social and Economic History, new series, ix (London, 1984), pp. 30, 150, describes the town's anchorites as hermits, while omitting any discussion of the hermitage 'enclosed by earthen walls' immediately outside the east gate. It served as a chapel and is documented from 1381 onward, when the townspeople shared the right to present the incumbent with the archdeacon of Norwich. F. Blomefield, *An essay towards a topographical history of the county of Norfolk*, 11 vols (London, 1805–10), viii, p. 513; King's Lynn Borough Archives, KL/C 50/625, 626, 634, C 59/25/5, 10.

8   V. Davis, 'The rule of Saint Paul, the first hermit, in late medieval England', in W.J. Sheils (ed.), *Monks, hermits and the ascetic tradition*, Studies in Church History 22 (Oxford, 1985), pp. 203–14.

9   BL, MS Sloane 1584, f. 93v. For extracts from a longer version of this rule, originally in Latin, see Jones, *Hermits and anchorites*, pp. 153–5.

10 Davis, 'The rule of Saint Paul', p. 203. For the widespread departure from extremes of asceticism, see G. Constable, 'Moderation and restraint in ascetic practices in the Middle Ages', in *idem*, *Culture and spirituality in medieval Europe* (Aldershot, 1996), pp. 315–27.

solitary contemplation in remote and inaccessible places, had been progressively urbanised; and, although some late medieval hermits continued to live in rural isolation, growing numbers flourished in busy, densely populated locations where they could be most useful and easily find support.[11]

Norwich's first documented hermitage comes to light at the very start of the fifteenth century at one such place, where the only access road into the city from the east, which brought traffic from the direction of Yarmouth and the coast, crossed the river Wensum (Map 4.1). Standing at the top of Bishopgate, right next to the turreted gateway with its portcullis, the hermitage belonged to the adjacent cathedral priory, whose gardener leased it out for a token annual rent of 4d. By 1419, however, the rent had risen to 1s 8d, which may perhaps denote a change of usage.[12] A local leet roll of 1432 refers to 'a certain hermit (*heremita*) who used to live there', after which point no more is heard about him or any possible successors.[13] It seems more than likely, given the location, that the hermit in question was responsible for maintaining the bridge, but we have no specific evidence of such activity, in marked contrast to the many legacies, royal letters of protection and indulgences offered to bridge and road hermits elsewhere.[14] The hermit who lived 'at the end of the bridge' in Chester was, for example, allowed to establish an oratory by the bishop of Lichfield in the 1360s, which would clearly have helped to augment the already considerable revenues to be collected there from travellers.[15]

Anthony Browne, the last hermit associated with Norwich, made a suitably dramatic exit from the city, being sentenced to hang for treason outside the guildhall in 1538. A former friar observant of Greenwich, 'of late takyng vpon hym as a hermyte', he had travelled to East Anglia to preach against the Act of Royal Supremacy and was duly hauled before the duke of Norfolk, whose Catholic faith rarely proved an obstacle to political expediency. Because a large crowd was expected to turn out in support of the condemned man, the bishop of Norwich (whose own conservative beliefs excited suspicion) was ordered to deliver a sermon at the scaffold explaining that 'this vnhappy folyshe fryer is well worthy to suffer and that his opinions be falls and

---

11 M.M. Sauer, 'The function of material and spiritual roads in the English eremitic tradition', in V. Allen and R. Evans (eds), *Roadworks: medieval Britain, medieval roads* (Manchester, 2016), pp. 166–7.

12 C. Noble (ed.), 'Norwich Cathedral Priory gardeners' accounts, 1329–1530', in *eadem*, C. Moreton and P. Rutledge (eds), *Farming and gardening in late medieval Norfolk*, NRS 61 (Norwich, 1997), pp. 37, 40, 42–3, 45–6, 49, 50, 52–3, 55–6, 58, 60, 61. According to John Kirkpatrick, *The streets and lanes of the city of Norwich*, ed. W. Hudson (Norwich, 1889), p. 71, the *domus heremite* was on the south side of the street near the gates, opposite a property of the prior and monks called 'le Tolhouse Place' in 1382–3.

13 NRO, DCN 79/2.

14 Sauer, 'English eremitic tradition', pp. 157–76; E.A. Jones, 'The hermits and anchorites of Oxfordshire', *Oxoniensis*, 63 (1998), pp. 51–77, on p. 55.

15 R.A. Wilson (ed.), *The second register of Bishop Robert de Stretton*, Collections for a history of Staffordshire, new series 8 (London, 1905), pp. 24, 38. For the close connection between bridges and hermits, see D. Harrison, *The bridges of medieval England: transport and society 400–1800* (Oxford, 2004), pp. 201–2.

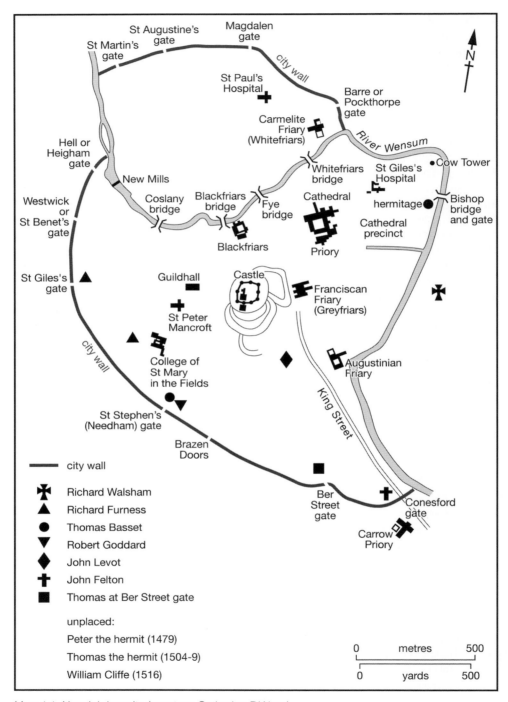

Map 4.1. Norwich hermits (courtesy Catherine D'Alton).

vntrewe'.[16] A similar ritual had taken place in Worcester at the execution of another dissident hermit; and we know that two more went on trial in Bristol and Chesterfield for denouncing Henry VIII's treatment of the Church. A fifth later stood accused of preaching 'sediciouslye' against the king's Six Articles at Gloucester in 1540.[17]

English hermits had long been associated with doctrinally challenging, if not overtly heretical, opinions, which had previously tended towards the evangelical persuasion. A parliamentary statute of 1389 requiring all hermits to carry letters of accreditation from their bishops was in part prompted by concerns that able-bodied vagrants, unwilling to work, were masquerading as hermits to defraud the public.[18] Taking up this theme, William Langland describes them as 'grete lobies [loafers]' heading off with loose women to Walsingham, where they could prey upon gullible pilgrims.[19] But there were also very real fears, as expressed at the London Blackfriars Council of 1382, about unlicensed preaching by itinerant religious reformers, such as the Lollard William Swinderby, who were often described as hermits.[20] It is interesting to note that the hitherto abundant flow of royal letters of protection enabling hermits to solicit alms for their own support effectively dries up during the 1380s, lest they might fall into the wrong hands.[21] As a bastion of orthodoxy, Norwich appears to have been unaffected by these developments, in part, no doubt, because of the close level of supervision that both the lay and ecclesiastic authorities could maintain there.[22] So far as we can tell, the resident hermits whose names can be identified between 1400 and the Dissolution conform more readily to the type of whom Langland clearly approved:

> In preieres and penaunce putten hem manye,
> Al for love of Our Lord lyveden ful streyte
> In hope to have heveneriche blisse.[23]

Who were these men? What do we know about them? How did they support themselves? Were they typical or, in keeping with Norwich's civic motto, did they

---

16 BL, MS Cotton, Cleopatra E.IV, ff. 122r–123v.
17 *LPFD*, VII (1534), no. 973; VIII (1535), no. 308; XV (1540), no. 183; TNA, SP1/95, f. 151r; SP1/134, f. 128r; Jones, *Hermits and anchorites*, pp. 178–80, 182–5.
18 *Statutes*, ii, 12 Richard II, cap. VII, p. 58.
19 William Langland, *The vision of Piers Plowman*, ed. A.V.C. Schmidt (London, 1995), p. 2; M. Godden, 'Plowmen and hermits in Langland's Piers Plowman', *The Review of English Studies*, 35 (1984), pp. 129–63; Jones, *Hermits and anchorites*, pp. 109–11.
20 R. Swanson, *Church and society in late medieval England* (Oxford, 1993), pp. 272, 334, 371–3; Jones, *Hermits and anchorites*, pp. 163–6.
21 One such letter, for example, offered protection in 1343 to Robert de Berton Benedich, chaplain and hermit of Cley by Blakeney Haven in Norfolk, 'who has not whereof to live unless relieved by the faithful, going to divers parts of the realm to seek for alms': *CPR, 1343–45*, p. 20.
22 In contrast, for instance, to the situation in some suburban villages: J. Plumtree, 'The curious incident of the hermit of Fisherwick', in C. Gunn and L. Herbert McAvey (eds), *Medieval anchorites in their communities* (Woodbridge, 2017), pp. 131–46.
23 Langland, *The vision of Piers Plowman*, p. 2.

'do different'? And, most important, what can they tell us about the devotional life of England's second city? It is at the outset important to stress that, although the following survey focuses upon ten individuals who are known to have lived as hermits in late medieval Norwich (in contrast to Tanner's higher total of fourteen), any attempt at counting heads remains conjectural and subject to further revision.[24] The identification of urban hermits and recluses can be problematic, especially as references are scattered and often tantalisingly incomplete. On the assumption that their executors would be personally acquainted with 'John the hermit' or 'the hermit in Ber Street', Norwich testators rarely bothered to furnish further details, which sometimes makes it impossible to distinguish one person from another.

Nor was disregard for convention necessarily a mark of eremitical status. The 'colourful' Thomas Scrope has been omitted from the following discussion, even though his behaviour as a young man certainly conformed to a pattern established by early medieval hermits such as Robert d'Arbrissel.[25] Scrope, whose family was closely connected with the eremitical revival in northern England, joined the Carmelite Order in Norwich, where he began wandering the streets as an apocalyptical preacher 'clad in a hair shirt and a sack and girded with an iron chain' during the 1420s.[26] If the firebrand d'Arbrissel seemed 'to lack only a stick to look like a lunatic' so far as the twelfth-century religious establishment was concerned,[27] reactions to Scrope during a period of nervous conformity may easily be imagined. He was confined to his friary by the Carmelite provincial and lived there under strict enclosure as an anchorite until 1450, when he left to become bishop of Dromore in Ireland. He eventually returned to a life of barefoot austerity and hellfire preaching in East Anglia as rector of Lowestoft, but he was never, strictly speaking, a hermit and was never described as one in his lifetime.[28]

We should, however, most certainly include the Benedictine monk Richard Walsham, whose fascinating case has hitherto attracted surprisingly little attention and was unknown to Tanner. After decades as a busy obedientiary at Norwich cathedral priory, Walsham experienced a period of mental and physical collapse that led him to petition Prior Molet in 1456 for permission to leave the cloister to live as a hermit. In recognition of his long service, Molet agreed, explaining that he was 'led, as we hear from him, by the spirit of God, [and] proposes to redeem this time, so that the Lord, coming even at the fourth watch, might find him vigilant'. Even so, because of

---

24 According to Tanner, *Church in late medieval Norwich*, p. 62 n. 32, a Robert Farnell 'hermit of Norwich' appears on a list of pilgrims staying at the English hospice in Rome in May 1514. Yet the source in question simply describes him as 'a hermit', without specifying any place of origin. The first pilgrim on the list is one Robert Pernell of Norwich, which may have led Tanner to assume that they were the same person: G. Hay, 'Pilgrims and the hospice', *Venerabile*, 21 (1962), pp. 109–44, reprinted in J. Allen (ed.), *The English hospice in Rome* (Leominster, 2005), pp. 99–144, on p. 142.

25 T. Licence, *Hermits and recluses in English society 950–1200* (Oxford, 2011), provides a classic study, which reveals how different late medieval hermits were from their predecessors.

26 Tanner, 'Religious practice', p. 139, describes Scrope as 'the most colourful' of Norwich's hermits.

27 G. Constable, *The reformation of the twelfth century* (Cambridge, 1996), p. 26.

28 For a succinct account of Scrope's life and writings, see R. Copsey, 'Scrope [Bradley], Thomas (d. 1492)', *ODNB*, vol. 49, p. 566.

his 'various illnesses', rumours began to circulate that Walsham was not departing voluntarily but had contracted leprosy and had thus been segregated from the community on medical grounds. In order to quash these unfounded allegations, Prior Molet arranged for his formal examination by a panel of physicians and surgeons, who duly pronounced him free of infection.[29] As was customary, they provided a certificate to this effect, which – remarkably – not only survives but also furnishes a detailed description of the arrangements made for Walsham's future accommodation. He was to live, appropriately for a hermit, just inside the great gate of St Leonard's priory, a cell of the mother house on a hill above Norwich, where he had previously served as sub-prior. His newly built residence boasted a garden full of produce (it had previously belonged to the cook) and carefully delineated rights of ingress and egress for himself and his servants. He was indeed residing at the Ritz Carlton end of the eremitic spectrum, being awarded a generous allowance of fuel, along with 'all the ale, wine, meat, fish and other victuals' to which a senior monk was entitled, ready for his attendants to prepare for him, à la carte, in the priory kitchens.[30]

Although the two men lived almost four centuries apart, Walsham's experience is remarkably similar to that of John, abbot of Fécamp (d. 1078), who, 'vexed by temptations and administrative duties', expressed a burning desire to become a hermit and atone for his sins.[31] It was not unusual for late medieval religious to take this step towards the end of their lives, or earlier, if they could secure approval. Thus, for example, Richard Gilbard, an Augustinian canon of Longleat, received a papal licence in 1399 'to choose and remain in any hermitage in the realm, in order to lead therein a solitary life'.[32] Less creditably, in the 1520s William Stapleton, a monk of St Benet Hulme in Norfolk, who palpably lacked any sense of vocation, obtained permission from his abbot to seek a dispensation to become a hermit, spending some time along the way in Norwich and Walsingham. He had fallen in with a gang of necromancers and treasure hunters, allegedly becoming embroiled in a plot against the duke of Norfolk, through which his picaresque adventures come to light. We can safely assume that he made little contribution to the spiritual life of the city, or indeed to its economy, as he failed miserably to locate any buried treasure there.[33]

---

29 Details of Walsham's busy career are provided by Joan Greatrex, *Biographical register of the English cathedral priories of the province of Canterbury, c. 1066–1540* (Oxford, 1997), pp. 568–9, who mistakenly states that 'he had contracted leprosy' by 1456. For his examination, see C. Rawcliffe, *Leprosy in medieval England* (Woodbridge, 2006), pp. 185–6.

30 NRO, DCN 35/7.

31 Dom J. Leclercq and J.-P. Bonnes, *Un maître de la vie spirituelle au XIe siècle: Jean de Fécamp* (Paris, 1946), pp. 19–29, and pp. 184–97 for the text of John's 'Lamentation'.

32 W.H. Bliss and J.A. Twemlow (eds), *Calendar of entries in the papal registers relating to Great Britain and Ireland: Papal letters, 1396–1404* (London, 1904), p. 200. The eremitical life may have proved too unstructured for some religious. In 1341 John de Flyctewyk, a former Benedictine, sought readmission to the order after spending less than a year as a hermit at Cripplegate in London: W.H. Bliss (ed.), *Calendar of entries in the papal registers relating to Great Britain and Ireland: Papal letters, 1305–1342* (London, 1895), p. 554.

33 *LPFD*, IV, part two (1526–8), no. 5096.

The church of St Leonard's priory housed a significant collection of relics and sacred images, which attracted a steady stream of pilgrims.[34] It is unlikely that Richard Walsham, an elderly invalid who embraced the contemplative aspects of the eremitic calling, had much to do with these visitors, although some hermits supported themselves as guides at shrines and he may have had younger, more active successors.[35] Pilgrims travelling to the popular shrine of St Walstan in the village of Bawburgh, on the other side of Norwich, were allegedly welcomed at a chapel next to the bridge by a hermit who celebrated mass for them there, before 'sprinkling them with hyssop and holy water' and conducting them, suitably cleansed, to the church where the holy relics lay.[36] Our only source for this anecdote, the Norfolk antiquary Frances Blomefield (d. 1752), does not, unfortunately, provide any corroborating evidence; and since, like many eighteenth-century antiquarians, he is prone to exaggerate the presence of hermits, we need to treat it with circumspection. His assumption that one of them managed the leper house outside the Magdalen gate is demonstrably unfounded:[37] some hospitals, such as those at Bicester, Earl Soham, Marlborough, Sherburn in Elmet and Southbroom near Devizes, appear to have been supported or even run by hermits, but there is no evidence of any such connection in Norwich.[38] The even more implausible claim that 'there were hermits dwelling in their cells in *all* the gates' (that is, a total of twelve at any one time) may come from a misreading of the will of the Norwich alderman and philanthropist William Setman, who in January 1429 left 12d to each of the city's (unnamed) hermits and a similar sum to every *leper* at the city gates.[39] Setman's will furnishes the first mention of Norwich's best-documented hermit, Richard Furness, who received a far larger legacy than any of the others. Indeed, at 40s it was twice the amount assigned to the anchoresses at Carrow abbey and in Conisford.

Furness had previously been residing as a hermit at St Giles's gates (*heremita nuper manens ad portas Sancti Egidii*), in one of the wealthiest parishes in Norwich, and had made such a favourable impression upon Setman that he was appointed to

---

34   M.R.V. Heale, 'Veneration and renovation at a small Norfolk priory: St Leonard's, Norwich, in the later Middle Ages', *Historical Research*, 76 (2003), pp. 431–49.

35   The most famous of these shrine keepers was Thomas Douchtie, 'the holye armite of Allarit', who introduced the cult of the Santa Casa of Loretto to Musselburgh in the sixteenth century. His chapel, built with enthusiastic support from the townspeople, drew enormous crowds, but he was later denounced as 'ane craftye preist or fenyeit fals armeit' by Protestant reformers. D. McRoberts, 'Hermits in medieval Scotland', *Innes Review*, 16 (1965), pp. 199–216, on pp. 209–10; D. Laing (ed.), *The poetical works of Sir David Lyndsay*, 2 vols (Edinburgh, 1871), i, pp. 324–5.

36   Blomefield, *Topographical history*, ii, p. 389.

37   Blomefield, *Topographical history*, iv, p. 438.

38   J.A. Twemlow (ed.), *Calendar of entries in the papal registers relating to Great Britain and Ireland: Papal letters, 1458–1471* (London, 1933), p. 501; *CPR, 1334–38*, p. 404; *1338–40*, pp. 49, 441; *VCH Wiltshire*, vol. III, pp. 342–3, 362; *VCH Yorkshire*, vol. III, p. 331. The hospital at Bicester, which was the project of a hermit 'of some independent means', may, however, never have become operative: Jones, 'The hermits and anchorites of Oxfordshire', pp. 58, 64–5.

39   Blomefield, *Topographical history*, iv, p. 167; Tanner, *Church in late medieval Norwich*, p. 242.

assist his executors, 'especially in the distribution of alms and other matters'. These men were redoubtable figures, headed by the master of St Giles's hospital and the dean of the College of St Mary in the Fields, the city's two elite institutions for secular clergy. It seems that Furness would have been called on to provide some necessary local knowledge about individually deserving cases, especially as Setman expected a healthy return on his spiritual investment and had no wish to encourage idlers, vagrants or other undesirables. He had left a munificent £40 for distribution in weekly handouts 'among the poor, and especially the lame, the blind, or the severely disabled remaining continuously in Norwich'. Furness, who presumably selected and paid the recipients, was to be rewarded for his labours at the executors' discretion.[40]

Just eight months later, in August 1429, the serving mayor of Norwich, Robert Baxter, another resident of St Giles's parish, drew up a will that underscores how much trust Furness could inspire among the city's richest merchants. First, Baxter set aside £20 from the sale of his goods, as well as the residue of his estate, for the hermit to spend as he saw fit on pious works for the health of his, the testator's, soul. This alone was a significant administrative – and spiritual – responsibility, but, in addition, Furness was promised £40 (the annual salary of a knight of the royal body) to make two important pilgrimages. He was to visit Rome, 'there going round fifteen times [three times the wounds of Christ] in a great circle', and then Jerusalem, 'in them doing what a true pilgrim does'.[41] On the evidence of this single legacy, Robert Swanson has posited the existence of a sub-category of hermits, who supported themselves as 'semi-professional pilgrims' by undertaking long-distance pilgrimages on behalf of others.[42] A case heard before the mayor and aldermen of London in 1412 certainly suggests that money was to be made in this way, even after the journey was safely over. It concerned a fraudulent hermit who, 'barefooted and with long hair, under the guise of sanctity', had attracted generous donations for six years by pretending to have travelled to Rome, Venice, Jerusalem and Seville.[43] A century later, the more reputable Henry Lofte went on pilgrimage as a hermit both to 'the sepulchre of Christ' in Jerusalem and to Rome, where he acquired various indulgences on behalf of the chapel of St James at Towton, Yorkshire.[44]

---

40   Tanner, *Church in late medieval Norwich*, pp. 242–4.

41   NRO, NCC, Surflete, ff. 86r–88r. For Baxter, see C. Hill, 'Politics and piety', in L. Clark and E. Danbury (eds), '*A verray parfit praktisour': essays presented to Carole Rawcliffe* (Woodbridge, 2017), pp. 128–34; J.S. Roskell, L. Clark and C. Rawcliffe (eds), *The Commons 1386–1421*, 4 vols (Stroud, 1993), ii, pp. 148–9. The sum involved would have allowed time for prolonged intercession. Also in 1429, Sir Gerald Braybroke left £50 ('and more yif hit nedeth') for three separate pilgrimages to Santiago, Rome and Jerusalem, where prayers and masses were to be said on his behalf: E.F. Jacob (ed.), *The register of Henry Chichele archbishop of Canterbury 1414–1443, II,* Canterbury and York Society 42 (Oxford, 1937), p. 411.

42   Swanson, *Church and society*, p. 272. The Latin rule of Pope Celestine discouraged 'gadding about' but sanctioned 'distant' pilgrimages made with a patron's approval: Jones, *Hermits and anchorites*, p. 155.

43   H.T. Riley (ed.), *Memorials of London and London life in the XIIIth, XIVth and XVth centuries* (London, 1868), p. 584.

44   *LPFD*, I, part one (1509–13), no. 885. See also above, n. 24.

Yet Furness was demonstrably far more than an eremitic mercenary who hired out his services to wealthy patrons. He had the option to appoint 'another suitable person' to leave England in his stead, which confirms how much confidence Baxter placed in his judgement as well as in his reliability. Indeed, Baxter's will confirms that the two men enjoyed a close relationship, in which Furness may have played the role of spiritual advisor and perhaps almoner to the deeply pious merchant. It is worth noting in this context that Baxter's daughter, Katherine, who married the wealthy bell-founder Peter Brasyer, left a personal bequest of 80s to Furness in her own will of 1457, this substantial sum standing in sharp contrast to the token legacies of 12d and 2s that she bequeathed to two other Norwich hermits.[45] Furness may perhaps have played some part in Katherine's early education, encouraging her to cultivate the piety so evident in her later life and in the circle of devout women among whom she then moved. At the very least, we have evidence of a long and sustained connection between Furness and one of fifteenth-century Norwich's most influential families.

The unanswered question remains: did Furness really undertake the long and hazardous journey to Jerusalem? Baxter died in 1431, and no more is heard of the hermit for over a decade, which is not itself proof that he spent time abroad. One item of circumstantial evidence discovered by Mary Erler is, however, suggestive, as it concerns 'a gold rynge that towched our lordys grave, as it is seid'.[46] This intriguing artefact belonged in 1498 to Katherine Moryell, whose sister, Christine Veyl, had supported Furness in his old age. The two women, who belonged to the civic elite, were left household goods, rather than jewellery, in his will, but it is possible, if far from certain, that he previously gave one of them the ring as a precious keepsake or was asked to take it with him on pilgrimage. Some hermits, such as John Scott of Jedburgh, are known to have brought relics home from the Holy Land, although Protestant authors were predictably scathing about the extravagant claims made for these stones, bones and 'date-tree leaves'.[47]

Whatever their destination, there can be no doubt that British hermits travelled widely at this time. Several of the royal licences to cross the sea and exchange currency entered in the Close Rolls during the late fourteenth and early fifteenth centuries were issued to men such as 'brother Thomas Basset hermite', who obtained two of these letters in August 1390 alone.[48] If he were still quite young at this point, Brother Thomas could have been the same person as Thomas Basset, hermit of St Stephen's parish in Norwich, who died there in 1435. This Thomas either came from or had close connections with Swainsthorpe, a village just south of the city, to whose parish church he left an image of St Anthony, one of the first hermits. His modest will, reflective of an austere lifestyle, is notable for its reference to his seal (*sigillum meum*), which suggests that, like Furness, he was the type of hermit who devoted himself to clerical activities rather than hard physical labour.[49]

---

45 NRO, NCC Reg. Brosyard, f. 58r. For Katherine Brasyer, see Hill, 'Politics and piety', pp. 136–7.

46 M.C. Erler, *Women, reading, and piety in late medieval England* (Cambridge, 2002), p. 74.

47 McRoberts, 'Hermits in medieval Scotland', p. 208.

48 *CCR, 1389–92*, p. 569; *1392–96*, p. 538.

49 NRO, NCC Reg. Surflete, f. 169r–v.

Furness reappears in 1446, at which point he had taken up residence at a place called 'Newbrygg'. Since at least 1428 the hermits there had attracted legacies from Norwich residents, Robert Baxter alone leaving a generous 20s to one of them named John Martyn.[50] Perhaps for this reason Norman Tanner assumed that 'Newbrygg' must be in Norwich, and included these various individuals in his survey of the city's anchorites and hermits. According to Francis Blomefield, the redundant church of St Margaret north of Blackfriars' bridge, later known as 'the new bridge', served as a hermitage from 1349, which would, on the face of things, lend credence to Tanner's assumption (Map 4.1).[51] But, as papal bulls and numerous other documentary sources make clear, the hermitage and chantry chapel of St Mary and St Lawrence of the New Bridge lay about twenty-eight miles south-west of Norwich at Ickburgh. It occupied an archetypically liminal situation on the Norfolk–Suffolk border, by a bridge over the river Wissey and on the site of a former leper hospital.[52] Furness did not stay there permanently and was back in Norwich within the next nine years. He then settled at a hermitage in Chapel Field, thereby consolidating his previous connections with the neighbouring College of St Mary, to which he eventually bequeathed a great psalter for use in the choir, and where he wished to be buried.[53]

Why did he go to New Bridge in the first place? Was he needed to put the house in order and ensure that a papal bull, originally issued in 1409, exempting it from tithes, was duly confirmed, as happened under his watch in 1452?[54] The hermits there were responsible for maintaining the road, bridge and drains adjacent to the river, and it may be that he was dispatched to deal with some infrastructural problem that hindered the passage of goods on their way to or from Norwich.[55] As David Dymond's study of the cloth trade in Lavenham reveals, wealthy local merchants paid handsomely to keep these arteries of commerce in working order.[56] A routine royal pardon issued to Furness in 1449 suggests that he had been busy acquiring property for the chapel and hermitage, probably with an eye to placing them both on a more secure financial footing.[57] He kept links with the place, leaving one of the hermits there his

50 NRO, NCC Reg. Surflete, ff. 26r (to 'the hermit de Newbrygg'), 86v (to John Martyn 'heremite de Newbrygg'); Reg. Wylbey, f. 131r (to Richard 'hermit at Newebryg').

51 Blomefield, *Topographical history*, iv, p. 474. See also Dunn, 'Hermits, anchorites and recluses', p. 23. M. Reddan, revised by A. Moss, 'The hermits and anchorites of London', in C.M. Barron and M. Davies (eds), *The religious houses of London and Middlesex* (London, 2007), pp. 235, 238, compounds the confusion by assuming that 'New Brigge' lay next to the London Blackfriars and that Katherine Mann, an anchoress at the Norwich Dominican friary, was enclosed there (but see Erler, *Women, reading, and piety*, pp. 100–06).

52 *VCH Norfolk*, vol. II, p. 440; NRO, BRA 833/14/1. Clay, *Hermits and anchorites*, pp. 232–3, identified the correct location.

53 NRO, NCC Reg. Brosyard, f. 1r; Reg. Jekkys, ff. 15v–16r; Tanner, *Church in late medieval Norwich*, pp. 233–4.

54 NRO, DN Reg. 6/11, f. 265r–v.

55 Blomefield, *Topographical history*, ii, pp. 239–41.

56 D. Dymond and A. Betterton, *Lavenham: 700 years of textile making* (Woodbridge, 1982), pp. 11, 67–71.

57 *CPR, 1446–52*, p. 208.

best overcoat, his hood and his scapular in his will of 1464.[58] Since, as we have seen, the assumption of the brown robe and white scapular, which had been blessed by the officiating bishop, marked the 'crucial part of the ceremony' for the institution of a hermit, this gift was especially poignant and replete with spiritual symbolism.[59]

Furness's will, made when he was sick and elderly, has been cited by historians of female learning and piety because of the evidence that it provides of local networks of devout women, most notably that headed by the formidable Margaret Purdans, to whom he left 'a cloth bearing the image of Christ'. (This was perhaps a copy of the vernicle venerated by pilgrims to St Peter's in Rome and possibly a souvenir of Furness's own visit.[60]) It also reflects his close relationship with his executor, the 'radical' and ascetic Richard Poringland, a distinguished Cambridge academic, who had been vicar of St Stephen's church in Norwich, but who eventually opted to serve there as a humble chaplain.[61] Poringland received a glossed psalter for life, with reversion to the nearby College of St Mary. It is important here to stress Furness's enduring attachment to the College, as it underscores the fact that he continued to move in the highest civic circles. He left small sums of money to each of the prebendaries, clerics and choristers there, while another of his testamentary bequests reveals that he had joined the prestigious fraternity of the Mass of the Name of Jesus in the city-centre church of St Peter Mancroft. The advowson of St Peter's belonged to the College, and it was where members of the aldermanic elite worshipped.[62]

So much is known about Furness that, rather like Dame Julian, he tends to attract the lion's share of attention. But at least seven other hermits, who have yet to be mentioned, lived in Norwich between the 1440s and 1516. They are far less well documented, possibly because some came from the ranks of the 'ordinary, obscure and "unsung" people' identified by David Dymond as a proper, but elusive, focus of local studies.[63] A few may even have found that they had no real vocation and soon abandoned the eremitic calling. The author of the devotional tract *Dives and Pauper* certainly believed that there were too many fair-weather anchorites and hermits, who 'withynyn fewe yerys comonly […] fallyn in reueryys or heresyys or they brekyn out for womanys loue or for orchod [boredom] of her lyf or be som gyle of the fend [devil]'.[64]

---

58 NRO, NCC Reg. Jekkys, ff. 15v–16r; Tanner, *Church in late medieval Norwich*, pp. 233–4.

59 Davis, 'The rule of St Paul', p. 209.

60 Erler, *Women, reading, and piety*, pp. 68–84; Hill, 'Politics and piety', pp. 134–7; *eadem, Women and religion in late medieval Norwich* (Woodbridge, 2010), pp. 35, 78, 113, 116. For the vernicle as an attraction in fifteenth-century Rome see John Capgrave, *Ye Solace of Pilgrimes*, ed. C.A. Mills (Oxford, 1911), p. 64. Significantly, the above-mentioned Katherine Moryell owned 'a varnacle that cam from Rome with the image paynted theron': NRO, NCC Reg. Multon, f. 90v.

61 Erler, *Women, reading, and piety*, pp. 75–82; Tanner, *Church in late medieval Norwich*, pp. 39, 41, 47–8, 124; NRO, NCC Reg. Gelour, ff. 91v–94v.

62 NRO, NCC Reg. Jekkys, ff. 15v–16r; Tanner, *Church in late medieval Norwich*, pp. 233–4; D. King, *The medieval stained glass of St Peter Mancroft Norwich* (Oxford, 2006), pp. liv, lvii, 147.

63 D. Dymond, *Researching and writing history: a practical guide for local historians* (Salisbury, 1999), pp. 65.

64 P. Heath Barnum (ed.), *Dives and pauper*, 2 vols in 3 parts: Early English Text Society original series 275, 280, 323 (Oxford, 1976–2004), ii, pp. 92–3.

Significantly, in the context of Norwich, which boasted so many anchoresses, the author maintained that women were less vulnerable to the temptations of hypocrisy, self-indulgence and vanity to which their male counterparts so often succumbed. It was, he observed, all too easy for these 'lewyd folys' to grow conceited when people flocked to them for spiritual guidance, hanging upon their every word.

Thomas, hermit at the Ber Street gates, who received a few modest legacies between 1446 and 1464,[65] and the obscure Peter 'hermyte', who appears just once in 1479,[66] may well have belonged to the ranks of the illiterate or less educated working men who were increasingly drawn to the eremitic life. Their presence in Norwich may thus reflect the value placed in late medieval society upon 'manual labour as a form of charitable spirituality',[67] although only one of our seven is definitely known to have undertaken this type of work, on the upkeep not of roads or bridges but of dykes and gates. In October 1483 the civic assembly agreed that one Robert Goddard, hermit, might have a dwelling (*mansum*) over the Needham gate, along with custody of the extramural ditches in St Stephen's ward, under the supervision of two designated officials. The state of a city's ditches was a matter of constant concern to the crown, as well as the local authorities, as the accumulation of dung and rubbish not only impeded the defences but also posed a risk to communal health. Since the Needham gate was the main entry point into Norwich from London and the south it was, moreover, essential to maintain appearances, so that the sight and stench of ditches piled high with filth would not repel important visitors.[68]

It might be expected that Robert's accommodation would come free in light of his uncongenial task, but the city drove a characteristically hard bargain, charging him an annual rent of 6s 8d and ordering him to repair the two rooms that he occupied.[69] Such arrangements may have been common. In 1315 a hermit priest living in the 'tourelle' on London Wall near Bishopsgate contracted with the mayor and aldermen to pay a similar rent, to spend 40s on structural improvements, to keep his lodgings watertight thereafter and 'always [...] properly to behave himself'.[70] Moral conduct likewise preoccupied the people of Maidenhead, who in 1423 required their new hermit not only to maintain the

---

65 NRO, NCC Reg. Wylbey, f. 78v; Reg. Brosyard, ff. 1v, 58v, 156v. He may well be the 'Thomas, hermit in Norwich' to whom Richard Furness left 4d in 1464: NRO, NCC Reg. Jekkys, ff. 15v–16r; Tanner, *Church in late medieval Norwich*, pp. 233–4.

66 NRO, NCC Reg. Awbreye, f. 21r.

67 Sauer, 'English eremitic tradition', p. 157.

68 Not coincidentally, public health measures of this kind were deemed to be 'godly and goodly' and cleanliness a reflection of spiritual as well as a physical health: C. Rawcliffe, 'Sickness and health', in Rawcliffe and Wilson (eds), *Medieval Norwich*, p. 310.

69 NRO, NCR, 16D/1, Assembly Proceedings, 1434–1491, f. 122r. According to Blomefield, *Topographical history*, iv, p. 165, these quarters had previously been home to Thomas Basset, who lived in this part of the city, and who did, indeed, leave one of his few bequests to the lepers living outside the Needham gate: NRO, NCC reg. Surflete, f. 169r.

70 Riley, *Memorials of London*, p. 117. A succession of anchorites later occupied the 'tourelle': M.C. Erler, 'A London anchorite, Simon Appulby: his *Fruyte of redempcyon*', *Viator*, 29 (1998), pp. 227–38, on p. 1 n. 3.

town's roads and bridges but also to remain chaste, praying, fasting and attending mass daily, while scrupulously avoiding taverns, entertainments 'and all other suspect placis of synne'. His oath, sworn during a public ceremony staged before the hermitage, was accompanied by a ritual blessing of the habit that he would wear while busy about his labours.[71] The Norwich authorities made no such stipulations, although it is unlikely that Goddard found many opportunities to rest idle. The chamberlain's accounts for 1483–4 record payments of 5d and 2d made to him for undertaking minor repairs to the gates at both St Stephen's and St Augustine's (on the other side of the city), which suggests that he may have assumed a more general roaming brief.[72]

Quite possibly the John Felton who appears as a hermit in Conisford between 1455 and 1478 was responsible for maintaining the gates there, but we can only speculate on this point. He did, however, receive modest legacies from Furness and members of his circle, such as Katherine Brasyer and Richard Poringland, which underscores the close and intimate nature of their network. The last of these bequests (a token 6d) came, significantly, from a local priest named John Spendlove, who sought burial at the College of St Mary in the Fields.[73]

Although he was not apparently in orders, it seems likely that John Levot, 'armyte', who had taken up residence somewhere in Ber Street by 1503, had enjoyed the benefits of a good education. The vicar of All Saints Ber Street then left him 3s 4d to pray for his soul;[74] and the will that he himself made six years later suggests that he came from a comfortable, if not necessarily affluent, background. He sought burial next to his sister in the parish churchyard and left small sums to his godchildren, as well as the nuns of Carrow priory, just outside the walls.[75] A John Levot was common sergeant of Norwich market in 1476 and may well have been a relative.[76] There is no doubt about the status of 'Ser William Clyffe, preste, heremyte', who witnessed a will in the parish of St Michael Mustowe in 1516 and, along with all the city's recluses, received a shilling from William Elsy, constable of Conisford Ward, in the same year.[77]

Legacies of a few shillings or pence were welcome, but not enough for even the most ascetic of hermits to live on, especially if they were engaged in hard manual labour. How did these men otherwise support themselves? It is clear from the wills of Thomas Basset, Richard Furness and John Levot that eremitic poverty was a relative concept, at least for those of higher social status or educational attainments. Levot left cash bequests of over 33s 4d, while setting aside an unspecified estate for 'dedes of pety and marcy to the most pleasure of God and profyte to my sowle'.[78] Like Basset,

---

71 Jones, *Hermits and anchorites*, pp. 139–43; *VCH Berkshire*, vol. II, p. 20.

72 NRO, NCR, 18A/3, f. 59r.

73 NRO, NCC Reg. Brosyard, ff. 1r, 58v, 156v; Reg. Jekkys, ff. 15v–16r; Reg. Gelour, ff. 92r, 183r.

74 NRO, NCC Reg. Popy, f. 548v.

75 NRO, NCC Reg. Spyltymber, f. 224v.

76 T. Hawes, *An index to Norwich city officers 1453–1835*, NRS 52 (Norwich, 1986), p. 96.

77 Tanner, *Church in late medieval Norwich*, pp. 202 n. 58, 231; NRO, NCC Reg. Bryggs, f. 19v. For Elsy, see Hawes, *An index to Norwich city officers*, p. 57.

78 NRO, NCC Reg. Spyltymber, f. 224v. His financial situation contrasts strikingly with that of Thomas Skutt, hermit of Eye in Suffolk, who on his death in 1525 left personal bequests

he had strong local roots and could probably draw upon long-standing familial and parochial connections in the Ber Street area. His sole executor was, however, the wealthy goldsmith and alderman, Thomas Clark, who may have been a favoured patron.[79] We should note, too, that our only information about the enigmatic 'Thomas hermyte' of early sixteenth-century Norwich derives from the wills of Sir Henry Heydon (d. 1504) and his flamboyantly pious widow Lady Anne (d. 1509). Each of them left him the handsome sum of 40s, while the latter made an ancillary bequest of the 'stuffe that perteyneth to his bedde to pray for my soule'.[80] If these prominent Norfolk landowners had not been funding him on a regular basis, they had at least helped to make him secure and comfortable.

As we have already seen, Christine Veyl, who moved in circles noted for their wealth and status as well as their piety, was keeper or '*custos*' of Richard Furness in his old age, which suggests that she provided him with the financial or material support that would previously have come from leading families such as the Setmans and the Baxters. An element of fashion as well as devotion may have entered into these arrangements, since many leading members of the aristocracy, including the Black Prince (d. 1376), Anthony, Earl Rivers (d. 1483), and Edward, duke of Buckingham (d. 1521), housed and maintained their own hermits.[81] The courtier Sir Bernard Brocas actually travelled overseas with his hermit, who joined him, perhaps as his confessor, when he was captain and controller of Calais in the 1380s.[82] Not surprisingly, the vernacular version of Pope Celestine's rule cited above required an aspirant hermit to be 'respectful [...] to his patron in whose accommodation he dwells'.[83]

The testamentary evidence from which much of our information about Norwich hermits derives indicates that bequests to these men came from a surprisingly small group of individuals, most of whom were prosperous, while some were very rich indeed. Only twelve of the 904 lay and clerical wills drawn up between 1370 and 1532

---

exceeding £24, largely to his four children under twenty. He had presumably become a hermit on the death of his wife and placed the money in trust for their use. A note at the foot of his will records that £30 was due to his estate from six different individuals: NRO, NCC, Reg. Attmere, f. 86r–v. Hermit wills are not uncommon. See, for example, that of Richard Newman (d. 1517), 'heremyte' of Bury St Edmunds, who was survived by a married daughter on whose behalf he had sold a tenement at Woolpit. His cash legacies came to 66s 8d and he owned a seal: SROB, IC500/2/6/41.

79   For Clark, see Hawes, *An index to Norwich city officers*, p. 37.

80   TNA, PROB 11/14/336, 11/16/563.

81   M.C.B. Dawes (ed.), *The register of Edward the Black Prince*, 4 vols (London, 1930–33), i, pp. 22, 94, 138; ii, p. 63; iii, p. 310; iv, pp. 48, 85, 380, 518; S. Bentley (ed.), *Excerpta historica* (London, 1831), p. 248; *LPFD*, III, part one (1519–23), no. 1285; III, part two (1521–3), no. 2145 (8). In a spectacular *coup de theatre*, Rivers entered the lists at a royal tournament in 1478 'armed in the habitt of a white hermite', complete with a mobile hermitage drawn on a pageant cart: W.H. Black (ed.), *Illustrations of ancient state and chivalry* (Edinburgh, 1839), p. 33.

82   *CCR, 1385–89*, p. 623. For Brocas, see Roskell, Clark and Rawcliffe (eds), *The Commons 1386–1421*, ii, pp. 359–62.

83   BL, MS Sloane 1584, f. 90v.

that Norman Tanner analysed in his study of the Church in late medieval Norwich include a legacy to one or more of the city's hermits, whereas a significantly larger total of 155 mention recluses.[84] It would be unwise to conclude that anchorites (who were far more numerous) exerted correspondingly greater popular appeal, since we have no idea how much support for hermits was forthcoming from ordinary people on an *ad hoc* daily basis, in the way of food, fuel and other basic necessities. Yet it does appear that specific personal or familial factors, beyond the demands of conventional piety, may have prompted a testator to contemplate this type of provision.

There is ample evidence elsewhere that successful merchants, and even those of artisan status, were actively sponsoring hermits and providing them with appropriate accommodation. In Pontefract, for example, in 1404 a mason and his wife gave Laurence Green, hermit and chaplain, the life tenancy of a dwelling that adjoined another hermitage situated in a neighbour's garden.[85] The idea of hermits congregating together cheek by jowl may seem strange to those of us who associate the eremitical life with solitude and contemplation in remote places. Yet it made complete sense in both a pragmatic and a spiritual context. As Tom Licence points out, few English hermits, however rustic, have ever lived completely alone, being accompanied by servants and attracting eager disciples from the outset.[86] By the later Middle Ages the concept of the 'solitary' life had, moreover, been effectively internalised – in an urban setting, at least, where companionship was actively encouraged. Richard Furness had a boy (*puer*) named John Sylver to care for him in his old age, while others relied upon their younger acolytes.[87] In 1353 William Lyouns, who had occupied the hermitage at Cripplegate, London, for eighteen years, complained to Edward III that he was 'broken with such bodily weakness through age that he [could] not personally attend to the rule and repair of the houses and buildings of the hermitage or seek his food elsewhere without the aid of another'. The king accordingly permitted Thomas de Saham, a chaplain, 'to dwell with and assist him' on the understanding that he would succeed Lyouns as hermit there for the rest of his life.[88] Such arrangements not only ensured that elderly hermits were well looked after but also enabled impressionable recruits to become acclimatised to their new lives without succumbing to the many tempting distractions described by the author of *Dives and Pauper*.[89]

A letter of 1423 from the mayor and leading inhabitants of Sudbury in Suffolk to the bishop of Norwich casts a fascinating light on this practice, which may well

---

84 Tanner, *Church in late medieval Norwich*, Appendix 7.

85 BL, Stowe Charter 469.

86 Licence, *Hermits and recluses*, pp. 16, 58–9, 98–100.

87 NRO, NCC Reg. Jekkys, ff. 15v–16r; Tanner, *Church in late medieval Norwich*, pp. 233–4.

88 *CPR, 1334–38*, p. 165; *1350–54*, p. 431. Not long afterwards, in 1372, a London scrivener left money to Friar Richard de Swepeston, a hermit who was living with Geoffrey, his companion, near the church of St Laurence Jewry: R.R. Sharpe (ed.), *Calendar of wills proved and enrolled in the court of husting, London*, 2 vols in 3 (London, 1889–90), ii, p. 147.

89 'Hyme owght nott to go alone yff he may gett a nother hermett with hyme or elles any other chyld or seruand [...] for dred of fallyng in temptacion off flestly lustes thorow vanites off the world': BL, MS Sloane 1584, f. 93.

have been adopted at Norwich. One Richard Appleby, 'a man as to oure conscience knowen a trewe membre of holy cherche and a gode gostly levere [good, pious man]', had sought admission to the order of hermits, only to be told that he must first find appropriate lodging 'in a solytary place where virtues myght increce and vices to be exiled'. To this end, the townsmen had arranged for him to live with their resident hermit, John Levyngton, in 'his solytarye place and heremytage' in the churchyard of St Gregory's.[90] Levyngton's reputation extended as far as Norwich, for he subsequently received a bequest of 40s from Furness's patron, Robert Baxter, in his will of 1429.[91] Since St Gregory's was associated with an adjacent college of priests, it would seem that he was in some respects very similar to Furness in the range of his ecclesiastical and aldermanic connections and the admiration that he so obviously inspired among the laity. Hermits, or at least the right kind of hermits, clearly ranked as a communal asset, whose mere presence brought spiritual benefits to all.

It is difficult to generalise about a group of men who ranged from the busy and well-connected priest Richard Furness to Robert Goddard, whose work on the city's gates and in its ditches conforms more closely to the conventional image of the late medieval hermit as a manual labourer of humble origins. As none of our men is known to have been the recipient of a papal or episcopal indulgence or of royal letters allowing him to raise money for particular projects it is impossible to tell how many of Norwich's other hermits undertook or helped to supervise work on the city's infrastructure.[92] Nor, curiously, do any of them appear to have been officially licensed to pursue their vocation. Indeed, only one hermit in the whole of our period, John Tourney, is on record as making his profession before the bishop of Norwich; and his letters testimonial were awarded as a personal favour to Sir Robert Radcliffe, Lord Fitzwalter, his presumed patron, in 1506.[93]

The elderly monk Richard Walsham, released by his prior to lead a life of prayer and contemplation in his comfortable hillside hermitage, is in many respects reminiscent of an earlier world, when hermits kept a (relative) distance from society, although not even he was spared the constant bustle of life at a busy shrine. More typical are individuals such as John Levot, who performed his pastoral ministry among people who had known him and his family for years. The assumption that

---

90   NRO, DN Reg. 5/9, f. 112r.

91   NRO, NCC, Reg. Surflete, f. 86v.

92   See, for example, the papal indulgence of 1443 to those who visited and gave alms for the repair of the pilgrim chapel of St Andrew at Stalham in Norfolk, where the hermit John Kylbourn lived: J.A. Twemlow (ed.), *Calendar of entries in the papal registers relating to Great Britain and Ireland: Papal letters, 1431–1447* (London, 1912), p. 333; and, more generally, Jones, *Hermits and anchorites*, pp. 114–17.

93   NRO, DN Reg. 9/14, f. 54r. The licensing of a hermit and the grant of an indulgence might go together, as in the case of Stephen Coye, who made his profession with great formality before Bishop Bekynton on 20 June 1445. An episcopal indulgence of forty days was issued on 16 July following to those who gave alms to him for the upkeep of the road between Bristol and Dundry: H.C. Maxwell-Lyte and M.C.B. Dawes (eds), *The register of Thomas Bekynton, bishop of Bath and Wells, 1443–1465*, 2 vols, Somerset Record Society 49–50 (London, 1934–5), i, nos 121, 132.

the late medieval hermit was not 'officially a member of the community' and derived much of his authority from the fact that he 'stood outside' the formal structure of the parish needs some modification, at least with regard to a city such as Norwich, whose hermits appear to have been closely integrated into parochial life.[94] And although Richard Furness soon outgrew the narrow confines of St Giles's, his original home, it is hard not to see him as a member of the establishment, distributing doles on behalf of wealthy aldermen and helping to shape the 'devout society' that attracted pious members of the civic elite. He was anything but detached.

It is telling, in this context, that we have no evidence of hermits living in the northern, less affluent, parts of the city, where they might potentially have been more useful. Nor do they seem to have attracted much in the way of donations there. St Paul's church and the adjacent hospital were dedicated jointly to the Apostle Paul and St Paul, 'the first hermit, who was the reputed patron of such diseased poor as were obliged to retire from the world as Paul did to his hermitage in the wilderness'.[95] Yet none of the known testators from this parish left anything to a hermit, named or otherwise.[96] Both Thomas Basset and Richard Furness made modest bequests to the sisters of the hospital, who pursued a quasi-religious vocation and enjoyed widespread support from the prominent citizens among whom Furness moved.[97] It seems, however, that the overwhelming focus of eremitical activity lay south of the river, in areas where individual patronage and collective approbation were more readily forthcoming (see Map 4.1). Significantly, in a city as ostentatiously religious as Norwich, no attempt seems to have been made by the ruling elite to establish a chapel, perhaps furnished with relics or a miraculous image, where prayers might be said by a hermit and donations collected for the upkeep of public works, as happened, for example, in Lynn, Maidenhead and Southampton.[98] On balance, we may conclude that Norwich's hermits relied less upon institutional encouragement than upon personal connections, akin to the ties of 'good lordship' that bound members of secular society in a network of mutual benefit and assistance.

---

94   Sauer, 'English eremitic tradition', p. 167.
95   Blomefield, *Topographical history*, iv, pp. 429–30.
96   The parishioners' wills were proved in a separate jurisdiction because St Paul's lay in Blofield Hundred: NRO, DCN/69.
97   NRO, NCC Reg. Surflete, f. 169r–v; Reg. Jekkys, ff. 15v–16r. For the hospital and its sisters see Hill, *Women and religion*, pp. 161–6 and C. Rawcliffe, *The hospitals of medieval Norwich*, Studies in East Anglian History 2 (Norwich, 1995), chapter two.
98   For the hermitage outside Southampton, whose incumbent shared with the townspeople the right to stage an annual fair, see *CPR, 1494–1509*, pp. 61–2; J. Silvester Davis, *A history of Southampton* (Southampton, 1883), pp. 230–1; and for Lynn and Maidenhead nn. 7 and 71 above.

Chapter 5

Glimpses of late medieval religion in Suffolk and elsewhere: evidence from the cult of King Henry VI

Heather Falvey

On 7 November 1490 two young girls were piling up straw in a barn. As the pile grew bigger and bigger, Marian Cowpar clambered on top of it and reached down to gather the straw being offered up on a pitchfork by her companion. Then, leaning over to take the next lot of straw, Marian fell forward onto the pitchfork, one prong puncturing her throat, the other piercing her jaw almost to her left ear; indeed, the latter prong went through her Adam's apple. The screams of the other girl brought neighbours running to the scene. Initially blood was gushing everywhere, and there was also internal bleeding; indeed, all feared that Marian had died. Then, inspired by the Holy Spirit, some of the crowd remembered the blessed King Henry and vowed to visit his tomb, whereupon the outflow of blood ceased and Marian was restored, without needing any medical assistance. Soon afterwards a group of neighbours who had witnessed the event, together with the healthy girl, visited the tomb at Windsor and there gave thanks to God for the miracle that had occurred.[1] When recorded at Windsor, the miracle was said to have taken place at 'Alborne', Suffolk. Knox and Leslie, editors of the English text of King Henry's miracles, noted that 'There does not appear to be any Albourne [*sic*] in Suffolk' and suggested that therefore it was either a mistake for Albourne in *Sussex*, near Cuckfield, or even Aldeburgh in Suffolk.[2] But *An historical atlas of Suffolk* indicates that there was a parish called 'Alnesbourn Priory' on the river Orwell, between Ipswich and Nacton.[3] It was this small parish that was the site of one of the recorded miracles attributed to Henry VI.[4]

---

1   The Latin text of the miracle was published in P. Grosjean (ed.), *Henrici VI Angliae Regis miracula postuma* (Subsidia Hagiographica, xxii, Brussels, 1935), pp. 246–7; earlier it was summarised in R. Knox and S. Leslie, *The miracles of King Henry VI: being an account and translation of twenty-three miracles taken from the manuscript in the British Museum (Royal 13c.viii) with Introduction by …* (Cambridge, 1923), pp. 187–8. It is miracle 134: I have produced my own translation. Note that in Grosjean both the lengthy introduction and the full Latin text of the miracles are paginated from page 1; in this chapter the pagination given for this book relates to the text of the miracles unless otherwise stated.

2   Knox and Leslie, *Miracles*, p. 187.

3   P. Northeast, '24. Religious Houses', in D. Dymond and E. Martin (eds), *An historical atlas of Suffolk*, 2nd edn, Suffolk Institute of Archaeology and History (Ipswich, 1989), p. 55.

4   J. Middleton-Stewart, *Inward purity and outward splendour: death and remembrance in the deanery of Dunwich, Suffolk, 1370–1547* (Woodbridge, 2001), p. 129 n. 76, indicates that two Suffolk

The other Suffolk miracle credited to the king was quite different and this *miraculé* can be identified in several other historical records.[5] Richard Swettock became rector of Bildeston in 1442.[6] The probate register 'Baldwyne' of the archdeaconry of Sudbury includes eight Bildeston wills of which this priest was either executor or witness.[7] He probably died in 1491, having been rector for nearly fifty years.[8] When his miracle occurred sir Richard was a very old man. He had become so deaf that, however close he stood, he was unable to hear the singing of clerks or the sound of pealing bells; indeed, over a period of ten weeks his hearing deteriorated even further. He was heartbroken because Lent was approaching 'when a rector ought to watch with a special diligence over the healing of the weaknesses of his flock'. As he knew that he was unfit to exercise the care of his flock he prayed to King Henry for help, promising to 'hasten even on foot to his holy shrine'. On Sunday his deafness had gone and he declared to all that his hearing had never been so good. The old priest may simply have been suffering from a severe build-up of wax which subsequently dispersed; nevertheless, he believed that his deafness had been cured as a result of his prayers to King Henry and, even at his great age, travelled, with some of his parishioners, all the way to the king's tomb at Windsor to give thanks and record his miracle.[9]

The cult of Henry VI

This chapter considers evidence for the cult of Henry VI, or lack of it, in various Suffolk parishes and at Bassingbourn (Cambridgeshire), St Albans (Hertfordshire) and Eversholt (Bedfordshire). In so doing it draws on details from some of David

---

miracles of Henry VI were reported: number 49 at Bildeston (of which more below) and the other at Alnesbourn.

5   Full Latin text in Grosjean, *Henrici VI*, pp. 127–8; brief summary in Knox and Leslie, *Miracles*, p. 111; miracle 49. This miracle has been translated in full and discussed in detail by the late Dr Lesley Boatwright: 'Henry VI cures a deaf clergyman', *Ricardian Bulletin* (March 2010), pp. 41–2; the author has briefly discussed it in H. Falvey, '*Miracles* in everyday life: the ordinary and the miraculous', *Ricardian Bulletin* (September 2012), pp. 44–7.

6   Lesley noted that David Dymond had supplied her with information concerning Swettock's incumbency at Bildeston; F.S. Growse, *Materials for a history of the parish of Bildeston …* (privately printed, revised edition 1892), p. 8 records that he was instituted in the church of Bildeston on 2 December 1442 at Hoxne, after the previous rector resigned.

7   P. Northeast (ed.), *Wills of the archdeaconry of Sudbury 1439–1474, part I, 1439–1461*, Suffolk Records Society XLIV (Woodbridge, 2011), nos 415, 744, 1486; P. Northeast and H. Falvey (eds), *Wills of the archdeaconry of Sudbury, 1439–1474: Wills from the register 'Baldwyne', Part II: 1461–1474*, Suffolk Records Society LIII (Woodbridge, 2010), nos 284, 303, 431, 720, 721.

8   On 14 March 1490/91 'William Coke, priest, was canonically instituted rector in the parish church "Bilston", vacant by the death of *dominus* Richard Swaetok the last rector there': Growse, *Bildeston*, p. 8. As he could not have been ordained priest until he was twenty-three, he was probably born in about 1419.

9   The miracle is undated but the account states that he recounted the miracle at Windsor on 7 October (year not given).

Dymond's publications, as well as other documentary evidence, to demonstrate not only the wide variety of images that might be present in late medieval parish churches but also the different strategies by which testators might seek assistance from King Henry, and indeed other saints.

The main documentary evidence for the king's cult is a collection of testimonies made by witnesses and *miraculés* recorded at Windsor during the late fifteenth century.[10] The first datable recorded miracle occurred in 1481 and the last in 1500.[11] Originally Henry VI had been interred at Chertsey Abbey, but in 1484 Richard III had the king's remains transferred to St George's Chapel, Windsor.[12] There an ornate tomb was constructed, situated to the right of the high altar and near to the shrine of Master John Schorn.[13] Popular devotion to Henry VI had commenced during the reign of Edward IV and in 1494 Henry VII 'took steps to glorify [his own] royal line' by applying to the pope for the canonisation of his Lancastrian forebear.[14] A papal bull was issued by Alexander VI instructing Cardinal Morton, archbishop of Canterbury, to appoint a commission to report on the miracles of Henry VI. Reports of miracles were gathered at Windsor, including details of some that had been reported at Chertsey, although ultimately Henry VI was never canonised. As the examples of Marian Cowpar's and Richard Swettock's miracles indicate, ordinary folk not only thought to, or were inspired to, call on the blessed Henry for assistance in times of trouble, accident or illness but also subsequently travelled to Windsor to give thanks at his tomb.[15] These miracles thus provide glimpses of faith, and, almost incidentally, of daily life, and of long-distance travel in the late medieval period.

---

10 For the cult and miracles of Henry VI, in addition to Grosjean, and Knox and Leslie, see, for example, L.A. Craig, 'Royalty, virtue and adversity: the cult of Henry VI', *Albion*, XXXV (2003), pp. 187–209; A. Hanham, 'Henry VI and his miracles', *The Ricardian*, XII/48 (March 2000), pp. 638–52; D. Piroyansky, *Martyrs in the making: political martyrdom in late medieval England* (Basingstoke, 2008), pp. 74–98; B. Spencer, 'King Henry of Windsor and the London pilgrim', in J. Bird, H. Chapman and J. Clark (eds), *Collectanea Londiniensia: studies in London archaeology and history presented to Ralph Merrifield*, London and Middlesex Archaeological Society special paper 2 (London, 1978), pp. 235–64.

11 For details of the dating and compilation of the miracles see Knox and Leslie, *Miracles*, pp. 16–29.

12 See, for example, R. Griffiths, 'The burials of King Henry VI at Chertsey and Windsor', in N. Saul and T. Tatton-Brown (eds), *St George's Chapel, Windsor: history and heritage* (Wimborne Minster, 2010), pp. 100–07.

13 For the tomb and its environs see T. Tatton-Brown, 'The constructional sequence and topography of the chapel and college buildings at St George's', in C. Richmond and E. Scarff (eds), *St George's chapel in the late Middle Ages*, Dean and Canons of Windsor (Windsor, 2001), pp. 3–38. For Master John Schorn see, for example, R. Marks, 'A late medieval pilgrimage cult: Master John Schorn of North Marston and Windsor', in L. Keen and E. Scarff (eds), *Windsor: Medieval archaeology, art and architecture of the Thames Valley*, British Archaeological Association, Conference Transactions, XXV (Leeds, 2002), pp. 192–207.

14 Knox and Leslie, *Miracles*, p. 3.

15 Eamon Duffy has written at length on the veneration of saints by late medieval people: E. Duffy, *The stripping of the altars: traditional religion in England 1400–1580* (New Haven and London, 1992), pp. 169–83.

So what was the appeal of Henry VI? Some historians have suggested that the cult was mainly a political phenomenon.[16] Undoubtedly the attempts to canonise him were politically motivated; indeed, two of the miracles occurred when victims' families preferred to call on Henry VI to cure 'the King's Evil' rather than take the victims to the reigning Yorkist monarch to be touched.[17] Nevertheless, most of the reported miracles relate to tragedies or difficulties that occurred during the course of daily life. In general, as Leigh Ann Craig has pointed out, 'Henry's devotees honored [*sic*] not only his piety and generosity, but also the positive example he set for those experiencing adversity'.[18] Eamon Duffy has argued that 'the English laity looked to the saints not primarily as exemplars or soul-friends, but as powerful helpers and healers in time of need.'[19] Indeed, despite the controversy surrounding the circumstances of his death, King Henry was not necessarily viewed as a martyr, but was counted among these holy helpers. Generally he was simply described as 'the blessed king Henry', but in a will written at St Albans he was, unusually, styled 'the blessed Henry king and martyr'.[20] His popularity can be demonstrated by the sheer number of pilgrim badges from his shrine at Windsor that have been discovered. In 1998 Brian Spencer noted that nearly 400 Henry VI pilgrim badges of differing styles had then been found; the only English pilgrimage site from which significantly more badges have survived is Canterbury, and that shrine was in existence for some 350 years, whereas the Windsor badges must have been generated in no more than fifty years.[21]

There are 174 recorded miracles attributed to Henry VI.[22] Whereas the surviving testimonies by witnesses and *miraculés* provide the most graphic evidence of the posthumous veneration of Henry VI, there are a number of other types of documentary record that provide further evidence of his cult, such as wills, inventories of church goods and churchwardens' accounts. As well as revealing devotion to Henry VI these documents shed light on other aspects of late medieval religion.[23] The terminal date

---

16 See, for example, J.W. McKenna, 'Piety and propaganda: the cult of King Henry VI', in B. Rowland (ed.), *Chaucer and Middle English studies in honour of Rossell Hope Robbins* (London, 1974), pp. 72–88; and the more balanced view in S. Walker, 'Political saints in later medieval England', in R.H. Britnell and A.J. Pollard (eds), *The McFarlane legacy: studies in late medieval politics and society* (Stroud, 1995), pp. 77–106.

17 Knox and Leslie, *Miracles*, no. 46 (Richard III) and no. 74, while Henry's tomb was at Chertsey, so probably Edward IV. These miracles inadvertently indicate that those two monarchs did touch of the King's Evil; such evidence is otherwise lacking for their reigns.

18 Craig, 'Royalty', p. 200.

19 Duffy, *Stripping of the altars*, p. 178.

20 See below for the discussion of the will of Isabel Lewis of St Peter's parish in St Albans.

21 B. Spencer, *Pilgrim souvenirs and secular badges. Museum of London medieval finds from excavations in London*, vol. 7 (London, 1998), pp. 189–92, at p. 189.

22 Grosjean's analysis of the original manuscript (BL MS Royal 13 C viii) shows that although the text, or heading notes, of 174 miracles have survived, the erratic numbering of the miracles in the manuscript indicate that originally at least 368 had been recorded. Grosjean, *Henrici VI*, pp. 25–30.

23 Various artefacts have also survived, such as the pilgrim badges from Windsor and paintings of Henry VI on rood screens: these have been discussed at length elsewhere. See, for example,

applied here is September 1538, when Thomas Cromwell's second set of Injunctions 'outlawed not merely pilgrimage, but virtually the entire manifestation of the cult of the saints'. From then on 'no candles, tapers, or images of wax [were] to be set before any image or picture': the only lights allowed were those by the rood-loft, before the sacrament and by the sepulchre.[24]

Saints' images at Bassingbourn

Dymond's introduction to his published transcript of the Bassingbourn churchwardens' book, and associated documents, demonstrates the value of such records and also the need to read them with care and understanding.[25] Within medieval parish churches were numerous altars and images dedicated not only to Our Lady, Jesus Christ, the Holy Trinity and, often, the patronal saint, but also to various other saints. As most images were destroyed during the Reformation historians are reliant on surviving documentary evidence to illuminate a parish church's interior. Recorded at Bassingbourn in April 1498 and revised in 1503 was an inventory of church goods. The amended inventory reveals the presence in the church of St Peter and St Paul of fifteen images of, for example, St Katherine and of the Annunciation of Our Lady (perhaps in alabaster); cloths 'pyctured' with 'ymages' of, for example, St Nicholas, St Peter and St Andrew; and images within tabernacles, such as those of St Katherine and St James.[26] The churchwardens' accounts reveal a further five images, presumably acquired after 1503.[27]

Richard Marks has described the way in which images were displayed in a church. 'They would have stood in their own designated space in the church and would have been raised on pedestals or brackets'. Some had flat backs, 'indicating that they were placed against a pillar or framed by a niche or a wooden tabernacle'.[28] Surviving at All Saints' Icklingham (Suffolk) is an 'elaborately decorated fourteenth-century niche or "tabernacle"', which, although considerably damaged, 'still shows the shadow of its original saintly image' (Plate 5.1).[29]

Although images were present in a parish church, how they had been acquired by the parish is not clear. While one might suppose that (relatively wealthy) testators might have bequeathed an image to their parish church, I have not found any unequivocal such bequests in the various volumes of published wills that I have consulted for this

---

Spencer, 'London pilgrim'; R. Marks, 'Images of Henry VI', in J. Stratford (ed.), *The Lancastrian court*, proceedings of the 2001 Harlaxton symposium; Harlaxton Medieval Studies XIII (Donington, 2003), pp. 111–24. Some of Marks' documentary evidence has been examined in detail in this chapter.

24 Duffy, *Stripping of the altars*, p. 407.

25 D. Dymond (ed.), *The churchwardens' book of Bassingbourn, Cambridgeshire 1496–c.1540*, Cambridgeshire Records Society 17 (Cambridge, 2004).

26 *Ibid.*, pp. 3, 9, 13, 20.

27 *Ibid.*, pp. 13, 19, 20, 58, 120, 139, 142.

28 Marks, 'Images of Henry VI', p. 121.

29 D. Dymond, *The business of the Suffolk parish, 1558–1625*, SIAH (Needham Market, 2018), p. 33, plate 19; quotation from text describing the plate.

chapter. There are, however, bequests to have images repaired or beautified, such as the bequest in 1501 of 3s 4d by Richard Sely of Bassingbourn for the painting of the images of St Nicholas and St Christopher; and the bequest in 1525 of 3s 4d by John Tryge of Bassingbourn for 'Saint Margaret heyd mending'.[30] We do know, however, that a parish might raise funds to purchase an image, as did Bassingbourn in 1521–2 when that parish finally took possession of an image of St George costing over £16, having commenced raising money for it in 1511.[31] Bassingbourn had also paid for the carving of an image of St Margaret sometime before February 1507.[32]

Very few English pre-Reformation images have survived, but many of those that have were brought together for the *Gothic* exhibition at the Victoria & Albert Museum in 2003 and are pictured in the exhibition's catalogue. These include St Christopher in alabaster; St George and the dragon in alabaster, and also in polychromed oak; St Margaret in sandstone; St Sitha in alabaster; and an alabaster relief of the Twelve Apostles.[33] And, for our purposes, the most important is a late fifteenth-century alabaster image of Henry VI (Plate 5.2). Regarding this image, Eleanor Townsend has noted that

> The orb and sceptre, as well as the crown, signify Henry's true kingship, asserted strongly under his anti-Yorkist successors, the Tudors. The inclusion of the heraldic beasts [a lion and an antelope] also constitutes a particular political statement and they were found on many images of Henry VI created after his death.[34]

The two beasts emphasised his Lancastrian royalty: the lion was the principal royal heraldic beast and he had an antelope on his heraldic badge, as had both his grandfather, Henry IV, and his father, Henry V. Nevertheless, this particular image is likely to have been a devotional statue.[35]

The cult of Henry VI at Walberswick (Suffolk)

There is no indication in the Bassingbourn accounts that the parish possessed an image of Henry VI, but churchwardens' accounts from elsewhere do record the presence of images or pictures of the king. For example, at Walberswick in 1497 Edmund Wryth was paid 3s 6d for 'Removynd [renovating] of Kyng Herry ys taball

---

30   Dymond (ed.), *Bassingbourn*, pp. 166, 177.

31   *Ibid.*, p. lxvii.

32   *Ibid.*, pp. 58–9.

33   R. Marks and P. Williamson (eds), *Gothic: art for England 1400–1547* (London, 2003), St Christopher (catalogue entry 283); St George & dragon (entries 84 and 284); St Margaret (entry 280 and plate 43); St Sitha (entry 281 and plate 28); 12 Apostles (entry 267).

34   *Ibid.*, catalogue entry 323 and plate 21; text by Eleanor Townsend. The statue is now held in the Rijksmuseum, Amsterdam; its provenance is unknown.

35   The statues of Henry VI at King's College, Cambridge, and Eton College are celebratory images of Henry as founder of these institutions rather than devotional images.

[his table, i.e. his picture] and other kosts'.[36] Much further on in those accounts, which recorded receipts separately, it is noted that in 1497 Marg[ar]yt Rowe had paid to the wardens 2s 10d 'of mony that was gatheryd be the maydynnys that be levyd of peytyng of kyng herry tabyll' and Margery Greyve had paid 3s 6d 'of the same gatheryng'.[37] This suggests that the young women of the parish were devotees of, or at the very least venerated, King Henry to the extent that they had collected a total of 6s 4d for the renovation of a painted picture of the king that was in the church; it seems that they were not providing something completely new.[38] One could speculate that there was a link between the repainting of the picture of King Henry at the cost of Walberswick's 'maydynnys' and young Marian Cowpar's miracle that had occurred some seven years previously at Alnesbourn, about thirty miles away. But two other records indicate that it was not just the maidens at Walberswick who favoured the blessed King Henry. In 1492 Thomas White of Walberswick had asked his executors to send 1d to 'Seynt Renyons of Skotland' the next time that a pilgrim went there, and also required a pilgrim to go to 'Kynge Herry of Wyndesore'.[39] In 1509 Margaret Pynne, wife (not widow) of John Pynne, required a pilgrim to go on her behalf to Our Lady of Grace, to 'Saynt Margaret of Eston Chapell' and to 'Kyng Herry of Wyndssore'.[40] As well as revealing other parishioners' devotion to Henry VI, these two Walberswick wills confirm that testators could choose which saints they wished to honour, or rather which they hoped would intercede for their soul.[41] As Eamon Duffy notes, bequests for 'surrogate pilgrimages' might be 'designed to discharge vows of pilgrimage undertaken by the testator themselves in earlier days, but for one reason or another unfulfilled'.[42] We cannot know why these particular pilgrimages were requested, but

---

36 R.W.M. Lewis (ed.), *Walberswick churchwardens' accounts, AD 1450–1499* (Ashford, 1947), p. 79. The word has been transcribed as 'Removynd': does it mean 'removing'; or even 'renewing' or 'renovating'?

37 *Ibid.*, p. 261.

38 The text seems to indicate that Wryth had taken down an existing table; perhaps it was to be more expensively painted. Lewis notes that a new parish church had been completed and hallowed in 1493 on site of a chapel of St Andrew: *ibid.*, p. iv.

39 SROI, IC AA2/3/152r, Thomas White of Walberswick. Presumably St Regulus, who brought St Andrew's bones to Scotland; the dedication of Walberswick church was to St Andrew.

40 SROI, IC AA2/5/80v–81r, Margaret Pynne of Walberswick. There is a possible link between the two wills: both testators appointed two executors, one of which was John Edmundes (although these might be two different men, as the wills were written seventeen years apart). There was a shrine to Our Lady of Grace just outside the west gate of the medieval town wall of Ipswich, which is marked by a plaque and a statue of Our Lady on Lady Lane. <http://stmaryattheelms. org.uk/st_mary_at_the_elms/Shrine.html>, accessed 19 November 2019. Perhaps 'Saynt Margaret of Eston chapell' was at All Saints, Easton? Or even at St Nicholas, Easton Bavents, now in the sea (north of Southwold, so not far from Walberswick)? See entries for those parishes on the Suffolk churches website <http://www.suffolkchurches.co.uk>, accessed 19 November 2019.

41 Middleton-Stewart mentioned briefly the connections between Walberswick and the cult of Henry VI: Middleton-Stewart, *Inward purity*, p. 129.

42 Duffy, *Stripping of the altars*, p. 194.

both testators wished to be represented at Windsor as well as at other sites, whether in Scotland or elsewhere in Suffolk.

The cult of Henry VI at St Albans

Some of the most frequent religious bequests in pre-Reformation wills were of money or wax for 'lights' within the parish church: that is, a candle or taper to burn before a particular image or picture, or before an altar dedicated to a particular saint. Indeed, Duffy explains that 'Before the altars and images lights were set, and the maintenance of these lights, especially during times of service, became the single most popular expression of piety in the wills of the late medieval laity'.[43] From collections of wills it is possible to determine in which parishes particular saints were venerated, although such investigations are, of course, dependent on survival of late medieval wills, which is patchy to say the least. Here I have made use (mostly) of published wills to consider the range of images within two parish churches, both of which possessed an image of King Henry; first, one of the parishes within the town of St Albans in Hertfordshire and, second, the rural parish of Eversholt in Bedfordshire.

Analysis of bequests in wills made by testators in the three urban parishes of St Albans (St Andrew's chapel in parish of the Abbey, St Michael and St Peter) between 1471 and 1500 reveals that just one will, that of Isabel Lewis, included a bequest for the maintenance of a light in honour of 'the blessed Henry king and martyr'.[44] This, nevertheless, indicates that at that time there was an image of King Henry in St Peter's church.[45] Of the 108 St Peter's wills, thirty included bequests to lights, images or altars.[46] Some simply made a bequest to the rood (or crucifix) light, the light of Our Lady and/

---

43 Duffy, *Stripping of the altars*, p. 134.

44 S. Flood (ed.), *St Albans wills 1471–1500*, Hertfordshire Record Society IX (Hitchin, 1993), p. 110, will no. 229, Isabel Lewis, lately wife of Robert (date of will printed as 24 May 1494; proved 12 May 1493 [sic]). The original is Hertfordshire Archives and Local Studies, 2AR68r, dated 24 May 1493. The date of the will seems to have been incorrectly recorded in the register because it was proved on 12 May 1493; perhaps the will was written on 24 *April* 1493. The published will is noted by Marks, 'Images of Henry VI', p. 115. No mention of anything relating to the cult of Henry VI was found in the published wills from the Hertfordshire parishes of Kings Langley and Sarratt, nor in the very extensive churchwardens' accounts of Bishops Stortford: Lionel M. Munby (ed.), *Life & death in Kings Langley 1498–1659* (Kings Langley, 1981); P. Buller and B. Buller (eds), *Pots, platters & ploughs: Sarratt wills & inventories 1435–1832* (Sarratt, 1982); S.S. Doree (ed.), *Early churchwardens' accounts of Bishops Stortford, 1431–1558*, Hertfordshire Record Society X (Hitchin, 1994).

45 The published version of the will simply records a light to 'blessed King Henry' but the original clearly states '*b[ea]ti Henric[i] Reg[is] & martir[is]*' ('the blessed Henry king and martyr').

46 It is difficult to ascertain the exact number of wills by parishioners of St Peter's: as there was no parochial churchyard for the abbey parish (St Andrew's) parishioners there usually requested burial in St Peter's churchyard. Of the 303 published wills, ten testators did not specify where they wished to be buried; 104 requested burial other than at St Peter's; eighty-one requested burial at St Peter's but were parishioners of St Andrew's; thus the author has calculated that 108 were wills of St Peter's parishioners.

or the Holy Trinity light (there was a guild of the Holy Trinity in the parish). A few others mentioned specific images, such as John Payes, a fletcher, who requested a 2d wax candle to burn before St Erasmus on the day of his death.[47] In complete contrast, in 1493 Isabel Lewis made bequests of 4d to each of fifteen particular lights and four specific altars. Omitting her bequests to various images of the Virgin, the rood and the Holy Trinity, Isabel's bequests included lights before images or altars of fourteen different saints; the other 107 testators of St Peter's parish mentioned only seven saints between them. Moreover, only five were common to both sets of bequests. Thus, without Isabel Lewis's will we would be unaware of eight images in St Peter's (King Henry, St Anne, St Clement, St Giles, St Mary Magdalen, St Nicholas, St Thomas of Canterbury and St Ursula) and of the altar of St Lawrence. The only two images that she did not mention were those of St Christopher and St Michael.[48] Without her will, our picture of late medieval St Peter's would be dimly lit, and historians of the cult of King Henry would be unaware of another location wherein he was venerated.[49] Furthermore, this collection of wills from St Peter's underlines the fact that religious bequests in wills might be highly individual, and not necessarily prompted by the cleric or scribe who actually wrote the will.

There is, indeed, another very faint link between St Albans and the cult of King Henry. In 1808 Henry Cook, an artist and printmaker, produced pictures of two paintings recently discovered in the parish church of St Michael in St Albans: one was of the Last Judgement, sometimes known as 'Doom', the other a crowned king's head. He described them thus:

> The greatest part [of the St Michael's doom] was Painted in Distemper upon the Wall, but the lower part, which is distinguished in the print by a semicircular Mark, was Painted in Oil Colors [*sic*] upon a Board shaped so as to fill up the Arch in the Wall. At the same time the Head of a King, believed to be that of Henry the 6th painted in Distemper upon Board, was found fixed to the Wall in the same Church.[50]

---

47   Flood, *St Albans wills*, will no. 78.

48   Flood assumed that the image of St Michael was in St Peter's: the stated place of burial was damaged and the testator mentioned the image of St Sithe which another had mentioned as being in St Peter's. (There is no mention of an image of St Michael in St Michael's parish church in wills from that parish.)

49   In his most recent book, Eamon Duffy states that there was an image of King Henry in St Albans Abbey: E. Duffy, *Royal books and holy bones: essays in medieval Christianity* (London, 2018), p. 196. This is not the case: the image was in St Peter's. Duffy cites as his source Marks, 'Images of Henry VI', but Marks only gives details of the image of Henry VI mentioned in the will of Isabel Lewis.

50   The doom painting is entitled 'A Representation of a Painting Discovered in the Church of St Michael, St Alban's, in the County of Hertford: in October 1808, upon taking down some Boards which had served as a cover or Lining of the Ancient Rood Loft between the Nave and Chancel of the Church': BL, Maps K.Top.15.49.z. The doom is remarkably simple and bears no resemblance to, for example, that in Holy Trinity, Coventry. I would suggest that the doom painting at St Michael's was a painted board erected in the reign of Mary, when such artefacts were used to replace rood paintings that had been white-washed over during the previous reign.

Cook produced a painting of the doom and an etching of the head of Henry VI. So, although none of the St Michael's wills mentioned a light to King Henry, there appears to have been a picture of him there apparently 'affixed to the Rood Loft over the Centre of a Painting representing the Last Judgement'.[51]

None of the miracles attributed to the king occurred in St Albans. The three recorded Hertfordshire miracles took place at Barnet, Berkhamsted and Elstree.[52] Although none of these was far distant from St Albans, it was perhaps the king's personal connections with the town that inspired the image in St Peter's and the picture in St Michael's: he had been present at both the first and second battles of St Albans (22 May 1455 and 17 February 1461), and he and his wife, Margaret of Anjou, had visited the town and the abbey on several occasions.[53]

The cult of Henry VI at Eversholt

Richard Marks identified two parishes in the neighbouring county of Bedfordshire that also possessed an image of Henry VI: Houghton Regis and Eversholt.[54] At Houghton Regis four testators specifically mentioned the image there of Henry VI.[55] The single Eversholt will that mentioned an image of Henry VI is that of William Barnewell, made in May 1533.[56] Whereas the only published late medieval Hertfordshire wills are those from St Albans, medieval and early sixteenth-century wills from Bedfordshire have been published in six volumes.[57] A thorough search of these revealed just eight other Eversholt wills written between 1480 and 1538.[58] Like Isabel Lewis' bequests, those of

---

51 The etching of the king's head is entitled 'A Copy of the Head of a King, believed to be that of Henry the 6.th painted in Distemper upon Board, which was discovered in October 1808 in the Church of St. Michael. St. Alban, in the County of Hertford, affixed to the Rood Loft over the Centre of a Painting representing the Last Judgement, which was discovered at the same time' (published in 1810): BL, Maps K.Top.15.49.aa. It has been reproduced in J.D. Lee (compiler), *A fifteenth century pilgrimage in honour of King Henry the sixth*, Henry VI Society (Southwark, 1975), p. 27.

52 *Miracles* 13, 54 and 147 in Knox and Leslie, *Miracles*, pp. 56–7, 113–14, 196.

53 See, for example, P. Burley, M. Elliott and H. Watson, *The battles of St Albans* (Barnsley, 2007).

54 Marks, 'Images of Henry VI', p. 115. Two other churches, St Paul's Bedford and Harlington, apparently had windows with representations of the king.

55 See H. Falvey, 'Illuminating late medieval religion: aspects of the cult of King Henry VI', *The Ricardian*, XXIX (2019), pp. 13–34.

56 Bedfordshire Archive Service, ABR/R3/183, ff.103v–104r.

57 Five volumes comprise wills from the archdeaconry of Bedford, the sixth comprises wills of Bedfordshire testators proved in the PCC. A.F. Cirket (ed.), *English Wills, 1498–1526*, BHRS 37 (Streatley, 1957); P. Bell (ed.), *Bedfordshire Wills, 1480–1519*, BHRS 45 (Bedford, 1966); P. Bell (ed.), *Bedfordshire Wills 1484–1533*, BHRS 76 (Bedford, 1997); P. Bell (ed.), *Bedfordshire Wills 1531–1539*, BFHS 3 (Bedford, 2005); P. Bell (ed.), *Bedfordshire Wills 1537–1545 and cases from the Archdeacon's Court*, BFHS 4 (Bedford, 2010); M. McGregor (ed.), *Bedfordshire Wills proved in the Prerogative Court of Canterbury, 1383–1548*, BHRS 58 (Bedford, 1979).

58 There were none in BHRS 37 and 58 or BFHS 4; three in BHRS 45 (William Gregory, will no. 45; Henry Plomer, no. 56; Thomas Bradwell, no. 59); two in BHRS 76 (Richard Sternall, no. 102;

William Barnewell were far more detailed than those of any of his fellow parishioners. In all he mentioned twenty-four lights, like Isabel Lewis giving 4d to each. Furthermore, just like the St Peter's parishioners, the other testators of St John the Baptist's, Eversholt, were far less detailed and generous in their bequests; indeed, four did not make any bequests to images or for lights.

Again omitting bequests to images of the Virgin and the rood, William Barnewell mentioned seventeen separate lights to saints' images, including two of St Catherine and two of St John; the other four testators (William Gregory, Henry Plomer, Richard Sternall and Roger Withebrede) just four. Moreover, all four of those saints were also mentioned by Barnewell; the only light in the church that he did not mention was that to 'All Souls'. Thus, without Barnewell's will we would be unaware not only of the image of Henry VI at Eversholt but also of twelve other saints' images: the church would be in almost total darkness.[59] Furthermore, Barnewell's will is again evidence of personal choice: he appointed as his executors his wife, Anne, and Richard Cowper. When Cowper made his own will in February 1536 he made no bequests to lights at all.[60] By the time that Anne made her will in March 1542 she was the widow of John Cowper and images of saints were no longer permitted in the church.[61] Moreover, William Barnewell's will had been witnessed by sir William Shepard, 'mi gostly father' (that is, his parish priest), John Jorden, Edward Deved, John Everhed and others. Just over a year later, in April 1534, Thomas Symond's will was witnessed by three of these men (sir William Shephirde 'mi gostly father', John Jorden, and John Evershed) and one other (William Gregory).[62] Like Richard Cowper, however, Symond made no bequests to lights despite his close connections with Barnewell's will. This confirms that while testators might be influenced in their religious bequests by their local cleric they exercised personal choice: it is highly likely that sir William Shepard had written both wills, but Barnewell and Symond had made very different bequests.

Why was there an image of King Henry at Eversholt? There is no obvious link between Eversholt and any of the recorded miracles: the only Bedfordshire miracle was at Luton (no. 48), some twelve miles away. Luton was, however, a market centre and at least seven Eversholt parishioners were members of the Guild of Holy Trinity, Luton: six were recorded as having a 'dirge' (*dirige*) said or sung by the guild for them after their death, and another, Ellyn Tylar, supplied two capons for the guild feast in 1545.[63] Perhaps Eversholt parishioners knew of the Luton miracle, but of course we do

---

Roger Withebrede, no. 264); and three in BFHS 3 (Thomas Symond, no. 150; Richard Cowper, no. 206; William Atslow, no. 220), William Barnewell's will is no. 104.

59   From the will of Henry Plomer of Eversholt, made in 1501, we also learn that there was a reliquary of St Hugh in that church.

60   Bell, *Bedfordshire Wills 1531–1539*, p. 113, will no. 206.

61   Bell, *Bedfordshire Wills 1537–1545*, p. 76, will no. 140.

62   Bell, *Bedfordshire Wills 1531–1539*, pp. 83–4, will no. 150.

63   B. Tearle (ed.), *The accounts of the guild of the Holy Trinity, Luton, 1526/7–1546/7* BHRS 91 (Woodbridge, 2012): Jone Draper (dirge), p. 89; Rychard Cooper (dirge), p. 114; Wylliam and Crystyan Slow (dirges), p. 160; Henry Draper (dirge), p. 169; William Gregory (dirge), p. 225; Ellyn Tylar (2 capons), p. 216.

not know when the Eversholt image was set up, and it is clear from the literature, and the above discussion, that Henry's cult was widely known and very popular.

What can we make of these wills of Isabel Lewis and William Barnewell? The obvious point is that these testators were apparently unique in their parishes regarding the details expressed in their wills, and that these two at least were making their own choices about their religious bequests. It is also striking that they were made forty years apart: one was written probably in early 1493 and the other in 1533, and thus the cult of Henry VI continued to flourish on the very eve of the Reformation (if one might be allowed the benefit of hindsight). That other testators were far less informative may have resulted from the promptings of their scribes: there is no reason to suppose that Lewis and Barnewell were any more educated than their fellow parishioners, perhaps just more determined, or more pious? We should simply be grateful that their wills are so revealing. In complete contrast, of the twelve Bassingbourn wills dated between 1494 and 1537 that Dymond published in his book only four mentioned images at all, and of these none named more than two.[64] To illustrate the number of images that there might be in a church, both in a rural setting and a small town, Eamon Duffy named the images within the churches of Stratton Strawless (Norfolk) and Faversham (Kent).[65] These are indeed long lists, not unlike those in the wills of Lewis and Barnewell, but he compiled them from bequests in *various wills* from those two parishes. Duffy's lists draw on the wills of numerous individuals making bequests to a small number of saints that cumulatively indicate a large number of images; on the other hand, the two wills from St Peter's and Eversholt indicate that *individuals* might request the intercession of numerous saints, including King Henry.

Saints' images at Long Melford (Suffolk)

As at Bassingbourn, within the records relating to Holy Trinity, Long Melford, is a pre-Reformation list of church goods.[66] This list was compiled in 1529 and annotated in 1541. It records the presence of twenty-three images and four altars; again, setting aside images of Christ, the Virgin, the Pietà and the Trinity, eighteen different saints were represented in images and would have had lights burning before them. In addition, and adding to the brightness within the church, in the Lady Chapel the image of the Virgin had attracted gifts of coats and girdles, and of jewels, i.e. beads and small silver and gold objects, that had been attached to the Virgin's 'apron'.[67] Again, as at Bassingbourn there is no evidence of an image of Henry VI at Long Melford. Considering only the fifteen published wills of Long Melford testators proved between 1461 and 1474, although several made

64 Dymond, *Bassingbourn*, pp. 157, 166, 175–6, 177.

65 Duffy, *Stripping of the altars*, pp. 155–6.

66 D. Dymond and C. Paine, *Five centuries of an English parish church: 'The state of Melford Church', Suffolk* (Cambridge, 2012), pp. 67–78.

67 Dymond and Paine, *Five centuries*, p. 70; on p. 182 they define this apron as 'an outer garment on an image of St Mary, to which votive offerings were fastened'.

bequests to the fabric of the church, none left money to the lights there, and only one, that of Thomas Sheppard, mentioned any of the images. In 1470 he left 20d to 'le payntyng' of the image of St Leonard, an image that was still there in 1529.[68]

Table 5.1 shows the various saints with images (lights) and/or altars present in the churches of Long Melford, St Peter's at St Albans, Bassingbourn and Eversholt, excluding those of Christ, the Virgin, the rood, the sepulchre, All Souls and the Trinity. These four parishes had a range of thirty-four different saints' images, or thirty-one excluding the unspecified St John and St Thomas and the image of St Michael & Our Lady. Separately, Long Melford had nineteen, St Peter's sixteen, Bassingbourn thirteen and Eversholt seventeen. Perhaps surprisingly, only three saints were common to all four: St Christopher, St Nicholas and St Catherine (assuming all four images were of the same St Catherine). And two had images of Henry VI. Table 5.1 demonstrates not only the number of images that might be found in parish churches within towns and villages in late medieval eastern England but also the wide choice available to parishioners when making bequests to lights or, indeed, when lighting candles to them during their lifetime. On the other hand, it is striking that the wills from Bassingbourn and Long Melford reveal very little about images and lights within those two churches, although admittedly the wills were only small samples from each parish, and from different date ranges. Nevertheless, without their inventories of church goods those two churches would appear almost devoid of images and set in darkness. The lesson to be emphasised here is that, as historians well know, negative evidence is dangerous: no mention of lights in late medieval parishioners' wills does not mean no images in their parish church.

A 'new' reference to the cult of Henry VI

During his search for images of Henry VI Richard Marks found references to numerous artefacts and wills that have enabled him to extend the limits of the 'territory of grace of Henry VI's cult'.[69] He also encouraged researchers to extend that 'territory', especially in areas not previously known to have connections with the cult. During the course of managing a group project to transcribe the probate register 'Milles' drawn up for the Prerogative Court of Canterbury the author has so far come across three wills from different parts of the country that refer to the cult, one of which is particularly relevant to Dymond's work.[70]

---

68   Northeast and Falvey, *Wills*, pp. 436–7, will no. 722.

69   Marks, 'Images of Henry VI', p. 112, title of sub-section; the phrase 'territory of grace' is taken from W.A. Christian, Jr., *Person and God in a Spanish valley*, revised edn (Princeton, 1989), p. 44.

70   The project is being undertaken by members of the Richard III Society. David has always been an advocate of group projects. A prime example of a publication resulting from such a project is D. Dymond (ed.), *Parson and people in a Suffolk village: Richard Cobbold's Wortham, 1824–77*, Wortham Research Group and Suffolk Family History Society (Wortham, 2007).

Table 5.1
Altars, images or representations of saints, or lights to those saints, at Long Melford, St Peter's parish St Albans, Bassingbourn and Eversholt.

Saint	Long Melford	St Peter's	Bassingbourn	Eversholt
King Henry		1		1
St Andrew	1		1	
St Anne	1	1		1
St Anthony	1		1	1
St Catherine	1	1	1	2
St Christopher	1	1	1	1
St Clement		1		1
St Dunstan			1	
St Edmund	1			
St Erasmus		1		
St George	1		1	
St Giles abbot		1		
St James	1	1		
St John [unspecified]*			1	2
St John the Baptist	1	1		
St John the Evangelist	1			
St Lawrence		1		
St Leonard	1			
St Loy	1			
St Margaret	1		1	1
Mary Magdalen	1	1		
St Michael		1		
St Michael & Our Lady*				1
St Nicholas	1	1	1	1
St Peter	1		1	
St Peter & St Paul			1	
St Roch				1
St Saviour	1			
St Sithe the Virgin	1	1		1
St Steven				1
St Sunday			1	1
St Thomas [unspecified]*	1			1
St Thomas of Canterbury		1		
St Ursula the Virgin		1	1	

Note: * denotes 'duplicate' images.

On 7 July 1489 Dame Margaret Darcy, widow of Thomas Darcy esquire, made her will at Bardwell, just outside Bury St Edmunds.[71] She was expecting to die at Bardwell but requested burial at All Saints, Maldon (Essex), next to her husband; the vicar of Bardwell would be recompensed accordingly for his lost burial fee. Her status of 'Dame' does not relate to her husband's status as an esquire but rather to her profession as a vowess after her husband's death. That she was a vowess can be inferred from the bequest of 'her profession Ryng to oure Lady of Walsingham'. Vowesses were usually widows who 'chose a life containing elements of both religious and lay states'.[72] Among her religious bequests she asked her servant Margaret Stamford to go on four particular pilgrimages on her behalf: 'to oure Lady of Owtyng, seint Willyam of Rowchestre, and to Kyng Henry, and to oure Lady of Walsingham'.[73] Presumably Margaret Stamford was expected to take Dame Margaret's profession ring with her to Walsingham and leave it there. The image of Our Lady in the Lady Chapel at Long Melford had nine rings of various shapes and sizes attached to it.[74] Perhaps Dame Margaret had previously desired, or even vowed, to go on those pilgrimages, but she was a widow with four under-age children: two boys, Roger and Thomas, both under twenty and two daughters, Elizabeth and Anne, both unmarried and the former under fourteen.[75] Nevertheless, her required pilgrimages included one to King Henry's tomb at Windsor, as well as others to Walsingham and Rochester.

There is a loose connection with Suffolk, one might say, as the testatrix made her will at Bardwell but requested burial at Maldon even if she were to die at Bardwell. There is, however, a much firmer link with Suffolk, and furthermore it is, in fact, with Long Melford: as two of her four executors Dame Margaret appointed 'myn uncle' John Clopton, esquire, and Edward Clopton, his son. John Clopton, the principal late medieval benefactor of Holy Trinity church, Long Melford, has been described as one of that church's heroes.[76] Dame Margaret was his niece by marriage: his wife had been born Alice Darcy. In his will, made in November 1494, John Clopton bequeathed items to Margaret's four children.[77] Another of Margaret's executors was Robert Crane,

---

71 TNA, PROB 11/8/289, Dame Margaret Darcy, widow; will dated 9 July 1489; probate granted in January 1490 (exact date not given). In several previous publications her name has been misread as Davy. See M. Erler, 'English vowed women at the end of the Middle Ages', *Mediaeval Studies*, 57 (1995), pp. 155–203, at p. 199; H. Harrod, 'On the mantle and ring of widowhood', *Archaeologia*, 40 (1866), pp. 307–10, at p. 309.

72 For the lives of vowesses, for example, M.C. Erler, 'Three fifteenth-century vowesses', in C.M. Barron and A.E. Sutton (eds), *Medieval London widows, 1300–1500* (London, 1994), pp. 165–84.

73 The first pilgrimage would have been to the statue of the Virgin Mary at All Saints, Ulting, Essex. See <http://www.essexviews.uk/photos/Essex%20Churches/Essex%20Churches%20U-Z/slides/Ulting-Church-Essex-1.html>, accessed 6 September 2019.

74 Dymond and Paine, *Five centuries*, p. 70.

75 TNA, PROB 11/8/289.

76 Dymond and Paine, *Five centuries*, p. ix.

77 The testament of John Clopton is TNA, PROB 11/11/266; reproduced in Dymond and Paine, *Five centuries*, pp. 51–8; the bequest to the four Darcy children (each to receive ten gold beads with a Paternoster) is on p. 55.

who was also one of Clopton's executors.[78] Furthermore, she bequeathed ten marks to her 'goode Awnte Amy [*recte* Anny] Momgomory': Anne, or Agnes, Montgomery was a sister of John Clopton and another of Clopton's executors.[79] It may therefore be suggested that through definite connections between Margaret Darcy and John Clopton there is a tenuous link between that parish and the cult of Henry VI, thus extending his 'territory of grace' and shedding further light on late medieval religion, in particular the variety of pilgrimages that might, and could, be requested. Surely Roger Martin, that stalwart traditionalist of Long Melford, who bemoaned the 'spoil' of Melford church following the Reformation, would have approved of the cult?[80]

Postscript

Simon Cotton's recent analysis of bequests to medieval Suffolk parish churches reveals three more testators who required a pilgrimage on their behalf to King Henry's tomb at Windsor. These three men were parishioners of Gislingham (John More, will dated 1493), Hacheston (Robert Colvyll, 1525) and Henstead (John Dorhunt, 1492).[81] More relevant here, however, is the bequest of Margaret Smyth of Hoxne of 13s 4d for 'the makyng of an ymage of king herry the vjth'.[82] Her desire to have this image made is all the more tantalising because her will was made in 1475, just four years after Henry's death and long before the transfer of his remains from Chertsey to Windsor.

---

78   Robert Crane married Katherine Darcy (presumably a relative of Dame Margaret's late husband) and also Anne Arundell; Crane died in 1500: Dymond and Paine, *Five centuries*, p. 56 n. 207.

79   *Ibid.*, p. 56 n. 207.

80   Two earlier editions of Dymond and Paine, *Five centuries*, were entitled *The spoil of Melford Church: the Reformation in a Suffolk parish* (Ipswich, 1989 and 1992).

81   S. Cotton, *Building the late mediaeval Suffolk parish church* (Needham Market, 2019), pp. 56, 57, 60. Cotton's book was published just before this book went to press.

82   Cotton, *Building*, p. 63; the reference for Margaret Smyth's will is Norfolk Record Office, NCC Hubert 75.

Chapter 6

The will of Robert Scolys, vicar of Southwold 1444–70

David Sherlock

I came across this unusual will while searching for references to medieval tiles in East Anglia and gladly dedicate its publication to David, whom I have known since we were both council members of the Suffolk Institute of Archaeology in 1968. As editor of the Institute's *Proceedings* I discovered David's very broad knowledge: who else could have published the excavation of a prehistoric burial mound and a medieval settlement in the same volume? Later, working in the north of England, I found his knowledge extended to Roman Britain, with his research into Roman bridges on Dere Street.[1] In addition, David's palaeography skill has helped me on many occasions.

Robert Scolys was a doctor of theology at Cambridge University by 1454 and became a professor of theology.[2] He must have been a man of some standing to have been named in the royal foundation charter for Christ's College in 1442, and he was admitted a fellow of Clare Hall (later Clare College) in 1448.[3] One of his gifts to Clare library is recorded in a college inventory as well as in his will.[4] A list of college benefactors states 'Mr Robert Stolys [*sic*] had chained in the said library Giles's commentary on the first book of *Sentences* which he gave with other scientific books but those are not chained' [*cathenavit in dicta libraria Egidium super primum sentenciarum quem librum cum aliis libris specialium scienciarum dedit Mr Robertus Stolys, sed non cathenantur*].[5] The gift of Giles's commentary on *Sentences* is also in his will, from where almost everything else known about Scolys is derived.

He combined his academic role with that of vicar of Reydon with Southwold, styled *ecclesia de Reydon cum Sowthwold*, from 1444, after the disastrous fire of *c*.1430

---

1   D. Dymond, 'Roman bridges on Dere Street, County Durham. With a general appendix on the evidence for bridges in Roman Britain', *Archaeological Journal*, 118 (1963), pp. 136–64.

2   A. Emden, *Biographical register of the university of Cambridge to 1500* (Cambridge, 1963), pp. 512–13.

3   W. Harrison and A. Lloyd, *Notes on the masters, fellows, scholars and exhibitioners of Clare College, Cambridge* (Cambridge, 1953), p. 23.

4   R.W. Hunt, 'Medieval inventories of Clare College library', *Transactions of the Cambridge Bibliographical Society*, 1 (1950), pp. 105–25, p. 111, inventory of c.1440, no. 23, *Alacenna in sua perspectiva*, on which see my discussion below. There is a thirteenth-century copy of this work inscribed in a fifteenth-century hand, *Liber iste est collegii Clare Hall*, which is now in Corpus Christi College, Oxford. Hunt, 'Medieval inventories', p. 124.

5   *Ibid.*, p. 118.

had destroyed Southwold's chapel.[6] The building and furbishing of the splendid new church on the site of the chapel was still not complete when he died in 1470, as some of his bequests towards its beautifying suggest. Scolys' vicarage was at Reydon, but he also had a *mansum* (dwelling-house) at Southwold.[7] He desired to be buried in Southwold church, which was by then regarded as the more important. As vicar he would have probably been buried in the chancel, but we do not know where and no memorial survives.

Transcription of the will[8]

In Dei nomine amen. Ego magister Robertus Scolys, theologie professor ac vicarius de Reydon cum Sowthwold, vi^{to} die mensis Junii anno Domini millessimo CCCC^{mo} lxx°, sano mentis et bona memorie condo testamentum meum in hunc modum. In primis lego animam meam Deo omnipotenti, Beate Marie, Beate Margarete, Beato Edmundo regi et marturo ac omnibus sanctis, corpusque meum sepeliendum infra sepulturam (5) ecclesie Sancti Edmunde de Sowthwold ut placuerit eis qui sepelient me. Item lego dicte ville de Sowthwold omnia armamenta mea ut in arcubus, sagittis, galiis, loricis, jakkis, salatis, lanceis, batayle axis ceteraque machinamenta mea ad defensionem in omne eventu dicte ville seu vendand' [*ink blot*] et disponantur circa reparationem dicte ecclesie de ecclesie [*sic*] de Sowthwold secundum quod eis placuerit, praeter unum jakke quod do et lego Johanni Godman et praeter unum salat et unum archum que do et lego Roberto (10) Godman. Item lego dicte ecclesie de Sowthwold unam Legendam Auream et minorem librum meum Magistrum Sentenciarum ac unum portiforium notatum pro choro. Item lego dicte ville unam crucem ligneam ad ponendum ubi voluerint. Item lego ad opus dicte ecclesie omnes tegulas quas habeo infra mansum meum. Item lego dicte ville unam tabulam de alabastro. Item lego dicte ville unum vestimentum nigrum ad celebrandum pro defunctis. Item do et lego dicte ville ad informandum (15) sacerdotes ibi degentes unam Dietam Salutis et unam Pupillam Oculi et Psalterium cum commune glosa. Item lego dicte ville unum librum exponentis difficilium verborum legendarum ympnorum, sequentiarum et aliorum verborum que frequenter utuntur in ecclesia et duo manualia abbreviatorum [*or* abbreviata]. Item do et lego ad fabricam decorum sancti crucifixi in dicta ecclesia xxij s. quod mihi debet Johannes Conyvere. Item lego eidem operi iiij s. quos mihi debet Thomas Fraunseys. Item lego fabrice seu emendationi ecclesie (20)

---

6   R. Wake, *Southwold and its vicinity* (Yarmouth, 1839), p. 88. The title *cum capella de Southwold* continued long after Scolys, and Southwold gained ecclesiastical independence from Reydon only in 1752. There is no church at Southwold recorded in Domesday Book. I am grateful to David Gill for information about the earlier chapel under the nave of Southwold church, which he has recently excavated.

7   A deed of 1458 mentions the south part of the chapel cemetery 'where in antient Time the Parish-Priest's Apartment [*camera*] stood': T. Gardner, *An historical account of Dunwich, Blithburgh, Southwold* (1754), pp. 209–10. This *camera* was presumably the predecessor of Scoly's *mansum*.

8   NRO, NCC, register of wills, 83 Betyns. I am very grateful to Dr Elisabeth Leedham-Green for much help with reading the Latin.

de Reydon xl d. quos mihi debet Ricardus Gardere et Radulphus Wattes pro decime parte. Item [lego] dicte ecclesie de Sowthwold xx d. quos mihi debet Georgius Bacown ad opus predicti crucifixi. Item do et lego librarie venerabilis collegii in Clare Halle omnes libros meos astronomicos et unum astrolabum. Item lego eidem aule Alacen In Perspectiva et Baconum in eadem. Item lego librarie Egidium super Primum Sententiarum. Item do et lego ecclesie Sancte Margarete de Reydon (25) totum calam [?] meam infra vicariam. Item do et lego ecclesie de Sowthwold omnia bona michi debita ratione administratione bonorum tenementi Helene Burgays praeter xxvi s. viij d. j quarta que dicta puella commorata cum Johannem Metesharp huiusmodi cum pervenerat ad congruam etatem nuptiarum. Huius autem testamenti facio, ordino et constituo executores meos magistrum Willelmum Jermothe, vicarium de Covehethe alias vocato Northal, Dominum Thomam Crowe (30), rectorem de Estone Bavent, Dominum Willelmum Hulverdale, sacerdotem parochialem de Sowthwold, quibus do et lego residuum bonorum meorum mobilium ac immobilium tam de functibus decimis oblatis et aliis perventibus ecclesie mea pertinentibus quam de aliis rebus de quibus testamenti predicti de iure seu consuetudine synodale iuxta tenorem eiusdem constitucione que incipit Walterus Suffeld ad dicta legata mea persolvenda ac debita mea ac etiam in (35) pios usus pro anima mea et pro animabus omnium quibus teneor iuxta eorum distressionem secundum quod vederint melius eos placere errogandum. Insuper volo quod dicti executores mei volunter aliqualiter de bonis meis supernis non legatis emere quos habeam pre aliis et meliori prece dummodo non multum numerantur primum datis et legatis sunt hic apud Sowthwold predictum die et anno superscriptis sub testimoniis Roberti Bysshop, Ricardi Joyye, Johannis Joyye, Roberti (40) Goodman et Johannis Goodman ac aliorum. Et ad fidem premissorum sigillum meum apposui.

Translation

In the name of God amen. I Master Robert Scolys, professor of theology and vicar of Reydon with Southwold, on the 6th day of the month of June in the year of our Lord 1470 being in sound mind and in good memory make my will in this mode.

Firstly, I bequeath my soul to almighty God, Blessed Mary, Blessed Margaret, Blessed Edmund, king and martyr, and all the saints, and my body is to be buried in a grave in the church of St Edmund of Southwold as it shall please those who bury me.

Item, I bequeath to the said town of Southwold all my armoury, namely bows, arrows, helmets, hauberks, jacks, sallets, lances, battle axes and the rest of my weaponry for defence in all event of the said town or to be sold and disposed of for the repair of the said church of the church [?] of Southwold, as it pleases them, except for one jack which I give and bequeath to John Goodman and except for one sallet and one bow which I give and bequeath to Robert Goodman.

Item, I bequeath to the said church of Southwold one *Golden Legend* and my minor book *Magister Sententiarum*, and one annotated breviary for the choir.

Item, I bequeath to the said town a wooden cross to place where they wish.

Item, I bequeath for the work of the said church all the tiles which I have at my house.

Item, I bequeath to the said town a retable of alabaster.

Item, I bequeath to the said town a black vestment for celebrating [Mass] for the dead.

Item, I give and bequeath to the said town for the information of priests officiating there one *Diet of Salvation*, one *Pupilla Oculi* and one glossed *Psalter*. I bequeath to the said town a book commenting on difficult words of hymns, sequences and other words which they frequently use in church and two abridged service book manuals.

Item, I give and bequeath towards the making of the decoration of the holy crucifix in the said church 22s which John Conyvere owes to me. Item, I bequeath to the same work 4s which Thomas Fraunseys owes to me.

Item, I bequeath to the fabric or repair of Reydon church 40d which Richard Gardere and Ralph Wattes owe me for small tithes.

Item, [I bequeath] to the said church of Southwold 20d which George Bacon owes to me for the work of the said crucifix.

Item, I give and bequeath to the library of the venerable college in Clare Hall all my astronomy books and an astrolabe. Item, I bequeath to the same hall Alacen's *In Perspectiva* and Bacon on the same. I bequeath to the library Giles's *Concerning the First Book of Sentences*.

Item, I give and bequeath to the church of St Margaret of Reydon all my sheaves of reed (?) at the vicarage. Item, I give and bequeath to the church of Southwold all the goods due to me by reason of the administration of the goods and tenement of Helen Burgays except for 26s 8¼d which the said girl living so to speak with Joan Metsharpe shall have, when she reaches the agreed age of marriage.

I make, ordain and constitute as my executors of this will Master William Jermouth, vicar of Covehithe, otherwise called Northales, Sir Thomas Crow, rector of Easton Bavent, and Sir William Hulverdale, parish priest of Southwold, to whom I give and bequeath the residue of my goods, moveable and immoveable, both of the fruits, tithes, offerings and other issues belonging to my church and of the other things of which the aforesaid will can be made of right, or according to the tenor of a certain synodal constitution beginning 'Walter Suffield', to pay my legacies and debts and also to distribute in pious uses for my soul and the souls of all those for whom I am bound according to their discretion, as they see best to please them. Furthermore I wish that my said executors concerning my liturgical things which I used to have may at their will in some way buy them before others and at a better price so long as they are not valued much more than those first given and bequeathed here at Southwold aforesaid, on the day and year written above, under the witnesses of Robert Bysshop, Richard Joyye, John Joyye, Robert Goodman and John Goodman and others. And to the witness of the above I have fixed my seal.

The will was proved by the official of the consistory court of Walter Suffield, bishop of Norwich, at Hoxne on 19 June 1470 with administration granted to the executors and the seal of the bishop appended.

Commentary

The bequests in Robert Scolys' will come under three headings: his armoury; his books; and his other bequests. His donations to the town of many church items, such as the vestment, the alabaster and service books, go to emphasise the close connection between church and secular at this time. Likewise, his armoury was to go towards the defence of the town 'in all event', or to be sold for the repair of the church.

Armoury

His formidable armoury included at least eight different items, all listed in the plural, so there was more than enough for one man.[9] There were bows and arrows. There were helmets and sallets, the latter a helmet with a tail piece to protect the neck made either in one piece or with a moveable visor. A hauberk was a mail shirt made of small, closely interlocked and riveted rings. It was worn by men-at-arms under plate armour or by common soldiers as a principal form of body armour, usually over a thickly padded coat. Less costly than the mail shirt was the jack, a body defence made of a large number of small metal plates stitched or riveted into a padded jacket of multiple layers of canvas or linen. A lance – often made of ash and about fourteen feet long – by Scolys' time usually meant a horseman's spear. Forms of battle axe included the poleaxe, an infantry weapon, its four- to five-foot shaft mounted with a head combining a thick spike, axe and hammer. For a shorter form we need look no further than the Southwold church clock-jack, a painted figure in late fifteenth-century armour striking a bell with his battle-axe reversed.

The chamber above the church porch (Plate 6.1), with its strong door, secret latch mechanism and iron-banded chest, could have safely held Scolys' arms and armour, as the chamber above Mendlesham church porch still holds armour today.[10] But why did a priest, whom one would judge to be a man of peace, own all these items, which he places right at the start of his will? Was there a threat to the peace of the town at this time? The 1460s had been turbulent years, with the threat of a Lancastrian invasion and civil war, while, judging by the Paston letters, local violence between competing magnates had been a serious problem in East Anglia. So the men of Southwold might have been called to muster to meet a range of dangers. The explanation for the vicar's ownership of the arms originates in 1369, in the orders of Edward III that required clergy to possess arms and to muster. Clergy were in the army raised against the Scots by Richard II in 1385, following royal summons for all clergy to be arrayed in arms, and they were listed among the rebel forces at the battle of Shrewsbury in 1403.[11] The evidence for their military activity consists of royal writs of array and the bishops' returns to these writs, some still preserved in the National Archives, ordering a bishop to 'cause all … ecclesiastical persons of your diocese whatsoever to be armed and arrayed, furnished with arms … so that they shall be ready with other [of] the king's lieges to march against the said enemies … '.[12] The returns give the number

9   For arms and armour of the period see A. Boardman, *The medieval soldier in the Wars of the Roses* (Stroud, 1998), pp. 118–54, and R. Woosnam-Savage, *Arms and armour of late medieval Europe* (Leeds, 2017). I am very grateful to Professor Matthew Strickland for help with references to arms, armour and the medieval clergy.

10 H.M. Cautley, *Suffolk churches and their treasures*, 5th edn (Woodbridge, 1982), pp. 329, 348. Perhaps the arms and armour remained there after Scolys' bequest because Gardner, *An historical account*, p. 209, says the chamber is 'the Arsenal for the warlike stores of the Town'.

11 M. Strickland and R. Hardy, *The great warbow* (Stroud, 2005), pp. 259, 263.

12 B. McNab, 'Obligations of the church in English society: military arrays of the clergy, 1369–1418', in W. Jordan, B. McNab and T. Ruiz (eds), *Order and innovation in the Middle Ages. Essays in honour of Joseph R. Strayer* (Princeton, 1976), pp. 293–314 and 516–22, p. 295.

of clergy arrayed according to the weapons with which they were furnished: the well-armed having lances (so probably mounted), hobelars (light cavalry), archers, and a fourth category that were armed with an assortment of weapons, including battle-axes.

Defence of the south against the French and of the north against the Scots were the perennial concerns of the kingdom, but Richard II ordered the abbot of Bury St Edmunds to proceed in person with all his men at arms, hobelars and archers to his estates on the coast of Suffolk, 'as heretofore used to be done by him and his predecessors in time of war', because he was informed that the French planned an invasion that summer with great force.[13] The last of these royal arrays of clergy was in 1418 and the returns for the Norwich diocese survive. They list 'armed men, all appearing with lances, hobelars, and archers arrayed with hauberks, bows and arrows, swords, shields and daggers'. A scale was established that determined the arms with which each was to be furnished and to appear in the array, according to the annual value of his benefice. Clergy with good livings were expected to have 'competent arms' for fighting on horseback, which would explain Scolys' possession of lances.[14] In 1463 Edward IV ordered the archbishop of York to assemble the clergy of his province in defensible array at Newcastle in January in order to help him resist a threatened Scottish invasion in support of the Lancastrians, and they were again ordered to muster at Durham in July.[15]

Despite canonical and traditional prohibitions on the bearing of arms and the shedding of blood by persons in holy orders (was this why there was no sword in Scolys' armoury?), the religious authorities in the later Middle Ages were willing to commit their clergy to the defence of the realm. A muster roll and clergy list survive for Holt hundred as late as *c*.1523.[16] The clergy are praised for their military training in Robert Reyce's *Breviary of Suffolk* of 1618.[17] In 1798, with another threat of French invasion, the vicar of Coddenham enlisted in the Suffolk Yeomanry with the approval of his bishop.[18] But, whatever the national position in 1470, Scolys donated his own arms to the town.

Books

To Southwold church Scolys left his *Golden Legend*. This was a collection of lives of saints compiled around the year 1260, widely read in the later Middle Ages and added to over the centuries. It had a strong influence on the imagery of poetry, painting and

---

13   *Ibid.*, p. 518 n. 22.

14   *Ibid.*, p. 306.

15   J. Raine (ed.), *The priory of Hexham, its chroniclers, endowments and annals*, 2 vols (Durham, 1864–5), vol. 1, pp. cvii–cviii.

16   B. Cozens-Hardy, 'A muster roll and clergy list in the hundred of Holt circa 1523', *Norfolk Archaeology*, 22 (1926), pp. 45–58.

17   F. Hervey (ed.), *The breviary of Suffolk by Robert Reyce, 1618* (London, 1902), p. 97.

18   M. Stone (ed.), *The diary of John Longe (1765–1834), Vicar of Coddenham*, Suffolk Records Society 51 (Woodbridge, 2008), p. li.

stained glass. Any such glass in Southwold church was doubtless destroyed when William Dowsing's men came in 1644, along with Scolys' alabaster and crucifix (see below).[19]

The *Magister Sententiarum*, 'Master of Sentences', by Peter Lombard (*c*.1100–1160), was an important theological work in four books (though Scolys called it his 'minor book') which became the standard textbook of theology, and for which Lombard earned the accolade *Magister*. Scolys left this to the church with an annotated breviary for the choir. But, apart from those bequeathed to Clare Hall (see below), he left all his other books to the town. A *Portiforium notatum* was a portable breviary containing daily prayers, annotated with music. The *Dieta Salutis*, 'Diet of Salvation', a daily office book by St Bonaventure, 1221–1274, would have been useful for priests officiating at Southwold. The *Pupilla Oculi* by John de Burgo, *c*.1386, was a book of instructions for parish priests, its full title being *Pupilla oculi omnibus sacerdotibus tam curatis quam non curatis summe necessaria per magistrum Johannem de Burgo cancellarium alme vniversitatis Cantabrigiensis et sacre theologie professorem compilata*; 'The Pupil of the Eye, for all priests both those with the cure of souls [that is, a benefice] and those without, of the chief things necessary, compiled through Master John de Burgo, chancellor of the nurturing university of Cambridge and professor of sacred theology'. Scolys also left to the town a glossed Psalter – the book of psalms with a general commentary; another book commenting on difficult words of hymns, sequences and other words frequently used in church; and two abridged service book manuals. These are anonymous, but as a former professor of theology Scolys could well have written some of them himself.

Many parish churches once had libraries and the books that Scolys bequeathed to Southwold were not rare. Assington had Peter Lombard's works and St James's, Bury St Edmunds, had Bonaventure's seven volumes, though these were in editions printed long after Scolys' time. As late as 1739 Coddenham vicarage had a library created for the 'free use, custody and perusal by the vicars of Coddenham for ever'.[20]

To Clare Hall Scolys left unspecified astronomical books (see my introduction above) and his astrolabe, an instrument for solving astronomical problems, as well as books by Alhacen, Bacon and Giles. Alhacen's 'Book of Optics' is the work by the Arabic writer Ibn al-Haytham, which was translated into Latin *c*.1200 as *De Aspectibus* and covered physics, anatomy and geometry. Roger Bacon, the Franciscan scholar (*c*.1220–1292), drew heavily on this for his own *Perspectiva* (*Book of Optics*), which was concerned with light, colour and vision, leading to the spiritual truths to be gained from their study.[21] Scolys also bequeathed to Clare his copy of the commentary by St Giles of Rome (1243–1316) on Book I of the *Sentences* by Peter Lombard (see above).

Other bequests

Scolys' other bequests included a wooden cross for the townsfolk to erect where they wished. John Lokles had already bequeathed 10s for making a cross in the

---

19   T. Cooper (ed.), *The journal of William Dowsing* (Woodbridge, 2001), p. 296.
20   A.E. Birkby, *Suffolk parochial libraries. A catalogue (London, 1976)*, pp. 19, 89, xvi.
21   D. Lindberg, *Roger Bacon and the origins of perspectiva in the Middle Ages* (Oxford, 1996).

churchyard in 1460, so if Scolys' cross was erected at the market place it might have been the one burnt in the town fire of 1659, which was replaced by a stone cross dated 1661.[22]

Whether the *tegulae* that Scolys had at his house and left to Southwold church were roof or floor tiles is unclear. The present church would seem always to have had a lead roof, but there may have been some other building adjoining it or in the churchyard that needed roof tiles. On the other hand, there survive areas of fifteenth-century floor tiles in the church to which he could have contributed. To St Margaret's, Reydon, he left the 40d owed to him in vicar's tithes and all the sheaves of reed – if this, not firewood, is the correct interpretation of *calam* – at his vicarage, suggesting that Reydon church was reed-thatched in his day.

An alabaster retable would have been carved and painted with a religious scene and placed above an altar, although Scolys bequeathed it to the town. It would have been made from Nottingham alabaster. From there, a prolific school of carvers in the Middle Ages exported such alabasters all over England and on the continent.[23]

In 1471, the year after Scolys' death, John Tyll bequeathed £20 *ad facturam unius vestimenti*.[24] Scolys' bequest of a black funeral vestment would have doubtless cost about the same to make, unless it was simply a cope for a priest to wear at a graveside in cold weather. Again, this was bequeathed to the town.

If the sacred crucifix was intended for inside the church it was presumably destroyed with the four vestry crosses by Dowsing's men in 1644.[25] Scolys also gave towards this cross the 4s and the 20d owed to him by two men. He bequeathed to St Edmund's what was due to him from the goods and tenement of Helen Burgays, except for 26s 8¼d that he reserved for a girl then living with Joan Metsharpe when she reached 'the agreed age of marriage'.

Robert Scolys was a man of many talents. Having been professor of theology at Cambridge with an interest in physics and astronomy, he fulfilled his duties as a parish priest, leaving books to help explain the faith to parishioners and townsfolk. He helped to look after the fabric of his two churches and he fulfilled his obligations for military array. His will shows the very close relationship between the sacred and secular in the Middle Ages.

---

22 SROI, archdeaconry of Suffolk wills, R2/44; Wake, *Southwold*, pp. 255–6. Anon., 'Ancient crosses of East Anglia', *East Anglian Notes & Queries*, new series 1 (1885), p. 75.

23 There are no alabasters from Southwold recorded in F.W. Cheetham, *English medieval alabasters* (Oxford, 1984).

24 Wake, *Southwold*, p. 250.

25 Cooper, *Dowsing*, p. 296.

Part II: Medieval trade and industry

Chapter 7

The fairs of late medieval Thetford[1]

Joanne Sear

Introduction

In the introduction to his transcription of the monastic accounts of the priory of St Mary, Thetford, which were published in two volumes by the Norfolk Record Society as *The register of Thetford Priory*, David Dymond explored the extensive use of fairs made by the priory (Plate 7.1) to procure a wide range of goods required by the monastic household.[2] Those fairs included the large international fair at Stourbridge Common in Cambridge, Ely Fair and a number of 'beast fairs', such as the horse fair at Woolpit, Reach fair and even the fair at St Faith's, just outside Norwich. The priory also visited a number of smaller fairs local to Thetford. Provincial fairs such as these were often short-lived, while many of those that maintained some degree of permanence declined and ultimately disappeared in the post-Black Death period.[3] Their documentary legacy largely consists of fragmentary references in scattered sources, which has made the study of provincial fairs difficult and largely ignored by historians. Despite this limited research, there is a general view that medieval fairs largely served their local hinterland and concentrated on the sale of wholesale produce, livestock and agricultural implements.[4]

Within a 'scrapbook' of records from the borough of Thetford held by Norfolk Record Office are a number of fair rolls listing the names of traders who paid tolls and customs at the provincial fairs of Thetford in the late thirteenth and early fourteenth centuries.[5] This paper uses these rolls to explore the geographical range of traders coming to the fairs, the nature of the goods and services provided by the fairs and their changing fortunes during a period that has often been identified as one which saw their decline.[6]

---

1   Thanks are due to Nick Amor, John S. Lee and Evelyn Lord for reading and commenting on a draft of this paper, to Keith Briggs for helping to identify some of the settlements referred to in the fair rolls, and to Max Satchell of the Cambridge Group for the History of Population and Social Structure (CAMPOP) for producing the maps.

2   D. Dymond (ed.), *The register of Thetford Priory, Part I 1482–1517*, NRS LX (Oxford, 1994), pp. 43–7.

3   J.S. Lee, *Cambridge and its economic region: 1450–1560* (Hatfield, 2005), p. 114.

4   E. Miller and J. Hatcher, *Medieval England: towns, commerce and crafts, 1086–1348* (London, 1995), p. 169.

5   NRO, T/C1/11.

6   See, for example, T.H. Lloyd, *The English wool trade in the middle ages* (Cambridge, 2005), p. 304.

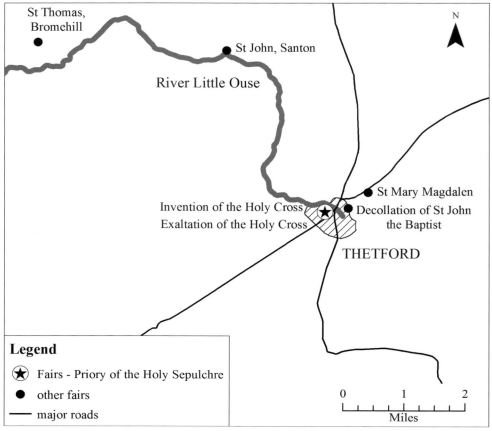

Map 7.1. Location of the Thetford fairs (courtesy Max Satchell). The course of the Little Ouse beyond Thetford cannot be identified with any certainty and has therefore not been plotted on this map.

Thetford fairs

Of the six fairs known to have been held in the vicinity of Thetford, the accounts of the priory of St Mary refer to only four that were visited by the priory. Of these, most visits were made to St Thomas's fair at Bromehill, which had originally been granted to the small Augustinian priory of Bromehill by Henry III in 1224 (although the charter was confirming existing practice).[7] It was held on the vigil and feast of the Translation of St Thomas the Martyr (6–7 July) at a location just across the county border from the Suffolk town of Brandon (five and a half miles from Thetford) and close to the Little Ouse. Frequent visits were also made to the fair of St Mary

---

7   Gazetteer of markets and fairs in England and Wales to 1516, <https://www.history.ac.uk/cmh/gaz/gazweb2.html>, accessed 10 January 2019.

Magdalen, which had been granted to the hospital of St Mary Magdalen in Thetford. This fair was held on 22 July at the hospital itself, which lay to the north of the town on the Norwich road. By contrast, the priory visited the fairs of the Invention of the Holy Cross (3 May) and the Exaltation of the Holy Cross (14 September) on only a handful of occasions. These fairs had both been granted to the priory of the Holy Sepulchre in Thetford by William, earl of Warrene, around the time that he founded the priory (soon after 1139) and were subsequently confirmed by Stephen. They were held at the fairstead, just to the south-west of the junction of the Brandon and London roads and close to the priory of the Holy Sepulchre, and were thus the only two of the six fairs held in and around Thetford that took place to the south of the Little Ouse and within the county of Suffolk.[8] Of the two fairs not referred to in *The register of Thetford Priory*, one was the fair of St John, Santon, which took place on 24 June, the feast of St John the Baptist, at the now-deserted settlement of Santon. It was probably held in or around the churchyard of St Helen's church and so is occasionally referred to in the rolls as '*Nundinas Sancte Elene*'.[9] This 'renaming' of the fair may also have been to avoid confusion with the last of the six, the fair of the Decollation of St John the Baptist, which had been granted to the hospital of the lepers of St John the Baptist in Thetford by Henry III in 1232 and was held annually on 29 August at the site of the hospital.[10] While the sites of two of these six fairs were outside Thetford, by 1288 the borough of Thetford had acquired rights over all of them such that tolls and customs from traders were paid to the mayor and burgesses of the town.

The location of these fairs is shown in Map 7.1 and it should be noted that they all lay close to the Little Ouse. The river played a vital role in the transport of goods and people to and from the fairs and provided a link to a huge fenland river network that permitted access into the Fens and western Norfolk, as well as to the east Midlands and, via Lynn, other ports in England and northern Europe. Access to river transport was essential to the success of medieval fairs and it is no coincidence that six of the great fairs of late medieval England were located on the same river network: Stamford on the Welland, Northampton on the Nene, St Ives on the Ouse and Bury St Edmunds on the Lark, while Lynn and Boston were port towns on the network.[11] While these fairs could be accessed by sea-going cargo vessels, smaller fairs such as those at Thetford were served by hulks and keels, which were lighter and easier to handle, and could incorporate oars as well as sails.[12]

---

8   C. Dallas, 'Excavations in Thetford by B.K. Davison between 1964 and 1970', *East Anglian Archaeology*, 62 (1993), p. 202.

9   Santon is a depopulated settlement that lay to the north of the river Little Ouse in the present-day parish of Lynford where a series of earthworks are all that remains of the settlement and its church; Norfolk Heritage Explorer <http://www.heritage.norfolk.gov.uk/record-details?MNF5684-Site-of-St-Helen%27s-Church-Santon>, accessed 26 February 2019.

10   Gazetteer of markets and fairs in England and Wales to 1516, <https://www.history.ac.uk/cmh/gaz/gazweb2.html>, accessed 10 January 2019.

11   E. Wedemeyer Moore, *The fairs of medieval England: an introductory study* (Toronto, 1985), p. 11.

12   *Ibid.*, pp. 11–12.

Table 7.1
Numbers recorded in the Thetford fair rolls.

	Invention of the Holy Cross	St John, Santon	St Thomas, Bromehill	St Mary Magdalen	St John, Thetford	Exaltation of the Holy Cross
	3 May	24 June	6–7 July	22 July	29 August	14 Sept
1288		38	51	80	23	19
1289	21					
1291		52	41			
1320		36	31	55	12	14
1321	11	33				
1322		35	44			
1324		33	31	22	14	5
1325	3					
1327		28	49	32	17	15
1328		22	53	39	9	13
1329		24	34			
Total	35	301	334	228	75	66

Although road transport was generally far less important than river transport for late medieval fairs, the Thetford fairs also benefited from the location of the town on the road linking Norwich to London. This road was significant; on the Gough map of *c*.1350 (which gives much detail about the river network), it appears as the only major road in East Anglia running from Norwich through Norfolk, Suffolk and Cambridgeshire and joining the Great North Road at Ware (in Hertfordshire). It went through the centre of Thetford and crossed the rivers Little Ouse (the county boundary between Norfolk and Suffolk) and Thet via the Town Bridge and the Nuns Bridge, both of which provided a steady income for the borough in the form of bridge tolls. In addition to connecting Norwich with London, the section of the road through East Anglia was a key transport route for travellers in and between the eastern counties.

The fair rolls

The fair rolls held by Norfolk Record Office are included within a 'scrapbook' of various documents from the borough of Thetford compiled by an eighteenth-century antiquarian, George Bird Burrell. While the scrapbook is fragmentary, the rolls themselves are a relatively complete record of the fairs and years identified in Table 7.1, which shows the number of names recorded on the fair rolls for these fairs and years.

Each roll lists the names of people, generally traders bringing goods for sale, paying various tolls at the fairs. The fairs are listed in the order in which they took place and most of the individual fair entries are separated out into three sections. The first of these lists the names of those paying a fair toll of 1d, with the amount recorded against their names. The second records those who paid various fines at the fair, together with a record of their payment; the fines levied ranged from 1d to 12d, although the nature of the offence is only occasionally recorded. The third section is usually headed '*Intrantes ibidem* [enterers to the place]' and is a list of people permitted to trade in the fair on the payment to the borough of an annual fee, known as a fine, occasionally recorded in the rolls as 1d, in line with similar payments recorded at other medieval towns.[13] Although most of the fair rolls list the names of payers under these three sections, in some the names are simply listed together, so that the numbers shown in Table 7.1 are a total of all the names recorded, with no distinction made between the different categories. It is also important to note that residents from the borough of Thetford were exempt from paying tolls at the fair, while certain goods were also excluded from tolls, so that the names of many traders would not have been recorded. Consequently, the numbers in Table 7.1 are not a complete record of all of the traders, but do give an indication of the varying levels of attendance. Many of the names listed on the rolls also record the home settlement of the trader (41 per cent). The occupations of some of the traders are also included (6.5 per cent), while some other surnames are clearly occupational (8 per cent).

In total, the fair rolls list the names of 1,144 people who attended the six Thetford fairs during the years indicated in Table 7.1. The numbers broadly suggest that over the whole of the period in question the fair of St Thomas, Bromehill, was the most well attended, followed by that of St John, Santon.[14] Of the fairs that took place within the town of Thetford, the fair of St Mary Magdalen was the most important, while those of the Invention of the Holy Cross, the Decollation of St John and the Exaltation of the Holy Cross were smaller events.

Geographical distribution of participants

The high number of home settlements listed in the rolls for the Thetford fairs allows for a study of the geographical distribution of participants. This also makes it possible to identify the transport links fair traders used to access the fairs and allows us to explore whether these fairs served just local and regional traders, as has been suggested by

---

13 Personal communication from John Lee and James Davis, 22 February 2019; R. Weeks, 'Making sense of the censarii: licensed traders in medieval sources', *Local Historian*, 34 (2004), pp. 113–17.

14 There are more extant rolls for these fairs than for those that took place within Thetford. The reason for this is unclear; while many fair rolls have obviously been lost, in some cases the rolls do not include entries for all of the fairs and it is impossible to know whether this was because the fair did not take place, the tolls were recorded on another roll, or for another reason.

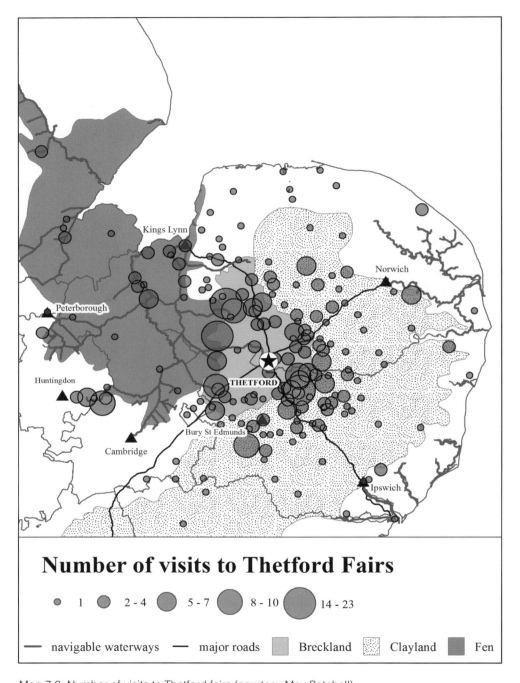

Map 7.2. Number of visits to Thetford fairs (courtesy Max Satchell).

various commentators, including Stephan Epstein, or whether they engaged in wider national or international commerce.[15]

The fair rolls list just over 200 places from which traders visited the fairs, of which it has been possible to identify 197. In very many cases, multiple visits were made to the fairs from these settlements; for example, twenty-three separate visits were made by men from Feltwell in Norfolk, while seven visits were made from St Ives in Huntingdonshire. The settlements, and the number of visits made by their residents, are recorded in Map 7.2.[16]

Most of the traders came from settlements in the hinterland of Thetford, up to a distance of around twenty miles. Unsurprisingly, as the fairs were held close to the border between Norfolk and Suffolk, this included places in both of these counties, although settlements in the Breckland region to the north and east of Thetford were particularly well represented. Other traders travelled further, but from places that could still just be regarded as regional; these included Wisbech and Swavesey (Cambridgeshire), Harwich and Thaxted (Essex), St Ives and Hemingford (Huntingdonshire) and Spalding, Fleet and Pinchbeck (Lincolnshire). A very few traders came from much further afield; one trader is recorded as coming from as far as Ireland, while others came from Hull, Chesterfield and Peterborough.

It is also evident from Map 7.2 that effective transport links played a key role in facilitating access to the fairs and that the fenland river network was of paramount importance. Many of the men who travelled even short distances probably relied on water transport, as, at this time, many of the nearby fen-edge settlements were linked to the natural watercourses by artificial waterways known as 'lodes', so that, in the words of Mark Bailey, 'most of the villages … had any number of small staithes and hithes to facilitate the loading and unloading of boats'.[17] The river network was even more vital to traders who came from further afield and some transport routes can be highlighted as significant.

The fairs were especially relevant to traders who came from a range of settlements in west Norfolk. Some of these came from places either on or close to the Great Ouse, including Lynn, Wiggenhall and Tilney, or its tributary, the Wissey, such as Oxborough, Foulden, Cressingham and Shipdham, and sailed via the Great Ouse to the Little Ouse and on to the fairs. Other men came from west Norfolk vills on the Little Ouse itself, such as Feltwell. A number of traders came from settlements near to the Nene on the west Norfolk/north Cambridgeshire

---

15   S. Epstein, 'Regional fairs, institutional innovation, and economic growth in late medieval Europe', *Economic History Review*, 47/3 (1994), p. 461.

16   A handful of occasional visits from traders from more distant settlements are not recorded in Map 7.2, including Ireland and Hull (one visit each); the waterways as shown on the map derive from M. Satchell, G. Newton and L. Shaw-Taylor, 'Navigable waterways of England and Wales time dynamic GIS 1600–1948' (2017) for the year 1600 with additions.

17   S. Oosthuizen, 'Cambridgeshire and the peat fen. Medieval rural settlement and commerce, c. AD 900–1300', in N. Christie and P. Stamper (eds), *Medieval rural settlement Britain and Ireland, AD 800–1600* (Oxford, 2012), p. 206; M. Bailey, *A marginal economy? East Anglian Breckland in the later Middle Ages* (Cambridge, 1986), p. 153.

Figure 7.1. Priory of the Holy Sepulchre, Thetford – granted two fairs in the twelfth century by its founder William, earl of Warrene (© Nicholas R. Amor).

border, including Wisbech, Elm, Upwell and Walpole, and accessed the fairs via the Nene and Well Creek, which provided a link to the Great Ouse. Traders also came to the fairs from west Cambridgeshire; a significant group of traders who visited Bromehill fair in particular were from settlements around St Ives, including places in both Huntingdonshire (such as Hemingford, Earith and St Ives itself) and Cambridgeshire (Swavesey and Over), and reached the fairs via a network that included both rivers (Great Ouse, Cam and Little Ouse) and channels (Old West River and Brandon Creek).[18]

Lynn was not only the home settlement of traders; it was an east coast port on the North Sea that lay at the mouth of the Great Ouse. As a seaport, it could be readily accessed by people travelling from much further afield. Any traders wishing to access the Thetford fairs via the port entered the Great Ouse at Lynn and sailed inland on the river before joining the Little Ouse for the journey to Santon, Bromehill or Thetford itself. This route was used by men from places on or near to other fenland rivers that flowed into the Wash. Traders from settlements including Spalding, Pinchbeck and Surfleet travelled via the Welland and the Wash to access the Great Ouse at Lynn, while the one visitor from Chesterfield made a similar journey via the Witham. This access point was also used by the few men who travelled significant distances; those from Ireland and Hull sailed around the English coast before entering the river network at Lynn. A few men also came to the fairs from various places on or close to the coast; while these settlements included places in both Suffolk and Essex, the majority were in north Norfolk, including Blakeney, Docking, Wells and Cley, from where it was possible to sail around the coast to Lynn and access the river network.[19]

Generally, roads were less important for accessing the fairs, but Map 7.2 indicates that some people used sections of the main road between Norwich and London for journeys to and from the Thetford fairs. Places on the road between Thetford and Norwich were especially well represented and included the Norfolk vills of Larling, Snetterton, Attleborough and Wymondham, while many other settlements, such as Kenninghall, Banham and Buckenham, were located just off the main road.[20] Fewer traders appear to have used this Norwich–London route from places south of Thetford, but men are recorded as coming from Kentford, Exning and Dalham, all of which were on or close to the road. Sections of the main road that ran between Ipswich and Lynn were also used, with traders travelling north to Thetford from Suffolk settlements

---

18 J. Edwards, 'The transport system of medieval England', PhD thesis (University of Salford, 1987), p. 222.

19 These traders were almost certainly bringing fish to sell at the fairs. Although there is limited evidence of this in the fair rolls, with only one man who can be specifically identified as trading in fish, a herring seller who visited Santon in 1321, in the early sixteenth century the priory bought a variety of fish, including mudfish, ling, cod fish and, on one occasion, whale at the fairs of Bromehill and St Mary Magdalene: D. Dymond (ed.), *The Register of Thetford Priory, Part II 1518–1540*, NRS LX (Oxford, 1995 and 1986), pp. 612, 660, 680, 699.

20 The rolls refer only to 'Bukenham' and do not specify whether this was Old Buckenham or New Buckenham.

Table 7.2
Occupations and occupational surnames recorded in the Thetford fair rolls.

	Invention of the Holy Cross, Thetford	*St John, Santon*	*St Thomas, Bromehill*	*St Mary Magdalen, Thetford*	*St John, Thetford*	*Exaltation of the Holy Cross, Thetford*
Agrarian or pastoral products	Hayward	Hayward Miller Warrener	Hayward Miller Shepherd	Hayward Miller Warrener	Hayward Miller Warrener	Hayward Poulterer
Agricultural services	Cooper Smith	Smith Roper Wright	Cooper Smith Roper Ironmonger	Cooper Smith Roper Wright	Smith Wright	Cooper Smith Saddler
Food, drink	Baker	Brewer Spicer Fisher	Brewer Baker Spicer	Brewer	Brewer	Brewer
Cloth, skins, clothing	Tanner	Shoemaker Barker Glover	Tailor Shoemaker Barker	Shoemaker Barker Skinner	Shoemaker Tanner	Shoemaker
Construction		Carpenter Plumber	Carpenter	Carpenter Mason		
Mercantile		Chapman Merchant	Chapman	Merchant		

such as Horringer, Lawshall and Shimpling, and south from Norfolk places including Shouldham and Swaffham.

The geographical distribution of traders suggests that, while the Thetford fairs catered largely for the region, their sphere of influence did extend nationally and probably internationally. Two aspects highlighted above support this assertion and demonstrate that the fairs were integrated into marketing networks wider than those serving simply the immediate hinterland. The first of these is the number of traders coming to the fairs from settlements in and around the coastal port of Lynn. Lynn had long been a collecting point for East Anglian grain, which was then shipped to London and the continent, and it was also the third most important port in England for the export of wool.[21] Many, though not all, of the merchants from Lynn and the

---

21 R. Britnell, *The commercialisation of English society* (Cambridge, 1996), pp. 87–8; Lloyd, *English wool trade*, p. 64.

surrounding area visited the July fairs of Bromehill and St Mary Magdalen, and the timing suggests that these traders were buying just-harvested winter barley and newly shorn wool fleeces to transport to Lynn for export. A number of names match those recorded as paying custom duties on goods moving to and from the port in 1322/23, but it is impossible to be certain that these were the same individuals; for example, Thomas Man paid 40s 9¼d on wool that left Lynn on 16 March 1323 on the ship of Allard the son of Cleyes, while a Thomas le Man visited the fair of St Mary Magdalen in 1328.[22] Some of these merchants are described as being '*de Hans* [of the Hanse]', denoting them as members of a short-lived Thetford merchant guild probably established for the purpose of trading in products such as barley and wool.[23] The second indication is the number of traders travelling from in and around St Ives, the site of a large, internationally important fair held at Easter. Many of these traders visited Bromehill fair and, as this was held in early July, it seems plausible to suggest that they were bringing goods bought earlier in the year at the larger fair to sell in the Thetford region. Fair networks, in which traders moved around fairs either buying goods for sale at subsequent fairs or selling goods already acquired, were known to have been in operation and the number of traders from the St Ives region visiting the Thetford fairs suggests that they formed part of such a network.[24]

Goods and services provided by the fairs

It has been contended that the goods traded at the small regional fairs such as those that took place in and around Thetford were predominantly wholesale produce, livestock and agricultural implements, although Richard Britnell notes that 'all sorts of other specialisations found an outlet in small fairs'.[25] No direct evidence of the goods sold at Thetford's medieval fairs in the pre-Black Death period has survived; however, as has been noted, the occupations of some of the traders who paid tolls at the fairs are recorded, while in many other cases the surnames are clearly occupational. The occupations that can be identified are shown in Table 7.2.

The poor soil of the Breckland region, in which Thetford lay, was such that it produced some grain, particularly barley, which was supplemented by the rearing of sheep and rabbits.[26] More productive soil lay to the west of Thetford (the Fens) and to the south-east (south Norfolk and the high Suffolk claylands). The occupational details confirm that the main focus of all of the fairs was on meeting the agricultural needs of these areas, in terms of both providing an outlet for produce and supplying a range of basic products required for agricultural activities. Some of the occupational details

---

22 D. Owen (ed.), *The making of King's Lynn: A documentary survey* (London, 1984), pp. 337–62.

23 'Hanse' was the term given to a merchant gild; these took various forms during the late medieval period, including, as was probably the case with the Thetford gild, associations of merchants within one town: see S. Ogilvie, *Institutions and trade: merchant guilds, 1000–1800* (Cambridge, 2011), pp. 19–30.

24 Epstein, 'Regional fairs', p. 468.

25 Britnell, *Commercialisation*, p. 89.

26 Bailey, *Marginal economy?*, p. 145.

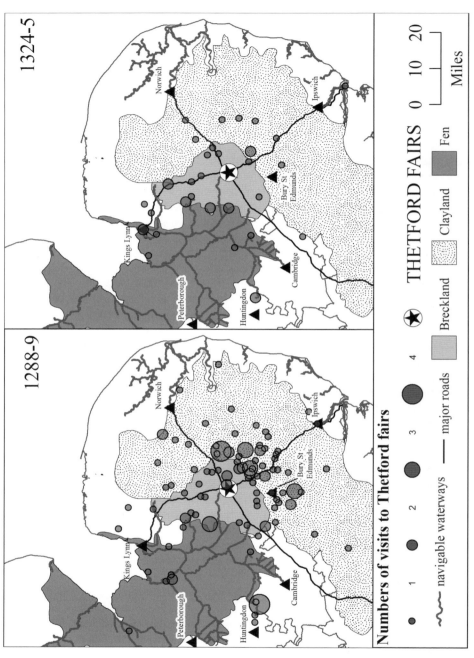

Map 7.3. Number of visits to Thetford fairs in 1288/9 and 1324/5 (courtesy Max Satchell).

indicate men who were engaged in selling agricultural goods, including a number referred to as 'le heyward', who visited the fairs from several different settlements, including Rickinghall and Drinkstone, and who were probably in the business of selling grain. Other occupations and associated names suggesting the sale of agricultural produce include those of miller, warrener, shepherd and poulterer, and the man referred to simply as 'Barlystraw' who, presumably, sold the byproduct of local barley production for animal bedding and possibly thatching. This function of the Thetford area as a dispersal point for agricultural produce is supported by other commentators: Mark Bailey noted that barley from the Norfolk manor of Langford was sent for sale at Santon fair, while Alan Crosby observed that Thetford had long been a trading centre for the export of regional agricultural produce.[27] The sale of meat and livestock at regional fairs has been noted by other observers, but there are no references to either butchers or to occupations that might have traded in larger animals, such as cattle or horses. This may reflect the fact that the Breckland area offered only poor grazing unsuitable for larger animals and had instead developed as a sheep- and rabbit-rearing region.[28] Other occupations recorded in the rolls were associated with agricultural activities and included smiths (at least thirty-three separate smiths can be identified), tanners or barkers (seven), coopers (five), ropers (five), wrights (four), ironmongers (two) and a saddler.

Traders also provided a range of other goods and services. Conviviality was evidently a feature, as brewers are recorded as paying the standard fair tolls, while a number of the fines recorded were for brewing. Roger Kinge (10d), Thomas Attedelfe (7d) and William Frost (9d) were all fined at Santon fair in 1288 and the sizeable fines suggest that large amounts of ale were involved. Bakers attended a number of the fairs and spicers are recorded at two of the larger fairs (Santon and Bromehill), including one from Ipswich who visited Bromehill in 1288. Surprisingly, while tailors are recorded only at the largest of the fairs, Bromehill, shoemakers visited all of the fairs with the exception of the Invention of the Holy Cross. The importance of leather for clothing and the carriage of liquid as well as for the harnessing of animals was such that tanners or barkers also visited all of the fairs except the Exaltation of the Holy Cross. There are also occasional mentions of crafts associated with building, including carpenters, a mason and a number of plumbers. Fairs were also known for attracting itinerant marketing and the rolls of Santon and Bromehill both record men identified as 'chapman'.

Decline of the fairs

In his work on the English wool trade in the Middle Ages T.H. Lloyd observed that, by 1300, fairs everywhere were in decline and, although his comments predominantly relate to the great fairs, many of the reasons were common to the smaller fairs.[29] The

---

27 Bailey, *Marginal economy?*, p. 149; Alan G. Crosby, *A history of Thetford* (Chichester, 1986), p. 14.

28 Bailey, *Marginal economy?*, p. 35.

29 Lloyd, *English wool trade*, p. 304; for a detailed exploration of fairs in the post-Black Death period see J.S. Lee, 'The role of fairs in late medieval England', in S. Rigby and M. Bailey (eds), *Town and countryside in the age of the Black Death* (Turnhout, 2012), pp. 407–37.

number of tollpayers recorded in Table 7.1 shows that, with the possible exception of Bromehill, fewer traders were visiting the fairs by the late 1320s than had done so forty years earlier, indicating a definite downturn. Some of the fairs seem to have been more affected than others, particularly those that took place within Thetford itself, which may reflect the general and ongoing decline in the population and prosperity of the borough.[30] Tollpayers at both St Mary Magdalen and St John had fallen by half over the period in question and although the reduction at the Exaltation of the Holy Cross was less significant (although only five people are recorded in 1324), tollpayers at its sister fair, the Invention of the Holy Cross, fell from twenty-one in 1289 to just three in 1325 and in subsequent years it does not appear in the fair rolls. Both the fairs held just outside Thetford saw an overall decline in numbers, although this was not as considerable as for the Thetford fairs. Tollpayers at Santon dropped from thirty-eight in 1288 to twenty-four in 1329, although this decline is more marked when compared with 1291, when fifty-two people are recorded as paying tolls. Although numbers at Bromehill fluctuated, the number of tollpayers was broadly maintained, with the highest number recorded in 1328, when fifty-three people paid some form of toll.

Overall, the number of tollpayers at the Thetford fairs fell quite considerably. In 1288/9 the names of 232 people were recorded on the rolls, but by 1324/5 only 108 names were listed.[31] This fall in numbers also appears to have affected the geographical distribution of fair traders (Map 7.3), which suggests that, although the decline was almost certainly due to a range of factors, one in particular was paramount. In 1288/9 men came to the fairs from settlements in and around Thetford as well as from much further afield. Although this basic pattern still existed by 1324/5 and the fall in numbers was in visitors from both near and far, traders from settlements to the west, south and, to a lesser extent, the north of Thetford had fallen quite considerably.[32] Broadly, this area corresponds with the south Norfolk and high Suffolk claylands, an area of moderately fertile soil that supported a mix of arable crops including barley, oats, legumes and wheat.[33] The period 1315–22 had seen an agrarian crisis, particularly in the years 1315–17, which saw back-to-back harvest failures and subsequent famine. Bruce Campbell and Cormac Ó Gráda noted that this had caused great hardship and significant excess mortality, particularly for those associated with agriculture, and that these years were characterised by the classic

---

30 Although the Domesday Book ranked Thetford as the sixth largest town in 1086, it was already in decline and this was exacerbated by the removal of the episcopal see of East Anglia from Thetford to Norwich in 1093. By the time of the Lay Subsidy of 1334 it was assessed for £16, well behind the city of Norwich (£94) and the two other Norfolk taxation boroughs of Great Yarmouth (£100) and Lynn (£50): R. Glasscock, *The lay subsidy of 1334* (Oxford, 1975), p. 192.

31 This is the latest year for which the rolls include tolls paid at all six of the fairs. No reference is made to the fair of the Invention of the Holy Cross after this date.

32 The waterways as shown on the map derive from Satchell, Newton and Shaw-Taylor, 'Navigable waterways'.

33 H. Hallam, 'Farming techniques: Eastern England', in H. Hallam (ed.), *The agrarian history of England and Wales: Vol. 2, 1042–1350* (Cambridge, 1988), pp. 294–303.

economic symptoms of famine, such as falling wages, petty land sales and rural-to-urban migration.[34] This period would have had a significant adverse effect on settlements within the claylands, which depended so heavily on arable farming, and it seems reasonable to conclude that these economic problems had a consequential impact on the Thetford fairs, with far fewer traders visiting from these settlements to sell their produce.

Conclusion

It is evident from *The register of Thetford Priory* that the pattern of decline that began in the early fourteenth century continued in the subsequent two centuries. The priory made regular visits to Bromehill fair, from which it bought a range of goods and services, and, to a lesser extent, to St Mary Magdalen.[35] Both the Invention of the Holy Cross and the Exaltation of the Holy Cross survived into the sixteenth century, although the priory's visits were very limited: only two visits are recorded to the Invention of the Holy Cross, in 1521 and 1528, and only one to the Exaltation of the Holy Cross, in 1525.[36] The *Register* contains no record of the priory visiting either of the two fairs dedicated to St John (Santon and Thetford), despite these having been moderately successful in the earlier period. While this cannot be considered as conclusive proof that they were no longer in operation, it does suggest that this may have been the case. In his list of fairs published in 1587 in *The description of England* William Harrison makes no reference to the existence of any of the Thetford fairs, although other sources confirm that Bromehill fair continued into the nineteenth century.[37]

The provincial fairs of late medieval England have left limited evidence and rarely feature in studies of trade and marketing during this period. While this paper relates only to six fairs in a confined geographical area, it demonstrates not only that they played an important role in the regional economy but that their influence extended much further afield. The evidence does confirm that much of their business was associated with meeting the needs of local agriculture, in terms of both the marketing of wholesale produce and the provision of related goods and services, but it also shows that other products could be obtained. Finally, the paper demonstrates the importance of good transport connections to traders in the late Middle Ages, particularly those offered by rivers.

---

34 B.M. Campbell and C. Ó Gráda, 'Harvest shortfalls, grain prices and famines in preindustrial England', *The Journal of Economic History*, 71/4 (2011), pp. 867–71.

35 Dymond, *Thetford Priory: Part I*, pp. 89, 130, 215, 229; Dymond, *Thetford Priory: Part II*, pp. 386, 402–03, 405, 420, 423, 457, 460–1, 476, 479–80, 495, 498–9, 513, 515, 531, 533, 564, 566, 579, 582, 597, 612–14, 616, 618, 630–1, 645, 646–8, 666, 680, 686, 699, 704–05, 721–3, 728, 737–8, 747.

36 Dymond, *Thetford Priory: Part II*, pp. 414, 496, 540.

37 G. Edelen (ed.), *The description of England: the classic contemporary account of Tudor social life by William Harrison* (London, 1994), pp. 392–7; G. Moore, *The history of Bromehill priory and fair: Weeting, Norfolk* (Weeting, 2002), pp. 50–3.

Chapter 8

Why did medieval industries succeed?
Early fourteenth-century Norfolk worsted
and late fifteenth-century Suffolk woollens[1]

Nicholas R. Amor

In the early 1980s David Dymond ran an extra-mural course in Lavenham that ultimately led to the publication of the classic study of that small south Suffolk town.[2] The project exemplified David's twin qualities as an inspiring teacher and as a learned and engaging author, while the volume told the history of the extraordinary, if short-lived, success of Lavenham as a centre of woollen cloth manufacture. It is a story that inspired the writer of this paper to study the medieval textile industry in East Anglia.

In seeking reasons for the success of cloth industries such as that of Lavenham, one must ask the right question. Not 'why was cloth produced there?' because the simple answer is that homespun was produced everywhere; but 'why did production grow to such an extent that it came to the attention of contemporary record keepers?' The medieval wool cloth industry had two principal products, worsteds and woollens. The manufacturing processes were different in important respects, as was the finished fabric. In particular, worsteds were generally lighter than woollens. The textile industry of Norfolk was primarily geared to the production of worsteds, and that of south Suffolk to woollens.

Sources

This paper draws on many different documentary sources, but statute merchant certificates (SMCs) and the plea rolls of the royal court of common pleas have been particularly valuable.[3] Edward I was keen to encourage alien merchants to trade in his realm for reasons of enlightened self-interest – he saw them as cash cows. A key element of his policy was to offer them sure and speedy justice in the recovery of their book debts. In order to achieve this, parliament enacted the Statutes of Acton Burrell (1283) and of Merchants (1285) which established 'statute merchant' registries, later known as

---

1   This paper is based on presentations delivered by the author to the Economic History Society conference in Belfast on 6 April 2019 and the Anglo-American conference in Worcester on 7 July 2019.

2   A. Betterton and D. Dymond, *Lavenham: industrial town* (Lavenham, 1989).

3   TNA, C 241 and CP 40.

staple courts, in leading towns, including Norwich. Anyone could register at such a registry any loan or other credit that they made available and, in the event of default, ask the registry to send to central government a certificate giving details of the debt and so initiate enforcement action against the assets of their debtor.

The plea rolls are probably our best source of information about late medieval private litigation. Between 70 and 80 per cent of pleas were debt actions for sums ranging from 40s to many thousands of pounds. These debt actions are evidence not only of who was dealing with whom, but also of who was providing credit to whom. As from 1413, they invariably gave the name, place of residence and occupation of the defendant; and, as well as the name, they often gave the place of residence and occupation of the claimant. This enables the historian to identify cloth-makers and those with whom they were in dispute, and those to or from whom they granted or took credit.

Measures of success

In both Norfolk and Suffolk the great 'wool churches' bear witness to the prosperity of their congregations in the late Middle Ages. That at Worstead is 'externally one of the dozen or so grandest Norfolk parish churches', while that at Lavenham is 'as interesting historically as it is rewarding architecturally' (Plates 8.1 and 8.2).[4] Some members of those congregations grew rich on the back of cloth manufacture. In Worstead, now a small settlement twelve miles north-east of Norwich, a rental of 1270 records that Reginald Dunnyng held half an acre of land; sixty years later four of his descendants were working as weavers in the village; fifty years after that a William Dunnyng was among the most heavily taxed of all village residents and was buying up land in Worstead, Westwick and North Walsham; and in the late fifteenth century the family were still resident and making cloth.[5] The Spryngs of Lavenham were even more successful. Thomas Spryng II was sufficiently prosperous to help fund the construction of the tower and vestry of Lavenham Church and endow scholarships at the universities of Oxford and Cambridge.[6] His son did even better. By the time of his death in 1523 Thomas Spryng III was perhaps the wealthiest commoner in England. The family ascent continued into the ranks of the gentry and even nobility. In ascribing reasons for industrial success the importance of individual talent and enterprise must never be discounted.[7]

The growth of the worsted industry in and around Worstead and of the woollens industry in south Suffolk is also evident in contemporary records of credit and debt.

---

4   N. Pevsner and B. Wilson, *The buildings of England, Norfolk 1: Norwich and north-east* (London, 1997), pp. 734–5; J. Bettley and N. Pevsner, *The buildings of England, Suffolk: west* (London, 2015), p. 351.

5   NRO, DCN 40/5, ff. 132r–135r; C.C. Fenwick (ed.), *The poll taxes of 1377, 1379 and 1381, part 2: Lincolnshire–Westmoreland* (Oxford, 2001), p. 165; TNA, CP 25/1/167/170; TNA, CP 40/886, f. 12v.

6   TNA, PROB 2/14.

7   Phillipp R. Schofield, 'Spring family (*per. c.*1400–*c.*1550)', *ODNB*, online edn, January 2008, <http://www.oxforddnb.com>, accessed 19 June 2019.

In Norfolk two sets of such records document the debts of the county's dyers; one dates from 1294 and records the book debts owing to woad merchants of Amiens that were arrested [confiscated] by the crown; the other, from the first half of the fourteenth century, records sums owing under SMCs, many of them due to those same Amiens merchants. The data is set out in Figure 8.1. The higher value debts are to the right and it is evident that the later ones, as recorded in the SMCs, were generally the more valuable. Those same SMCs record rising levels of credit flowing into Worstead and its surrounding villages, much of it granted to dyers and weavers. In late fifteenth-century Suffolk the growth of cloth-making is evident from the growing number of clothiers cited in the plea rolls. The data is set out in Figure 8.2. Five plea rolls from the ten years either side of 1490 cited 133 different clothiers, far more than any other county in England.[8] So what lay behind the success of these two industries, separated in time and manufacturing quite different products? If we can identify factors that they had in common, then we may be nearer to answering the question 'Why did medieval industries succeed?'

Versatility

Both Norfolk worsted and Suffolk woollens were versatile fabrics that were manufactured in a range of qualities and, particularly in the case of worsted, could be put to a variety of uses. Several sources between the 1290s and the 1330s give prices per ell (forty-five inches) for lengths of worsted that range from less than 3d to as much as 2s 5d.[9] To an extent this may be explained by differences in width, although Munro contended that early worsted was invariably a narrow cloth.[10] But it also reflects differences in quality that are corroborated by examination of fragments recovered by archaeologists working on the Thames Embankment in London.[11] Worsted could be used for bedding, coverlets, hangings and curtains, as well as religious dress and everyday wear such as stockings, robes and coats. Plantagenet kings bought worsted to cloth their armies and also, as an act of charity, to provide coverlets for the bedding of students at Cambridge University.[12]

Although statute law required that each Suffolk broadcloth weigh at least thirty-eight pounds (weight being a rough guide to quality), Suffolk woollens sold in a range

---

8   TNA, CP 40/871, 891, 911, 931, 951.

9   NRO, DCN 1/5/3, 4, 5, 6, 8, 10; TNA, E 101/379/12, E/101/382/2, E 154/1/18A; J. Burtt, 'Account of the expenses of John of Brabant and Thomas and Henry of Lancaster A.D. 1292–3', *Camden Miscellany*, 2 (1853), pp. 1–18 at p. 8.

10   J. Munro, 'Three centuries of luxury textile consumption in the Low Countries and England, 1330–1570: trends and comparisons of real values of woollen broadcloths (then and now)', in K.V. Pedersen and M.B. Nosch (eds), *The medieval broadcloth: changing trends in fashions, manufacturing and consumption* (Oxford, 2009), pp. 1–73 at p. 4.

11   E. Crowfoot, F. Pritchard and K. Staniland, *Textiles and clothing 1150–1450* (London, 1992; repr. Woodbridge, 2001), pp. 36–7.

12   TNA, E 361/3/9, 13.

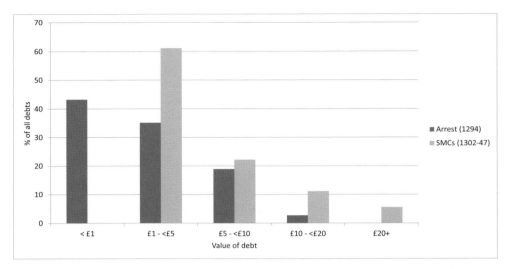

Figure 8.1. Value of dye-related Norfolk debts. In the period 1305–09 the mean value of all Norfolk SMCs was £17. *Sources:* TNA, E 106/3/6, C 241; P. Nightingale, *Enterprise, money and credit before the Black Death* (Cham, 2018), p. 191.

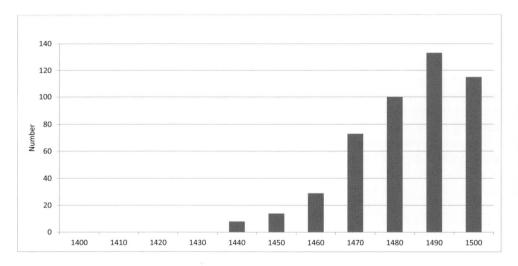

Figure 8.2. Numbers of Suffolk clothiers. Each column records the number of Suffolk clothiers in the twenty years centred on the given date. *Source*: TNA, CP 40/716, 736, 756, 776, 796, 814, 834, 853, 871, 891, 911, 931, 951, 971, 990.

of different prices.[13] Some were manufactured from fine premium-quality wools bought in the Cotswolds and Welsh Marches, others from much coarser wools sourced locally from Breckland. In 1414 John Sutton shipped from Ipswich 600 straits (short, narrow cloths) worth 6s 8d each and another 500 worth 5s 6d each; 200 cogware (coarse narrow cloths, possibly originally of Coggeshall, Essex) worth 4s 10d each; 200 matsales (cloths of Mattishall, Norfolk) worth 4s each; twenty broadcloths worth 30s each; and 200 broad dozens (broad cloths, originally twelve yards long) worth 14s each.[14] Later in the century John Rainham of Nayland manufactured broadcloths worth £3 each, and Nicholas Gosselyn of Lavenham vesses (lower-quality broad cloths) worth only 36s each. Both Norfolk and Suffolk craftsmen could cut the cloth to suit the purse.[15]

Rural-based industries

The industries in both counties were based in the countryside. Rural enterprise thrived in the absence of urban regulation and expense, and cloth-makers enjoyed greater operational freedom. As early as 1270, surname evidence identifies cloth-workers in the village of Worstead. A 1327 petition by worsted weavers against state regulation of their craft named eighty-two men, spread across at least nine villages.[16] Twenty-two – nearly 40 per cent of the fifty-eight for whom a residence is legible – came from Worstead itself. All the weavers lived within a six-mile radius of that village. Among the dyers we looked at earlier, eight came from Worstead. A third of the inward credit flowing into Tunstead Hundred, as recorded in SMCs, went to Worstead. Of the twenty-six SMCs addressed to Worstead debtors, five were issued against the weaver Henry Martolf, at least one more was issued against a weaver and three were issued against dyers. The sum of all these numbers is that, before the Black Death, Worstead was, without doubt, the epicentre of the industry that bears its name.[17]

Although Lavenham is the best known of the Suffolk 'wool towns', the textile industry was far less concentrated in one centre than it had been in Norfolk, or indeed than it was in many contemporary cloth-making counties. This multi-focal nature of the county's textile production can be traced back to the late thirteenth century, and by 1500 at least eight small towns and villages in south Suffolk were home to significant numbers of clothiers: Lavenham, Long Melford, Nayland, Stoke-by-Nayland and Sudbury in the hundred of Babergh; Bildeston and Hadleigh in the hundred of Cosford and East Bergholt in the hundred of Samford. A nationwide search of late fifteenth-century plea rolls shows that they heavily outnumbered those in any other county in England and almost certainly produced more cloth.[18]

---

13 *Statutes*, 2, pp. 424–5.
14 TNA, E 122/51/39.
15 TNA, PROB 2/87; TNA, PROB 11/8/360.
16 TNA, C 145/104, m. 3.2.
17 TNA, C 241/61/11, C 241/71/28, C 241/90/69, C 241/95/41, C 241/97/60, C 241/101/27, C 241/103/184, C 241/104/32, C 241/112/260, C 241/157/104.
18 N.R. Amor, *From wool to cloth: the triumph of the Suffolk clothier* (Bungay, 2016), pp. 222–39.

The clothier was the fifteenth-century archetypal figure in the rural industry. According to Carus-Wilson he

> had not to suffer a constant drain on his purse for local taxation, pageants, liveries, and all the burdens of public office. Nor had he to submit to the industrial controls that bound the city manufacturer. He was free to employ what workers he pleased [and] to offer whatever wages would secure them.[19]

The same nationwide search reveals that just over a third of cloth-finishers – that is, dyers and shearmen – lived in the greater towns of England; and just over a fifth of cloth-producers – spinsters, card-makers, weavers and fullers; but only one in twelve clothiers did so. And it was the clothier who had become the driving force in the growth of late medieval textile manufacture.[20]

Availability of labour

In the late thirteenth century Norfolk was the most heavily populated county in England, home to nearly half a million people, the majority of whom enjoyed personal freedom.[21] Manure-intensive and highly productive methods of arable husbandry generally helped support the masses, but they were very vulnerable to poor harvests. In his analysis of the 'agrarian problem' in Norfolk, Campbell rightly stresses that 'no other county was so congested'.[22] In Worstead itself two-thirds of local holdings were of less than five acres, including those of cloth-workers and of men such as Reginald Dunnyng, who fathered dynasties of weavers.[23] This land hunger meant two things: most peasants struggled to grow enough food for themselves and their families and so were in desperate need of other income; and an army of impoverished men and women was available to undertake the labour-intensive work of cloth-making. The surviving poll tax lists of 1379 and 1381 show just how many of them in Worstead and its surrounding villages took up the challenge.[24]

By the late fifteenth century population pressure had been relieved by the demographic collapse that followed the Black Death and successive epidemics of plague. This catastrophe initially released large areas of land on to the market and pushed marginal soils out of cultivation. In the longer term it had two consequences:

---

19 E. Carus-Wilson, 'The woollen industry', in M.M. Postan and E. Miller (eds), *The Cambridge economic history of Europe: trade and industry in the Middle Ages* (Cambridge, 1952, repr. 1987), pp. 614–90 at p. 684.

20 Amor, *From wool to cloth*, p. 54.

21 S. Broadberry, B.M.S. Campbell, A. Klein, M. Overton and B. van Leeuwen, *British economic growth 1270–1870* (Cambridge, 2015), p. 25.

22 B.M.S. Campbell, 'The agrarian problem in the early fourteenth century', *Past and Present*, 188 (2005), pp. 3–70 at pp. 66–9.

23 NRO, DCN 40/5, ff. 132r–135r; E. Martin and M. Satchell, *Wheare most inclosures be. East Anglian fields: history, morphology and management* (Ipswich, 2008), p. 80.

24 Fenwick, *The poll taxes*, pp. 159–71, 196–9.

a switch from arable to pastoral farming that by the 1420s was well underway, followed by the engrossment and enclosure of holdings that had the effect of concentrating land ownership in fewer hands. Studies of Monks Eleigh and Thorney (near Stowmarket) show this in progress.[25] The incomes of those with little or no land were further depressed by a general economic malaise, known as the Great Slump, which coincided with the start of the county's industrial growth spurt. Suffolk peasants confronted similar problems and challenges to those faced by their Norfolk forebears two centuries before, and appear to have responded in the same way by turning to craft activity. A rental of 1441/42 for the manor of Melford Hall in Long Melford lists tenants in Hall Street, at least eleven of whom were fullers.[26] Their holdings were tiny, certainly not big enough to support subsistence agriculture, with only three holding more than an acre and none more than two. An analysis of acres per taxpayer, based on the subsidy of 1524, shows that many of the most heavily populated Suffolk parishes were not those that had been most overcrowded in 1327 (the previous date for which lists of taxpayers survive), but those, such as Bildeston, Hadleigh, Lavenham and Nayland, where textile manufacture was most intense. They had been successful in attracting the labour force that their clothiers required.[27]

Industrial organisation

Craft guilds in medieval East Anglia were uncommon. This did not prevent cloth-makers from organising themselves to protect and further their interests and from finding novel ways of doing so. In the early fourteenth-century Norfolk worsted industry tensions grew between mercers, who wanted to buy and sell by the ell and know for certain what they were buying, and weavers, who fought for the right to manufacture as they wished. In particular, they wanted to produce piece-goods to satisfy particular orders rather than bolts of cloth of specific length. And many of them wanted to do so on cheaply made vertical looms that would not meet the standards of strict regulation. These tensions came to a head in 1327, when the crown-appointed local alnager, Robert Poley, became heavy-handed in seizing cloth that did not comply with regulations. Two SMCs may record fines of £100 and £200 that he imposed and sought to enforce against recalcitrant weavers.[28] They did not take this lying down, but fought back with impressive and concerted industrial action. The appointment of successive royal commissions of inquiry, petition and counter-petition led to ultimate victory for the weavers. As we have already seen, one of those petitions provides our best evidence of where they were carrying on their craft. No wonder that Edward III later grumbled about this episode: 'various quarrels were brought to us every day'. In 1329 Poley was dismissed and the sheriff of Norfolk ordered to proclaim that the

---

25 TNA, CP 25/1/224/114–16; CCA DCc-Register/B; N.R. Amor, 'Late medieval enclosure – A study of Thorney, near Stowmarket, Suffolk', *PSIA*, 41 (2006), pp. 175–97.

26 SROB, J/523.

27 H. Todd and D. Dymond, 'Population densities, 1327 and 1524', in D. Dymond and E. Martin (eds), *An historical atlas of Suffolk* (Ipswich, 1988; repr. 1989 and 1999), pp. 80–3.

28 TNA, C 241/100/2, 5.

weavers and workers of worsteds might work and sell their cloths without assay. Thereafter, for the rest of the Middle Ages worsteds remained outside the jurisdiction of the alnager.[29]

In late fifteenth-century Suffolk, richer clothiers turned to the putting-out system to enable them to boost production and meet the growing demand of domestic and overseas markets. They bought the wool; distributed it to and paid the wages of those workers who, in their own homes, turned it into cloth; marketed and sold the cloth, increasingly through London; and pocketed the profit. Looking back on this development, Karl Marx was to write in *Das Kapital* that 'the prelude to the revolution that laid the foundation to the capitalist mode of production was played in the last third of the fifteenth and the first decade of the sixteenth century. A mass of free proletarians was hurled on the labour market … '.[30] For several later economic historians the clothiers who employed these free proletarians were the pioneers of modern capitalism.[31] In his will Thomas Spryng II bequeathed 100 marks (£66.67) to his spinners, weavers and fullers. He was either extraordinarily generous or had a lot of people working for him. His fellow townsman Thomas Sturmyn left 2d to each of his spinners in Glemsford and Stoke-by-Clare. This gift tells us not only about the normal rate of testamentary reward for cloth workers, but also about the hinterland from which they were drawn. Stoke-by-Clare is nearly twelve miles from Lavenham, a much longer journey in the 1490s than it is today.[32]

Commercialisation

In the Middle Ages crosses sprang up across East Anglia to signal the creation of new markets, and those at Binham and Lavenham still stand (Plates 8.3 and 8.4). The number of earliest references to village markets in Norfolk and Suffolk peaked in the second half of the thirteenth century, while England's silver currency, earned by wool exports, reached its maximum value in the first quarter of the fourteenth. Both phenomena were signs of the increasing commercialisation of English society. By 1300 East Anglia had the densest networks of weekly markets in the kingdom. David Dymond was the first to map those of Norfolk. If, as Bacton suggested, peasants could travel six and a half miles from home and the same distance back in a day then in parts of north Norfolk they could visit a market every day of the working week. In parts of south Suffolk they enjoyed almost as much choice. For the first time in recorded history ordinary people had regular contact with those who lived beyond the boundary of their own parish and the more fortunate ones had spare cash to spend

---

29 *Rot. Parl.*, ii, 204; *CFR, 1327–37*, p. 32; *CPR, 1327–30*, pp. 297–8, 424; A.F. Sutton, 'The early linen and worsted industry of Norfolk and the evolution of the London mercers company', *Norfolk Archaeology*, 40 (1989), pp. 201–25 at pp. 207–9.

30 K. Marx, *Capital: a critique of political economy*, 3 vols (Chicago, 1926), vol. I, p. 789.

31 R.H. Tawney, *Religion and the rise of capitalism* (Middlesex, 1938), pp. 79–80; E. Power, *The wool trade in English medieval history* (Oxford, 1941), p. 4; R. Hilton, 'Capitalism – what's in a name?' in R. Hilton (ed.), *The transition from feudalism to capitalism* (London, 1978), p. 156.

32 TNA, PROB 11/7/352, 11/10/42.

on cloth. It cannot be a coincidence that this period saw the early growth of textile manufacture in both counties.[33]

In Tunstead Hundred three market charters were granted between 1225 and 1260 to Broomholm, Horning and the village of Tunstead; the earliest reference to the market at North Walsham dates from 1274/75; and in 1336 a fourth charter was granted to Worstead. This market quickly attracted so much business that within three years the earl of Huntingdon was complaining about its detrimental impact on his one at nearby Sutton.[34] In Babergh Hundred, Lavenham, Long Melford, Nayland and Stoke-by-Nayland all received market charters between 1227 and 1303. The market at Long Melford appears to have had a similar impact on one at Clare as Worstead's had on Sutton's.[35]

As well as enjoying easy access to markets, cloth-makers benefited from good transport links. Worstead and North Walsham lie near the heads of navigation of the rivers Bure and Ant and their output could be carried by boat to the port of Great Yarmouth.[36] Ships that already carried corn from Norfolk's intensive grain fields down the east coast to London could also carry worsted. The river Stour served Suffolk clothmakers in the same way. The waterman Thomas Lukat clearly enjoyed a sufficiently close relationship with the Nayland clothier Stephen Raynham to visit him in his dying days and act as one of the witnesses to his will.[37] South Suffolk was also within a few days' ride of London by cart. For local carriers taking Lavenham cloth overland to the City, the earl of Oxford had, as early as 1329, secured exemption from all tolls that might otherwise have been payable en route.[38]

Trade networks

It is trite but true that in business it is not so much what you know as who you know. Relationships of trust and confidence with customers are essential to success. Cloth-makers of both Norfolk and Suffolk forged close ties with two particular groups – the German merchants of the Hanseatic League and London mercers – who were instrumental in selling their wares both domestically and overseas.

The German Hanse was a political and commercial league of towns, from Gdansk in the east to Cologne in the west, whose merchants dominated much of north European trade from the late twelfth century. Among the earliest records of their business with England are alien customs accounts that record their exports and imports. These are studded with references to worsted. For instance, in April 1311 ten consignments

---

33 D. Dymond, 'Medieval and later markets', in P. Wade-Martins and J. Everett (eds), *An historical atlas of Norfolk* (Norwich, 1993), pp. 76–7; Gazetteer of markets and fairs in England and Wales to 1516, <https://www.history.ac.uk/cmh/gaz/gazweb2.html>, accessed 19 June 2019.

34 *RLC*, ii, p. 67; *CChR, 1226–57*, 309; *CChR, 1257–1300*, p. 26; *Hundred Rolls*, I, p. 533; *CChR, 1326–41*, pp. 353, 463.

35 *CChR, 1226–57*, pp. 12–13, 209, 475; *CChR, 1300–26*, p. 36; *CRR, 1234–7*, p. 202.

36 J. Campbell, 'Norwich', in M.D. Lobel and W.H. Johns (eds), *The atlas of historic towns, Vol. 2 Bristol, Cambridge, Coventry, Norwich* (London, 1975), pp. 1–25 at p. 14.

37 TNA, PROB 11/18/55.

38 *CChR, 1326–41*, p. 122.

worth in total £193 were shipped from Great Yarmouth, of which the two most valuable belonged respectively to Rykewyn and Christian of Cologne.[39] Moving forward over a century, merchants of Cologne were major figures in the export of Suffolk woollens from Colchester and Ipswich. In the mid-1400s they regularly shipped more than a thousand whole cloths each year (or equivalent in narrow ones) and in 1446/47 the number peaked at 5,105. This would have accounted for most of the cloth produced in north Essex and south Suffolk that year.[40] Remarkably, there is very little evidence of their trade in either SMCs or the plea rolls. A search of twenty rolls recording tens of thousands of pleas between 1430 and 1470 has found only three disputes between a Hanse merchant and a Suffolk cloth-maker, with a total value of just £38, the price of perhaps twelve broadcloths and a tiny fraction of the value of their cloth trade.[41] A similar search of the borough records of Ipswich has found only one such dispute, which arose when, on 12 June 1461, the merchant Hans Sandowe bought nine broadcloths from William Warner but failed to pay him the full £21.[42] The explanation for this paucity of records is probably cash. The Hanse merchants not only exported cloth but also imported a wide range of merchandise, accounting for over 60 per cent in value of goods arriving in mid-fifteenth-century Ipswich.[43] So they had ready money with which to buy the woollens and, even if statute had not restricted denizens from granting them credit, very rarely would they have had needed to give or take credit. In a parliamentary petition of 1455 the Commons, whose number included aggrieved English merchants, complained that 'marchaunt straungers [...] have custumably used to ryde aboute for to bye Wollen Clothes [...] in every partie of the same Reame [...] the said Marchaunds [...] have redie money and therewith at the ferst hande bye Wollen Clothes'.[44]

The relationship between East Anglia's cloth-makers and London's mercers was, despite the occasional quarrel referred to above, perhaps an even closer one. In Norfolk the same land hunger that had encouraged peasants to turn to weaving for a second income forced many to move away. The harvest failures of the mid-1290s and particularly of 1315–17 made rural–urban migration more urgent and quickened the flow of humanity 'in a desperate quest for food and alms'.[45] The most enterprising went to London to become mercers. The second largest cluster of such immigrants came from around Worstead. For instance, by 1292 a Robert de Worstead was working in the capital city as a mercer and, in 1318, was numbered among 'the more powerful and better class of' men. Sutton has identified seven mercers from Tunstead Hundred alone, among them Simon and John de Worstead, who both served as wardens of the company. References to London mercers selling worsted or holding it in stock are

---

39   TNA, E 122/148/13.

40   E.M. Carus-Wilson and Olive Colman (eds), *England's export trade 1275–1547* (Oxford, 1963), pp. 94–102.

41   TNA, CP 40/748, m. 363v (AALT IMG 1759); TNA, CP 40/796, m. 9v (AALT IMG 861).

42   SROI, C/2/10/1/2.

43   TNA, E 122/52/42–8.

44   *Rot. Parl.*, v, pp. 334–5.

45   B.M.S. Campbell and C. Ó Gráda, 'Harvest shortfalls, grain prices, and famines in preindustrial England', *The Journal of Economic History*, 71/4 (2011), pp. 859–86 at p. 871.

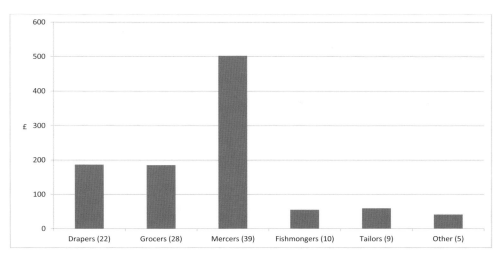

Figure 8.3. Value of litigation between Suffolk clothiers and London merchants, 1440–1500. Each column records the value of litigation between Suffolk clothiers and members of that company and the number of disputes is stated at the bottom. *Source*: TNA, CP 40/716, 732, 736, 756, 758, 768, 788, 796, 807, 814, 826, 834, 837, 841, 853, 861, 871, 883, 885A, 887, 888, 889, 890, 891, 895, 907, 911, 919, 931, 943, 951.

commonplace.[46] When Richard Feverer (alias Elsing – a Norfolk village) died in 1332 his inventory included twenty-two items of worsted piece-goods as well as bolts.[47] London mercers were also big players in the export of worsted. On the eve of the Black Death, in early February 1349, one of them, Henry de Cawston, exported 300 cloths from the City. As with Hanse merchants, there is very little sign of this trade in SMCs. Before the Black Death just twelve certificates were issued by London mercers against Norfolk debtors and only one was issued by a Norfolk creditor against a London mercer. None of these mercers had a toponymic name linking them to Tunstead Hundred, and none of the Norfolk men was resident there. SMCs issued by and against Norwich merchants suggest that they may have acted as middle-men between cloth-makers and mercers – twelve of the SMCs against Worstead debtors were issued by Norwich men. In addition, extended family links between Norfolk and London may have created trust and confidence that often made credit, or at least the formal recording of credit, unnecessary.[48]

By the end of the fifteenth century London had become the most important market for Suffolk clothiers and, within the City, mercers were their most valuable customers. The value of disputes taken from thirty-one plea rolls between Suffolk clothiers and members of London livery companies is shown in Figure 8.3. Far more disputes were

46   A.F. Sutton, *The mercery of London: trade, goods and people, 1130–1578* (Aldershot, 2005), pp. 54–7, 82–3, 555.
47   TNA, E 154/1/18A, mm. 1–2.
48   TNA, C 241.

with mercers than with members of any other company and, at over £500, mercers accounted for nearly half the total value of the litigation. The mean value of their disputes was nearly £13, significantly more than the others. Almost certainly, most of these pleas arose from advance or deferred payments for cloth and nearly three-quarters of the credit thus recorded flowed from London to Suffolk. Clothiers were heavily dependent on mercers for the cash flow that enabled them to keep their businesses afloat, but the continuing success of those enterprises kept the cash taps running.

Conclusion

There do appear to have been several common factors in the success of Norfolk worsteds and Suffolk woollens. The talent and enterprise of individuals was one. The versatility of both fabrics, but particularly of worsted, helped capture different market sectors. Both industries were based in the countryside, which allowed cloth-makers to operate free of urban restraint and to recruit the requisite labour force. They organised themselves in a way that defended and promoted their business interests. The commercialisation of English society created a framework and infrastructure within which their enterprises could prosper. East Anglian cloth-makers made friends in the right places and this enabled them to market and sell their products well beyond the boundaries of their own region.

Chapter 9

Artisans and peri-urban development: a case study from the domestic building industry in the late Middle Ages

Alan Rogers

David Dymond's use of artefacts (especially buildings) and documents in his historical studies, bridging archaeology and history, is well known; his use of geographical concepts, space and relationships in his landscape studies is less recognised. This paper seeks to draw on all three disciplines in an analysis of the late medieval domestic building industry to suggest that, around major towns, rural-based artisans benefited from the patronage of wealthy urban-based landlords. The argument is based on the recently published account book of successive wardens of Browne's Hospital, Stamford. Attention among artisanal historians of the late Middle Ages has of late focused more on identities, how they were perceived by contemporaries, than on the processes involved. While this has revived the debate about the rural–urban location of many industries, it is still true, as Thirsk said many years ago, that 'not enough is known about local economies'.[1]

The medieval building industry has been well served by historians, and accounts of building projects have been published. But the evidence so far comes from major works under the supervision of master masons, such as castles, cathedrals and abbeys;[2] little is known about the ordinary domestic builder working on small-scale

---

1   J. Thirsk, 'Industries in the countryside', in J. Thirsk, *The rural economy of England* (London, 1984) p. 219; J. Lee, *The medieval clothier* (Woodbridge, 2019), repeats traditional arguments about the rural location of industries. The starting point is J. Harvey, *Medieval craftsmen* (London, 1975). More recent studies include C. Dyer, P. Coss and C. Wickham (eds), *Rodney Hilton's Middle Ages: an exploration of historical themes* (Oxford, 2007); G. Rosser, 'The five guildsmen', in S.H. Rigby and A.J. Minnis (eds), *Historians on Chaucer: the 'General Prologue' to the Canterbury Tales* (Oxford, 2014), pp. 247–61; M.A. Pappano and N.R. Rice, 'Medieval and early modern artisan culture', *Journal of Medieval and Early Modern Studies*, 43/3 (2013), pp. 473–85; L.H. Cooper, *Artisan and narrative craft in late medieval England* (Cambridge, 2011); J. Cherry, *Medieval crafts: a book of days* (London, 1993). See also P. Belford, 'English industrial landscapes: divergence, convergence and perceptions of identity', in A. Horning and M. Palmer (eds), *Crossing paths or sharing tracks* (Woodbridge, 2009); L. Klapste and P. Sommer (eds), *Arts and crafts in medieval environments, Ruralia* vi (Turnhout, 2007).

2   W.D. Simpson (ed.), *The building accounts of Tattershall Castle, 1434–1472*, Lincoln Record Society 55 (Lincoln, 1960); A. Rogers, 'Building accounts for Pontefract Castle, Michaelmas

building and repairs of houses, barns and walls. In the records of Browne's Hospital, Stamford, we have an opportunity to see how a regional domestic building industry worked over a period of some twenty years, 1495–1518.

The Hospital estates and the obligations of the warden

Browne's Hospital was founded between 1475 and 1494 by William Browne of Stamford, merchant of the Calais staple, and after his death (1489) by his brother-in-law and executor Thomas Stokes, rector of Easton on the Hill. The Hospital was endowed with estates scattered across south Lincolnshire, east Rutland and north Northamptonshire: two manors and some thirty farms and rented properties were held by the warden. Responsibility for the repairs of most of these properties fell to the warden as landlord, and details of this work were recorded in the surviving account book of the first four wardens of the Hospital.[3] Most of the properties underwent extensive repair. To take just one example, North Luffenham Bede Farm (Plate 9.1), with its fifteenth-century hall and cross wing, belonged to William Browne and then to the Hospital. It had major repairs in 1500–01 and 1507–08 and minor maintenance work on six other occasions to both the main building and to its louvre, kiln and dovecote.

The sources

The account book contains a detailed account of expenditure from 1495 to 1518. The largest sum spent each year was on '*reparations*' to the Hospital's properties. The accounting process for these repairs is clear. After the work had been completed, a

---

1406–Michaelmas 1407', *Journal of British Archaeological Association*, 166 (2013), pp. 140–56; A. Hamilton Thompson, 'Building accounts of Kirby Muxloe Castle 1480–84', *Transactions of the Leicestershire Architectural and Archaeological Society*, 11 (1913–20), pp. 193–345, available at <http://www.gatehousegazetteer.info/English%20sites/1772.html>, accessed 30 April 2013; for ecclesiastical accounts see J. Raine (ed.), *The fabric rolls of York Minster* (Durham, 1859); A.M. Erskine (ed.), *The accounts of the fabric of Exeter Cathedral 1279–1353*, Devon and Cornwall Record Society 24 (Exeter, 1981); C.A. Stanford (ed.), *Building accounts of Savoy Hospital, London 1512–1520* (Woodbridge, 2015). One of the most important recent surveys of the value of high-status building accounts for domestic building is J. Rimmer, 'A re-assessment of the use of building accounts for the study of medieval urban houses', 2011, available at <https://www.arct.cam.ac.uk/Downloads/ichs/vol-3-2599-2612-rimmer.pdf>, accessed 19 November 2019; see works cited in this paper. L.F. Salzmann, *Building in England down to 1540* (Oxford, 1952) is still the starting point for any discussion of this industry, but see also H. Swanson, *Building craftsmen in late medieval York* (York, 1983); D. Knoop and G.P. Jones, *The medieval mason* (Manchester, 1967); D. Parsons, 'Stone', in J. Blair and N. Ramsay (eds), *English medieval industries: craftsmen, techniques, products* (London, 2003), pp. 1–27.

3   Bodleian Library, Rawlinson Ms. B. 352, edited A. Rogers, *The wardens: Managing a late medieval hospital: Browne's Hospital, Stamford 1495–1518* (Bury St Edmunds, 2013); for foundation, N. Hill and A. Rogers, *Guild, hospital and alderman: new light on the foundation of Browne's Hospital. Stamford 1475–1509* (Bury St Edmunds, 2013).

bill was drawn up by the person overseeing the repair, specifying the craftsmen and the work undertaken. Payment may have been made directly on site, in which case the bill is recording such payments; alternatively, payment was made by the warden after receiving the bill.[4]

These bills seem to have been copied into the book faithfully. At times, the name of the craftsman employed is not recorded; for example:

Item iiij masons ij days	iijs iiijd
Item to a thakkar [thatcher] ij deys and to hys servar of ye sam	xvjd

But many craftsmen are named, as for example:

Item to wynpeny the mason for settyng in off a window with hys server	xiiijd
Item I paid to hygen and john wrygt for makyng a window j day	xijd

On occasion, the residence of the builder is also given:

Item to Rawlyn lokkey off wyrthorp sklatter iij days and half xxd

From this source it is possible to compile a list of the various builders employed and (in many cases) their residences.

This list can be compared with the contemporary Stamford Borough Hall Book, which records the admission to the freedom of those who traded from within the town between 1465 and 1657. These lists appear to be comprehensive; efforts were made from time to time to bring them up to date. So we can be reasonably certain that we have an almost complete list of craftsmen licensed to work in the town, although from time to time a man is enrolled without his occupation being stated:

John Tyard free born in the borough will give nil fine and was sworn	
Thomas Grace admitted to freedom … and will give for fine	js [1s]

Out of 326 freemen enrolled between 1465 and 1518, one in six (fifty-two) had no occupation listed; 274 craftsmen with occupations were registered as freemen of the borough in this period.[5]

---

4 One such bill survives; it is undated but seems to belong to the years immediately preceding the account book, when the hospital and its estates were in the hand of Thomas Stokes before being vested in the warden: TNA, SP 46/123/57. It is for work done in Stamford on the 'New Tavern'; transcribed in Rogers, *The wardens*, p. 36.

5 Stamford Town Hall borough records, Hall Book I (hereafter HBI). It was rather badly kept and there is a gap from 1492 to 1494. The years from 1465 to 1492 have been transcribed and edited by A. Rogers, *William Browne's town: the Stamford Hall Book vol. I: 1465–1492*, Stamford Survey Group (Stamford, 2005). The years from 1494 onwards have been transcribed by John Hartley and are in the process of final editing. All references after f. 50 are from this unpublished transcript. I am grateful to John Hartley for his willingness to share this transcript and other information.

Stamford builders

The building industry is represented in this cadre of artisans. Between 1465 and 1518 thirteen masons were enrolled, some 5 per cent of all craftsmen. In a town with so much stone building, this is few for forty-three years. Some masons clearly worked from the town without being admitted to the freedom: William Mason of St Clements parish, Stamford, was employed extensively by the wardens but his admission cannot be traced.[6] Twelve carpenter-wrights were admitted, with three carvers and one sawyer. Ten freemen slaters can be identified. There were no thatchers; two plumbers, one plasterer and two painters were enrolled. The number of smiths and brasiers (seventeen) suggests a stronger iron industry than building industry. These relatively small numbers suggest not only that there were unlicensed craftsmen in the town but also that we need to look elsewhere for such artisans.

The Hospital accounts help here. A total of eighty-two building craftsmen are named. Of these, the location is not given for thirty artisans. Occasionally the name of a craftsman employed by the wardens was not given but the location was recorded: 'the thatcher of Belmesthorpe', for example. The accounts reveal that four out of every five craftsmen used by the wardens resided in the neighbouring villages around Stamford. It is possible that some of the named but unlocated builders came from the town, but none of these can be traced in the Hall Book.

The village craftsmen

Four building crafts, masons, carpenters/wrights, slaters and thatchers – as listed in Table 9.1 – feature mainly in the accounts and were used extensively. Of the rest, plumbers were employed nine times but none is located except 'the plommar of seynt andrew parysch', twice. Much the same is true of the smiths: the 'smyth of seynt mary parysch' is the only located smith recorded.

Successive wardens employed only one of the thirteen freemen masons, four of the twelve enrolled carpenters and none of the ten freemen slaters. Most of the work was done by builders from outside the town. And sometimes from a considerable distance: the only named plasterer used, Harry Plaisterer of Oakham, worked in Stamford (four times) and Stretton, a distance in each case of about eleven miles. So, it is clearly not for reasons of convenience that the wardens used village craftsmen. They were often sent from one side of the town to the other, across the river Welland – from Casterton to Barnack, for example, or from Belmesthorpe (a hamlet in Ryhall parish) to Easton on the Hill. And many were brought into the town to work there. When one considers the time taken to travel across the district (the distances involved are not great, five to eight miles, but almost all journeys would need to cross the river Welland at Stamford bridge or causeway), carrying tools and perhaps some materials,[7] and allowing for

---

6   He may of course have used a different surname, rather than his occupation, when admitted.
7   The accounts are full of payments for deliveries of cartloads of building material throughout the district; the total spent on carriage exceeded all other expenditure. The craftsmen themselves may have used donkeys or ponies for carriage of their own goods and tools.

Table 9.1
Building workers featured in Stamford hospital accounts.

Named or located artisans	Urban	Rural	No known location	Total
Masons	2	13	6	21
Carpenters/wrights/sawyers	5	9	8	22
Slaters	2	10	2	14
Thatchers	-	2	-	2
Total	9	34	16	59

the short winter days and long summer days, the amount of work on site must have varied considerably.

The craftsmen were not confined to their own specialisms. While daubing of partition walls was undertaken at times by labourers, wrights and masons also engaged in lathing and pargetting:

Item to wyllam mason for lathyng and dawbyng at the seyd particion j day   vjd [6d]
Item to ij masons vij deys for makkyng up of walls and for pargentyng
ye dowf' hows [pargetting of the dove house]   vijs [7s]

Rates of pay

An analysis of the payments that can be clearly identified over this period of twenty-two years is revealing (Table 9.2). In the contracts listed, daily rates predominated other than for the carpenter-wrights. Out of all the payments made to them (217), masons received three-quarters in day rates, slightly increasing as the time passed, and thatchers and slaters had nearly two-thirds of all payments in day rates. On the other hand, carpenters and wrights were paid at piece rate for rather more than half of their contracts. The few contracts for plumbers, glaziers and smiths show that they were always paid piece rate, while plasterers at first were paid piece rate but later day rates.[8] There is no sign of any difference between winter and summer rates.

---

8   Some payments included the wages of the 'server' and the exact division between them cannot be determined. Some payments are so anomalous that they have been omitted from this survey; these may have included other costs, such as materials. For example, in 1497–8 one wright was paid 2s 8d for two and a half days – just over 12d per day, double the normal rate. Some of these may be errors in writing the accounts. On rates of pay, see C. Dyer and S.A.C. Penn, 'Wages and earnings in late medieval England: evidence from the enforcement of the labour laws', in C. Dyer, *Everyday life in medieval England* (London, 1994), pp. 167–90; H. Swanson, *Medieval artisans: an urban class in late medieval England* (Oxford, 1989), pp. 82–97.

Table 9.2
Payments made by Stamford hospital to each craft.

	Masons	Carpenters/wrights	Thatchers	Slaters
Piece rate payments	59	111	34	49
Day rate payments	158	102	60	75
Day rates as % of all payments	73	48	64	60

Masons

Twenty-one masons were identified either by name or place. These were not itinerant masons as depicted in most studies but permanently resident builders, working on local domestic and farm sites. The locations of four unnamed masons are known, two 'of Ufford' and two from Oakham. The locations of six of the seventeen named masons are unknown – some of these may be Stamford-based, but they were not freemen. Some masons were used only in their own locality, but mostly they were used some distance away. Thus, while a Barnack mason was used in Barnack with a mason from Stamford, a Casterton mason with a mason of Stamford went to Barnack, some six miles across the river through the town. A Wittering mason was used in Stamford and Barnack, and the Ufford masons were used in Stamford, Pilsgate and Barnack. Two masons from Oakham were brought over to Stamford; the Easton masons were used almost exclusively in Stamford.

The majority of masons, then, were recruited from outside the town and many were brought in to work in the town. We know of one other mason in the town, Nettleton (a tenant of the Hospital) in St Martin, who was not used, unless he was one of the unnamed masons employed – which is unlikely, for local artisans would have been known and therefore named in the accounts.

As previously mentioned, some three-quarters of all the contracts given to masons were for day rates. Whether from town or village, they were generally paid at the same rates: at first, 5d per day, gradually rising to 6d, the change appearing about 1502 (perhaps with the change of warden). The difference is unlikely to have been seasonal, as for the first five years almost all were at the rate of 5d per day, and after 1506 all payments (except two) were at 6d per day. There appears to have been no difference between jobs in Stamford and in the villages, but it is possible that masons who lived in the place where they were asked to work were paid less. John Elys, mason in Warmington, on two different occasions was paid only 3d per day for a total of ten days' work; several (unnamed) masons were paid at 4d per day. Richard Uffington, mason, was paid 6d per day while working in Barnack, while his fellow mason Gee, who came from Barnack itself, was paid 5d per day for what seems to have been the same job. On the other hand, Wimpeny of Swayfield was paid 6d per day for work in his own village.

Carpenters

Carpenters in traditional societies were of different kinds. *Joiners* were often wealthy house and barn builders, employing other workmen. *Wrights* made substantial items ranging from carts (cartwright, wheelwright and so on) to milling machinery (mill wrights), and items within buildings, such as doors and windows. *Carvers* may of course have been carvers of stone or of wood; wood carvers made smaller items, from small tools to buckets, platters and bowls – usually working on their own. In the Hospital accounts, the terms carpenter and wright are used interchangeably, and carver appears only as a surname. *Sawyers* were not often distinguished from carpenters but were named on three occasions; they were used only in the Hospital yard, although (unnamed and unlocated) sawyers were also paid for work done at Swayfield, Stretton and Wothorpe. They almost always worked in pairs.[9]

Twenty-two carpenter-wrights and sawyers were identified by place or name. Four of the eleven carpenter freemen enrolled between 1465 and 1518 and one other carpenter/sawyer from Stamford were used; none of the three freemen sawyers was employed by name. Nine came from outside of the town. They were used intensively, often at considerable distances, frequently forming partnerships across the villages and with Stamford-based craftsmen. John Hygen, carpenter, of Ryhall and John Wright of 'Belmysthorp' wright almost always worked together; Hygen also worked with a freeman of Stamford and others. Presumably the heavy building work involved needed two carpenters as well as their 'servers'. Hygen seems to have become the wright of preference for the Hospital.

Rather less than a half of all payments to carpenter-wrights were at day rates – piece rate was more normal. Although carpenters on occasion had day wages adjusted to suit the task (that is, deductions or in some cases small additions were made), during this period, the named carpenter-wrights were paid 6d per day; only John Wright junior in 1495 (one task), Thomas Benson wright in 1507 (one task) and Thomas Abbot for one of his ten employments were paid at 5d per day, which does not suggest winter payments. Of the day wages of unnamed wrights or carpenters, a third (sixteen) were at 5d, the remainder (thirty-three) were at 6d.

Thatchers

Only two thatchers are identified in the accounts, although clearly more were employed. One (unnamed) from Belmesthorpe was sent across the river to work in Easton; but on the whole Robert Kesten of Wothorpe, a tenant of the Hospital, had a near monopoly of the thatching work of the Hospital estate. He worked in Stamford, Wothorpe, St Martin, Easton, Barholme and Pilsgate, and some of the unattributed thatching work was probably his. He normally worked with one or more servers and could also turn his hand to hedging. There are no known thatchers in Stamford itself. Kesten, like most of the unnamed thatchers, was paid 5d per day. From about 1506, some were paid 6d per day. There are more anomalies here, presumably related to the size of the task involved.

---

9   J. Blair and N. Ramsay (eds), *English medieval industries: craftsmen, techniques, products* (London, 2003), pp. 2, 382, 386; Swanson, *Medieval artisans*, p. 86.

Slaters

The Stamford area is a major centre for roof slates, which came from pits at Collyweston, Wothorpe and Easton. There are many purchases of slate from the pits, including the Hospital's own pits, and many slaters provided slates in bulk. Of the fourteen slaters identified by name or location, all but three came from Wothorpe or Easton. Three lived in the town, the slater 'yat dwell in peter paryche' and Robert Slater 'yat dwellyd at ye boyr'. A third, John Wylson, was one of the ten freemen-slaters in the town: he worked only inside the town. They frequently worked in groups, especially Rawlyn Lokkey of Wothorpe, the most used slater. Much of their work was in Stamford and St Martin, but the neighbouring villages of Easton, Wothorpe, Pilsgate and Barnack also saw them at work. Lokkey and Hawkyn were always paid 6d, but Wilson only 5d. Of the unnamed slaters, most were paid 6d; only in 1500 and 1515 were some paid 5d. Several payments were for more irregular sums, from 4½d to 8d per day – perhaps including the server and probably adjusted for the work to be done.

Some factors influencing the location of building workers in rural areas

The majority of the building workmen employed by the wardens came from centres outside of Stamford (Map 9.1), which raises the question: why were they there? It is important to remember that even if these men were living only a mile or so outside the town, many of the town's opportunities for commercial activities and obligations of taxes, guild expenses at festivals and trading regulations no longer applied to them.

Rurally based industry has attracted the attention of historians for many years, at both macro- and micro-levels. It has been recognised that 'in many localities … craftsmen … outnumbered the men living mainly by agriculture'. Most of the focus has been on textiles and associated crafts (gloves, hemp, lace, stockings, hats, baskets), together with some iron and woodwork. The building industries have featured less frequently.[10]

---

10 D.C. Coleman, 'Proto-industrialization: a concept too many', *Economic History Review*, 36 (1983), pp. 435–48; E.B. Fryde, 'Peasant rebellion and peasant discontents', in E. Miller (ed.), *Agrarian history of England and Wales*, vol. iii, 1348–1500 (Cambridge, 1991), pp. 744–819, at p. 775; L. Poos, *A rural society after the Black Death: Essex 1350–1525* (Cambridge, 1991); J. Whittle, 'Individualism and the family-land bond: a re-assessment of land transfer patterns among the English peasantry c1270–1580', *Past and Present*, 160 (1998), pp. 25–63. Thirsk, 'Industries in the countryside', pp. 230–1, cites knitting; making of baskets, hats, gloves and lace; wooden platters and trenchers; Swanson, *Medieval artisans*, p. 2, lists smiths, carpenters and weavers, miners, glass-blowers and charcoal burners; J. Thirsk (ed.), *Agrarian history of England and Wales*, vol. iv, 1500–1640 (Cambridge, 1967), pp. 425–9, lists cloth, gloves, hemp, iron, lace, leather, linen, pottery, stockings, woodwork. M. Bailey, *Medieval Suffolk: an economic and social history* (Woodbridge, 2007), p. 153, lists smiths, leather workers, tailors, carpenters and thatchers. Carus-Wilson and Bridbury debated the town and country divide vigorously in relation to the cloth industry: A.R. Bridbury, *Medieval English clothmaking: an economic survey* (Farnham, 1982 edn); E.M. Carus-Wilson, 'Evidences of industrial growth on some fifteenth-century manors', reprinted in E.M. Carus-Wilson (ed.), *Essays in economic history*, Economic History Society, vol. ii (London,

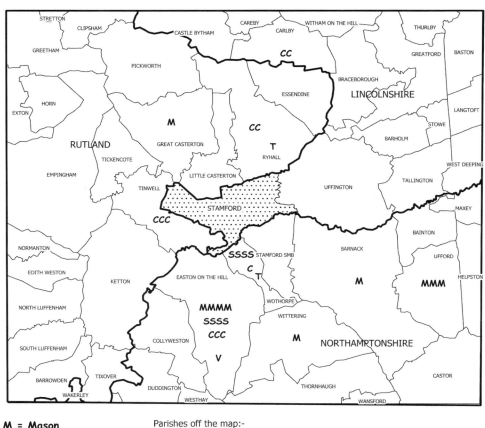

M = Mason
C = Carpenter or Wright
S = Slater
T = Thatcher
V = Carver

Parishes off the map:-

Oakham has 2 masons and 1 plasterer
Swayfield has 1 mason and 1 carpenter
Warmington has 1 mason and 1 carpenter

Drawn by David Addy
Using QGIS 3.8

Map 9.1. Location of late medieval building trades around Stamford (courtesy David Addy).

Some of the reasons given for the location of industrial activities in rural areas do not appear to apply to the area around Stamford. Blair and Ramsay have suggested that 'town and gild attitudes drove industry … into the countryside. … No such controls existed in the countryside where working hours and wage rates were unrestricted and the expense of gild membership and civic pageantry could be avoided.' But in late medieval Stamford, the powerful guilds were parish or socio-religious ones,

---

1962), pp. 151–67; E.M. Carus-Wilson, 'The woollen industry before 1550', in E. Crittall (ed.), *A history of the county of Wiltshire*, vol. iv (Oxford, 1959), pp. 115–47.

such as the guilds of St Katherine or All Saints, to which craftsmen of various kinds belonged; there were no craft guilds. Such associations in Stamford as existed for the Corpus Christi pageants provided by the different crafts in the town at the order of the town council were, as elsewhere, 'an arm of civic administration'; regulation of the trades by searchers of the markets was controlled by the borough council.[11] And such regulations as were imposed by the town council appear to have been confined to the town itself; how far the searchers of the market went out of the town to places such as Barnack or Easton on the Hill to inspect work done by Stamford carpenters, masons and slaters is not known. Nevertheless, some of the obligations and costs that freemen incurred may at the least have deterred some from seeking to be admitted to the freedom of the town. Nor was it the freedom to set their own wages that led them to settle in rural contexts. There is no evidence that 'low wages' due to surplus labour existed in this region;[12] for, as these accounts show, there was no difference in wages between rural and urban building workers.

Rather, many rural areas were characterised by a long-standing natural diversification of peasant economies, taking advantage of surplus produce (such as cheese-making, baking, brewing and so on) and spare time left by seasonal farming. Peasant families (especially children) often had spare time from work on their land and could do other work, exploiting all resources, natural and human, on 'by-employments'. Equally, a diversity of livelihoods was in many cases essential for survival: 'a degree of occupational specialization should not be expected in the Middle Ages … almost every settlement contained holdings too small to provide for the needs of a family without supplementation of income by earnings in … industry.'[13]

Thus most village communities had their own service industries. 'The appearance on the rural scene of … small teams of artisans widened employment in the villages and gave many a man frustrated by the insufficient resources of his agricultural holding an occupation and a means of living.' The association between land and

---

11   Blair and Ramsay, *Medieval industries*, pp. xxiv–xxv; see also 'It is alleged that their [craft guilds'] attitude was one of the prime factors which … in later medieval England … drove industry from the town to exploit freer conditions in the countryside', J.L. Bolton, *The medieval English economy 1150–1500* (London, 1980), pp. 264–7. See A. Rogers (ed.), *The act book of St Katherine's Gild, Stamford, 1480–1534* (Bury St Edmunds, 2011); A. Rogers, *Noble merchant: William Browne c1410–1489* and *Stamford in the fifteenth century* (Bury St Edmunds, 2015), pp. 187, 201, 223–5, 246–52; Swanson, *Medieval artisans*, pp. 5–6, 142; Rogers, *William Browne's Town*, p. 137.

12   Swanson, *Medieval artisans*, p. 142.

13   I. Blanchard, 'The miner and the agricultural community in late medieval England', *Agricultural History Review*, 20 (1972), p. 104. See J. Birrel, 'Peasant craftsmen in the medieval forest', *Agricultural History Review*, 17 (1969), pp. 91–107; J.Z. Titow, *English rural society 1200–1350* (London, 1969), p. 92; Thirsk, 'Industries in the countryside', p. 232; Thirsk, *Agrarian history*, pp. 425–9; E. Miller and J. Hatcher, *Medieval England: rural society and economic change 1086–1348* (Harlow, 1978), p. 250; Swanson notes 'multiple occupations', *Medieval artisans*, pp. 4–6; D. Hurst, 'Medieval industry in the West Midlands', West Midlands Regional Research Framework for Archaeology (Birmingham, n.d.), p. 3, available at <www.birmingham.ac.uk/documents/college-artslaw/caha/wmrrfa/5/derekhurst.doc>, accessed 19 November 2019; Dyer, *Everyday life*, pp. 7–8.

craft worked both ways: some village artisans were 'part-time cultivators' and some small landholders engaged at times in artisanal activities. For some non-agricultural activities, such as textiles, much of the work was part-time and seasonal. The early development of towns with their specialisms did not kill village industries: Bailey has suggested that in parts of rural Suffolk between 12 per cent and 20 per cent of the economically active population could have been 'those whose primary employment was earned from skilled or semi-skilled craftswork'. Hilton pointed out that every excavation of medieval rural sites produces a crop of artefacts not all of which came from urban specialists.[14] Most villages would have had a local mason, carpenter and roofer nearby.

The location of industry was, of course, dictated in part by its need for access to resources (wood, stone for walls and roofs, straw for thatching, fuel and clay for pottery, tiles and brickmaking and so on). Many of the masons and slaters employed by the wardens were close to their supply of stone; and the region around Stamford was noted for its forests, enough to encourage the development of a thriving woodwork industry. But not all – there were masons in villages without stone and many in Stamford itself.[15]

An important factor in the case of Stamford would seem to have been space. To run a carpentry business, especially that of joiner and wright, required a substantial area for a 'yard'; masons, too, required a yard in which to work and keep materials. The warden knew this, for he used the plot behind the Hospital for storing building materials and for working timber, and he had a substantial barn and yard in Scotgate. The small burgage tenements of Stamford[16] could not provide space for all crafts. While there were a number of barns in the town, there must always have been a lack of space – or, at least, space would be more easily (and perhaps more cheaply) available in the rural communities around the town.

In addition, the royal taxation system that assessed the town tradesmen at one tenth of movables and those in rural areas at one fifteenth – although the sums had become to some extent customary – was probably significant. But this is still largely unexplored territory; as Harvey points out, the rural taxation system is still obscure, with 'some smallholders being assessed more highly than peasants with standard customary holdings'.[17]

---

14 G. Duby, *Rural economy and country life in the medieval West* (London, 1968), p. 154; C. Platt, *Land and people in medieval Lincolnshire*, History of Lincolnshire iv (Lincoln, 1985), p. 120; R.S. Hilton, *Medieval society* (London, 1966), pp. 206–7, 214; Bailey, *Medieval Suffolk*, pp. 153–4. The number of keys for locks found on sites cannot all have been bought in town markets: Platt, *Land and people*, p. 122.

15 Bolton, *Medieval English economy*, p. 272; Rogers, *Noble merchant*, p. 71. For local woodcraft, see *VCH Rutland*, vol. I, p. 233, Uppingham trenchers.

16 RCHM, *The town of Stamford* (London, 1977); a range of medieval tenements along the north side of St Paul's Street shows how small the burgage tenements in parts of Stamford were.

17 B. Harvey, 'Population trends in England 1300–1348', *Transactions of the Royal Historical Society*, 16 (1966), p. 29; see M. Jurkowski, C.L. Smith and D. Crook, *Lay taxes in England and Wales 1188–1688* (London, 1998), p. xxix.

But, in the end, explanations in terms of access to raw materials, spare labour, space and rural advantages over the towns are not enough to account for the location of rural industries. At the heart lies much personal initiative. This would have been a development over many years, probably not even noticed at the time; the outcome of many individual decisions. Inertia probably played a part: as long as the work kept coming in, as long as there were local markets to sell the produce and landlords, lay and clerical, with work to be done, rural tradesmen would continue to flourish. Rural industrial employment was of much more than 'marginal significance';[18] for numerous men and women it was a major occupation and contributed to the local economy substantially.

Concentrations of rural craftsmen

Such factors do not, however, explain the concentration of tradesmen around a town such as Stamford. There would, of course, have been jobbing builders in more remote villages, but the concentration we see around Stamford seems to call for further explanation. It was, I suggest, the result of the fact that the town possessed a range of patrons for building work – landlords such as William Browne and other lay and ecclesiastical lords and their agents with property scattered throughout the region that required repairs and with resources to pay for them. Those building craftsmen who lived close to any major town benefited naturally from such patronage, prospering more than more remote fellow-tradesmen. Proximity to a town may on the one hand have encouraged what Bailey calls 'the leaking of ... expertise from the established boroughs', while at the same time it may have increased the demand for crafts and trades that the town could not fulfil completely, and this in turn led to greater specialisation.[19] The peri-urban fringe of towns such as Stamford would have prospered from the proximity of the town's wealth.

Yet, these workmen were not evenly distributed among the neighbouring villages. Wothorpe had a significant number, mainly slaters and a thatcher. Ryhall also had a number, both in the main village and in the smaller settlement of Belmesthorpe. A major concentration was in the parish of Easton on the Hill: here were no fewer than four slaters, three masons, two wrights and a carpenter. These three parishes also supplied much of the material the wardens' builders used. (The fact that these concentrations occur in villages removed from the river suggests that transport of materials by river was not a major factor at this time.)

In Easton on the Hill we have what is perhaps an example of the 'semi-farming, semi-industrial communities' to which Thirsk drew attention.[20] For her, domestic

---

18 J. Hare, 'Pensford and the growth of the cloth industry in late medieval Somerset', *Somerset Archaeology and Natural History*, 147 (2004), p. 177; Titow, *English rural society*, p. 92.

19 Bailey, *Medieval Suffolk*, pp. 153, 298.

20 Thirsk, 'Industries in the countryside', p. 232; see also Thirsk, *Agrarian history*, pp. 12–14; 'the location of handicraft industries is not altogether haphazard, but is associated with certain types of farming community and certain kinds of social organization.'

Plate 2.1. Cellarer's Chequer (counting house), Barnwell Priory, Cambridge. It dates from the thirteenth century, and stands at the junction of Priory Road and Beche Road, Cambridge. As second only to the prior, the cellarer had responsibility for storing food and other supplies (© Joanne Sear).

Plate 3.1. Stained glass image of Robert de Skelton, merchant, at St Denys, Walmgate, York (© J.A. Frost).

Plate 3.2. Stained glass image of a merchant visiting the sick and the elderly, popularly taken to be Nicholas Blackburn, senior, at All Saints, North Street, York (© J.A. Frost).

Plate 3.3. Stained glass image of Robert Semer, cleric, at St Martin, Coney Street, York (© J.A. Frost).

Plate 3.4. Stained glass image of John Walker, cleric, at Holy Trinity, Goodramgate, York (© J.A. Frost).

Plate 3.5. Stained glass image from possible guild, at St Michael-le-Belfrey, York (© J.A. Frost).

Plate 5.1. A niche next to the east window of the south aisle, at All Saints' Icklingham, Suffolk. It shows the 'shadow' of an image (© Michael Durrant).

Plate 5.2. Late fifteenth-century devotional alabaster image of Henry VI (© Rijksmuseum, Amsterdam, reference BK-18310).

Plate 6.1. Porch of Southwold church. The room above may have been used to store the arms and armour of the fifteenth-century vicar Robert Scolys (© Bob Carr).

Plate 7.1. The priory of St Mary, Thetford, made extensive use of local fairs to procure a wide range of goods (© Nicholas R. Amor).

Plate 8.1. Worstead church, Norfolk, a memorial to industrial success and 'externally one of the dozen or so grandest Norfolk parish churches' (© Nicholas R. Amor).

Plate 8.2. Lavenham church, Suffolk: the archetypal Suffolk 'wool church', 'as interesting historically as it is rewarding architecturally' (© Nicholas R. Amor).

Plate 8.3. Binham market cross, Norfolk. Erected in the fifteenth century, it marks the site of one of many medieval markets first recorded in the thirteenth century (© Nicholas R. Amor).

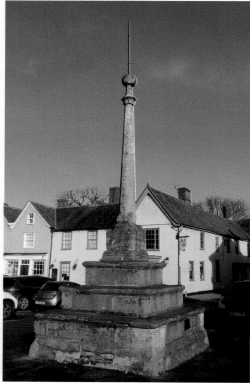

Plate 8.4. Lavenham market cross, Suffolk, first set up in 1501 under the will of the clothier William Jacob (© Nicholas R. Amor).

Plate 9.1. North Luffenham Bede Farm, with its fifteenth-century hall and cross wing. It belonged to William Browne and then to the hospital he founded (© Nick Hill).

Plate 13.1. The Plomesgate Union workhouse at Wickham Market, one of the workhouses built in 1836/7 to meet the requirements of the New Poor Law (© Ray Whitehand).

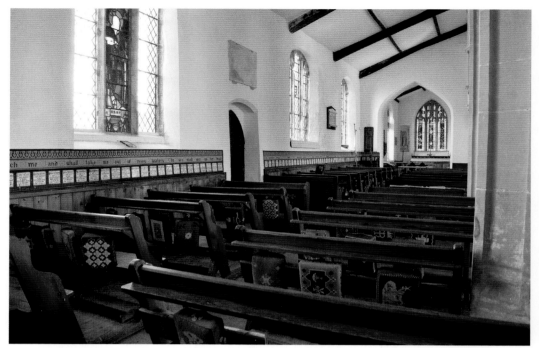

Plate 16.1. Frieze of commemorative tiles inside Brightlingsea church installed from the 1870s by Canon Arthur Pertwee to remember local mariners lost at sea (© Sean O'Dell).

Plate 16.2. Frieze of commemorative tiles inside Brightlingsea church: two tiles remember a father and son both named David Day and both lost at sea in the same vessel on 9 December 1872 (© Sean O'Dell).

industry was located in pastoral areas with plentiful labour and spare time, where there was not enough return on agriculture, and where weak manorial control allowed greater freedom for industries to develop. There were two manors in Easton, one held by the king and the other by Tattershall College, both absentee landlords: the estate was held by 'a series of non-resident noblemen [with] no manor house, the only dwelling of consequence being a copyhold'.[21]

But, as Mark Bailey says, 'it is no longer satisfactory to seek a simple or single explanation of economic change ... [it is] a highly complex process involving a range of variables acting together'; the interaction between agriculture and industrial development is multi-faceted. For example, while the existence of significant numbers of small holdings may in some places have encouraged the development of alternative forms of livelihoods, equally the availability of alternative forms of work in 'petty crafts and by-employment' may have encouraged the development of small holdings. Strong manorial control did not necessarily exclude the development of alternative livelihoods; the more effective manorial courts of some landholders may have encouraged such development; as Mark Bailey has commented, 'the very high proportion of smallholdings was possible precisely because the availability of non-farm employment was greater here than elsewhere'.[22]

The parishes around Stamford in the early sixteenth century were marked by subdivision into small settlements and absentee landlords. Out of twenty-six parishes, only two (Collyweston and Peakirk) were nuclear. Two other manors were emerging with influential resident landlords: Milton, where the family of FitzWilliam was making their main residence; and Tolethorpe, the newly created home of Christopher Browne of Stamford. All the other parishes were subdivided into small hamlets and separate estates. Even Maxey, where the castle had seen the long-term residence of Lady Margaret Beauchamp (mother of Lady Margaret Beaufort), was now highly subdivided, the castle leased from at least the late 1490s.[23]

And much of the area was in the hands of absentee landlords, members of the nobility, old and new, and church institutions, especially Peterborough Abbey, with lands either leased or managed by bailiffs or stewards. The region had space available for development and had non-resident landlords. At the same time, parts of the region around Stamford were subject to enclosure for pasture – Christopher Browne and other members of his family were among those accused in Star Chamber of enclosure – and in the light of rural redundancies some manorial lords may have encouraged alternative livelihoods.[24]

---

21 RCHM, *An inventory of the historical monuments of the county of Northamptonshire* (London, 1985).

22 Bailey, *Medieval Suffolk*, p. 153; see also pp. 300–01; N.R. Amor, *From wool to cloth: the triumph of the Suffolk clothier* (Bungay, 2016), pp. 82–3.

23 This paragraph is based on an analysis of the manorial and sub-manorial structures of all the parishes circling Stamford as described in *VCH Northants*, vol. III and *VCH Rutland*, Vols I and II.

24 *VCH Rutland*, vol. I, p. 221; see Amor, *From wool to cloth*, pp. 63–4; Swanson, *Medieval artisans*, p. 143 speaks of the accumulation of holdings.

Conclusion

The picture that emerges of the region around late medieval Stamford is one where industry was not confined to the urban area. The region must be taken as a whole when examining its economy. Joan Thirsk pointed this out for a later period when looking at marketing and the cloth industry; the accounts of Browne's Hospital extend this picture to the building industry in an earlier period.[25] Around this town, as presumably around most larger towns, there grew up an area of semi-industrialised villages supported in large part by the patronage of town residents. It was not a case of villages relying on the town for prosperity; it was a symbiotic relationship in which town patrons such as the wardens of Browne's Hospital relied on out-of-town craftsmen to get their work done.

---

25   J. Thirsk, 'Stamford in the sixteenth and seventeenth centuries', in A. Rogers (ed.), *The making of Stamford* (Leicester, 1965), pp. 58–75.

Part III: Early modern

Chapter 10

'Villaines enough': political and personal feuding within Thetford Corporation, 1658–1700

Alan G. Crosby

Introduction

David Dymond's magnificent two-volume edition of the register of Thetford Priory is a major contribution not only to our knowledge and understanding of late medieval monastic houses but also to the history of East Anglia and the town of Thetford itself. The dissolution of the priory and Thetford's nine other religious foundations had a calamitous effect: 'now the pilgrims are "abhorryd, exesepulsyd and sette apart for ever, wherby a grett nombyr of peopyll … by idylld and lyke to be browght ynto extreme beggarye"'.[1] Over a century later, when the great priory had become one of the 'bare, ruin'd choirs',[2] Thetford was still in decline. But one aspect of its civic life was full of vigour: the fierce arguments that raged in its scandal-ridden Corporation.

This paper looks at the turbulent and bitterly divisive politics of the Corporation in the period from the death of Oliver Cromwell in September 1658 to the Glorious Revolution of December 1688, when deep-seated political and religious differences were exacerbated by the conflicting personalities of key figures. The experience of Thetford emphasises the importance of looking at the local dimension and demonstrates how channels of communication operated between the centre and the periphery in the later Stuart period. I offer this paper to David with my warmest thanks for many years of personal friendship, and with gratitude for his immense contribution to local and regional history in East Anglia and throughout this country for well over half a century.

Background

The restoration of the monarchy in May 1660, following a four-year experiment in republican government and seven more years of quasi-monarchical protectorate, ushered in a period of recrimination and retribution. During the previous eleven years institutions such as the Church of England had been abolished or reordered and

---

1   From a petition to the Privy Council by the mayor of Thetford in 1539, transcribed in T. Martin, *The history of the town of Thetford in the counties of Norfolk and Suffolk from the earliest accounts to the present time* (London, 1779).

2   William Shakespeare, sonnet 73, line 4 (1609).

radical restructuring was imposed on legal and governmental frameworks. Those changes were now to be reversed and undone, and further turmoil was inevitable. Between 1649 and 1656 there had been intense pressure for the removal of royalists and religious conservatives from positions of power and influence and their replacement by radicals and dissenters. That process petered out in 1657–8: the momentum of the revolution failed, providing an opportunity for conservative forces to regroup. With the gradual collapse of the Commonwealth between September 1658 and May 1659 traditionalists were able to reassert themselves, setting the stage for a sweeping counter-reaction once the position of the restored monarchy was consolidated in mid-1660.

The primary objective of the counter-revolution was to purge dissenters from national and local institutions of all sorts – removing 'Oliverians' from positions of authority,[3] cleansing the newly recreated Church of England by ejecting dissenting ministers, and trying to ensure that the political composition of parliament accorded with the requirements of the crown. These strategies were implemented using legislation, collectively known as the Clarendon Code, that clamped down upon the activities of dissenters in the Church, government and politics. A key weapon was the 1661 Corporation Act, which required that all members of borough corporations should formally acknowledge the Church of England and the king's place as its supreme governor and (to demonstrate that allegiance) receive holy communion in an Anglican place of worship at least once each year. The consequence of the Clarendon Code was that during the reign of Charles II there was frequent aggressive action against groups and individuals, and acrimonious and bitter debate between hostile factions. The extreme political and social tensions continued during the reign of James II, which culminated in the Glorious Revolution. In individual communities these purges, ejections, conflicts and personal vendettas were of major significance, because in a comparatively decentralised state much of importance was still determined at local level.

The changes under the Commonwealth and the post-Restoration counter-reaction were especially contentious in boroughs where the corporation was the parliamentary electorate. One such was Thetford,[4] which received its charter of incorporation from Elizabeth in 1574. Thence until 1835 the borough was governed, under the terms of that charter, by a council of thirty-one comprising the mayor, ten aldermen (or senior or principal burgesses) and twenty common councilmen, often termed 'the commonalty'. This was a self-perpetuating oligarchy: vacant aldermanic places were filled by nomination from among the commonalty, and vacancies in the commonalty by appointment from among the freemen of the town. The mayor was chosen each year from two men whose names were put forward, from among their number, by the aldermen and voted for by the commonalty and aldermen. With a total of only

3   The parish register of Alburgh (Norfolk) includes the burial entry for 'John Wright an old Oliverian' on 22 December 1720 (NA, PD 196/2).

4   The background to the town and its society, economy and governance in the Stuart period is given in Alan G. Crosby, *A history of Thetford* (Chichester, 1986), especially ch. 4 'Thetford 1540–1700'.

thirty-one individuals there was much scope for nepotism, venality and manipulation. Thetford was a parliamentary borough, first enfranchised in 1529 under the influence of Thomas Howard, 3rd duke of Norfolk, for whom it would potentially be a pocket seat. From 1547 onwards it returned two members to each parliament and, under the charter of 1574, the electorate comprised the thirty-one members of the Corporation, the composition of which was therefore politically crucial.

The Corporation 1658–60

At the Restoration the character and composition of the Corporation were very different from the position ten years before. The assembly book for 1647–59,[5] which records all changes in membership, shows that a major turnover had taken place. Only twelve of the thirty-one members in 1659 had been on the Corporation in 1647, and ten had been appointed in a single mayoral year, 1658–9. There had been twenty-six new admissions to the commonalty between 1647 and 1659, sixteen being explicitly the result of the death of a sitting councillor or the elevation of a common councilman to replace a deceased burgess. Four admissions were unquestionably the result of members of the commonalty being forcibly deprived of their places. The usual pretext was that, as in the case of the royalist and twice mayor Henry Daveny in October 1650, he had 'lately gone to live out of this Borough'. The remaining six instances are doubtful, since the assembly books give no reason for the admission, but deaths were reliably recorded so it is probable that the ejection of an existing councillor was the reason. It is also apparent that in the later 1650s vacancies, whether caused by death or ejection, were not filled promptly but were 'saved up', probably for political advantage. During the mass intake of 1658–9 all but one of the ten vacancies resulted from the death of a councillor, but they were spread over the preceding three years. During the two mayoral years from 1655 to 1657 there were four new councillors, and one councillor was elevated to be a principal burgess. But then came three admissions on one day, 18 September 1658, with one each in October and February, three in March and two in April. Thus, almost half the commonalty took office in the eight months from September 1658.

The common councilmen admitted in 1658–9 shaped the administration of Thetford for a quarter of a century, their subsequent actions suggesting that this amounted to a *coup d'etat* by the Anglican Tory faction, as it began to reassert itself following ten years of dissenter supremacy. An inner group of the intake was extremely active during the early 1660s in enforcing religious conformity and cooperating with the crown in purging the Corporation. There are pointers to a planned takeover – for example, several of the incomers were closely related by blood or marriage. Thus, Thomas Drewery was the son-in-law of the group's *de facto* leader Burrage Martin. The subsequent progress of some was exceptionally swift: John Kendall was admitted as a common councilman on 16 February 1659, became a principal burgess forty-nine days later and was chosen as mayor in September 1660. Indeed, the strength of the new intake is shown by the mayoral list:

5   NA, T/C 1/5: all quotations and data in this section relate to that source.

1659 Thomas White (elevated to burgess 1657)
1660 John Kendall (admitted 1659)
1661 Osmond Clarke (admitted 1659)
1662 Burrage Martin (admitted 1659)[6]

The Anglican Tories regained control in 1658–9 and over the next three years consolidated their position, with important posts being occupied by men who had been on the Corporation for a very short time. They lasted a long time. In the early 1680s survivors of the group were among those pushing for the surrender of the borough charter to the king, while Burrage Martin was prominent in events throughout the period until he died, still a member of the Corporation, in March 1688.

The crisis of 1664

The assembly book covering the period November 1659 to March 1682 is lost – possibly the result of deliberate destruction – so we know little about what was happening within the Corporation during that period. Episodes such as the purging of corporations in 1661 by the king's commissioners, employing the Act of that year and other statutory weapons, must have been very significant in Thetford, but their precise impact cannot be assessed. The purges undoubtedly produced major disruption, although partisan evidence put forward by the Anglicans twenty years later suggests that some councillors during the 1660s and 1670s adopted nominal conformity by taking sacrament in the Church of England as infrequently as they could.

During the summer and autumn of 1664, however, tensions within the Corporation were sufficiently strong to generate a serious and damaging public dispute that is externally documented. The trigger was a proposal from the leading Tories, under Burrage Martin, to renew the charter of 1574. Their rationale was that a new charter from the crown would name the principal burgesses, perhaps even the common councillors, and those individuals would unquestionably be steadfast supporters of the government. In December 1664 John Piddock of Fersfield near Diss testified that

> about Midsumer last past ... att the house of one Mr George Cook in Thetford [he] mett with Mr Thomas Snellinge one of the burgesses of the Corporation ther, who (beinge in discourse about their Charter with this informant) told him, that they (meaninge the rest of the Corporation) were about renewinge their charter.[7]

The matter caused much controversy in the town. 'Reasons against Renewing the Charter', an anonymous petition on the subject, lambasted the Corporation generally: 'the Mayor's power does too much domineer over them and tyranize over all other

---

6   A full list of mayors of Thetford in the second half of the seventeenth century is given in Hamon le Strange (ed.), *Norfolk official lists from the earliest period to the present day* (Norwich, 1890), pp. 230–1.

7   Raynham Hall MSS: Attic: Townshend family (papers of Sir Horatio Townshend, 1st Viscount): my thanks to Susan Maddock for clarifying the referencing system of the Raynham Hall archives.

inhabitants ... the present power is made use of only for sinister ends and private gain'. It was claimed that the Corporation comprised men of inferior status: 'there are twenty of them not worth an hundred pounds a year, half of them can neither write nor read'.[8]

The accuracy of these claims is impossible to ascertain, though it is certainly true that in this small town the members of the Corporation were generally small tradesmen and craftsmen: in 1682, for example, they included a carpenter, a plumber and glazier, a brickmaker, an ironmonger and a butcher.

Thomas Cropley, the town clerk, who had been appointed before 1658, was openly hostile to the proposal to renew the charter, making his views very clear: he 'did rudelie and uncivilly affront the Major of the said Borough'.[9] As a result the Corporation determined to be rid of him, and an order was made 'for the puttinge of Mr Thomas Cropley out of his Towne Clarkes place'.[10] Cropley argued that the Corporation had no power to do this, since he served for life. The mayor, Edmund Hunt, endorsed that view, saying that it was 'well-knowinge that by the Charter the Mayor & Burgesses had nothing to doe with the Town Clarkes place'.[11]

Word of the quarrel reached the Privy Council, which on 21 October 1664 instructed the lord lieutenant of Norfolk, Sir Horatio Townshend (Baron Townshend), to go to Thetford and resolve the acrimonious dispute.[12] He did so in person, and made efforts to conciliate: 'I propounded to the Major, that Thomas Cropley should make a publique in their open Court, declaring his sorrow for the said affront, and humbly begging the pardon of both the said Major, and all the Corporacion, to which the Major did readily consent and agree'.[13] Edmund Hunt was politically and temperamentally a moderate and modest man. His acceptance of this compromise was completely unpalatable to the strong-willed partisan group that had been admitted in the late 1650s. According to Townshend, 'Mr Burrage Martin, with the rest of the Burgesses, did absolutely and peremptorily refuse to accept either of the submission or Thomas Cropley, saying that they would have nothing to doe with either, lett Mr Major doe what hee would'.[14] A witness, Christopher Wyndutt of Methwold, yeoman, alleged in December 1664 that

> the next day after the Right Honourable the Lord Townshend, Lord Leiutenant
> of the County of Norfolke was att the Guyldehall in Thetford, endeavouringe to
> composse the differences between the then Mayor ther & one Thomas Croplye
> the towne clark ... Mr. Thomas White, one of the burgesses of Thetford did, att

---

8   NA, BL/GT/12.

9   Copy of Mss report from Sir Horatio Townshend (Viscount Townshend) to the Privy council,
    bound in front of NA, T/C2/6 (henceforth Townshend NA, T/C2/6).

10 *Ibid*.

11 *Ibid*.

12 It is perhaps indicative of the almost complete withdrawal of the dukes of Norfolk from county
    affairs at the time of the Civil War that they played no part in the borough's post-Restoration
    municipal or parliamentary politics.

13 Townshend NA, T/C2/6.

14 *Ibid*.

his owne house [say] that before the above named Croplye should ever be town-clarke agayne ther, or that they should not have a new charter, it should cost a thousand, and a thousand & a thousand pound; further sayeinge; that if they did not, our Children after us, would rue it.[15]

Townshend, in a further attempt to conciliate the parties, 'offered Mr Martin, or any of the said Burgesses ... for their better satisfacion ... that they should have the penning of the submission themselves'. Again his efforts were rejected, and he therefore personally wrote the submission to be made by Cropley and took it to the assembly meeting the next day. Nobody would agree to read it out in open session, so Cropley was brought into the meeting and read it aloud himself. The mayor, Edmund Hunt, then accepted the submission, but 'Mr Martin with the rest of the Burgesses (as formerly) did declare their aversenesse and unwillingnesse to accept either the submission or any other way that could be propounded, by way of accomodacion, saying that Cropley should never have anything to doe there'.[16]

Townshend was incensed by the public lecture he received from Burrage Martin, who

protested against what I had done, telling mee in a very insolent manner, that it was unreasonable; upon which I tould him I hoped it would not appeare so to any body but himselfe, And to let him see, that I was not ashamed of what I had done, I did desire that it may be entered into their Book, in perpetuam memoriam, to which the Major was very willing, but Mr Martin tould him that nothing could be entred in their Booke, without their consent, upon which I desired Mr Major to put it to the vote, and it was carried in the negative with a great deale of scorne.[17]

The lord lieutenant and the mayor then left the Guildhall, declaring loudly that there was no more to be said. Burrage Martin, who evidently never knew when to hold his tongue, followed them 'downe into the yard, and in a very high reproachfull Manner, told Mr Major there was, or hee had something else to doe'. Townshend left Thetford in a high fury, later reporting to the Privy Council that he had 'suffered very much, by their reproachfull Language, & false representacions of my carriage in this affaire'.[18] He having departed, the group led by Martin went to the house of Edmund Hunt, whose daughter Elizabeth subsequently testified that

upon the Nynth day of November last past shee being in the kitchin in her said fathers house ... heard diverse persons [pass] thorough the Hall ... up the Stayers and soe on to the Chamber, where her said father was in bed, and she hearinge some noyse & disturbance above ... enquired what was the matter,

---

15   Raynham Hall MSS: Attic: Townshend family (papers of Sir Horatio Townshend, 1st Viscount). The reference to thousands of pounds was dramatic hyperbole, as a charter usually cost £100.

16   Townshend NA, T/C2/6.

17   That book was of course the missing volume of the minutes of the corporation.

18   Townshend NA, T/C2/6.

where her fathers maid Servant told her that Mr Martin Mr Tyrrell Mr Clarke Mr John Hunt Mr Thomas White & Mr Cock were gone up into her fathers Chamber.[19]

Townshend later reported that they gave the mayor 'very rude and uncivill Language for being perswaded by mee to a friendly reconciliacion'. The gang ordered Hunt immediately to swear into office his successor, Robert Tyrrell, who had been chosen at the September meeting. It seems that the conspirators sought to subvert the borough constitution by dismissing Hunt ahead of the due date. He protested and, when told to administer the oath to Tyrrell, 'the Mayor being in Bedd refused to doe, But whether he would consent or not the words of the oath were read … at the same instant by one of them, Since which time the said New elect hath acted as Mayor of the said Corporation'.[20]

With the authority of the Privy Council, Townshend ordered the arrest of Tyrrell, Burrage Martin, Osmond Clarke, John Hunt, Thomas White, Bartholomew Snelling and John Cock. The six were at first imprisoned, but were quickly released after sending Townshend an obsequious petition acknowledging that they had

> carried themselves very Irreverently and misbeseeming that Duty they owe into his Majestie … and that we or some of us have since agravated our misdemeanors by saying that what your Lordship did … was unreasonable … for which our Miscarriages and disrespective behaviours wee are most hartily sorry, and doe not in the least desire to Justifie or extenuate the same, But doe humbly Crave that your Lordship will be pleased to remitt your petitioners faults and pardon them.[21]

Edmund Hunt testified to the lord lieutenant's officer at Bury St Edmunds in December 1664,[22] explaining that until the summer he had been 'relyeinge solely upon the direcions and Judgment of the said Mr Martin not only in the prosecucion of [the Cropley affair] but of all other transaccions as he was Mayor'. Thus an old man, who had first been mayor as long ago as 1639 and who was politically neutral, was chosen in 1663 because of his pliancy and susceptibility to pressure. Burrage Martin was rightly confident that Hunt would do their bidding: not until the arrival of Townshend did the latter seem to realise the gravity of what was happening. Hunt said that

> he at last perceivinge the false and malitious practizes of the said Martin, did forbeare any further to be over ruled by him, but did declyne his advice or to be further diverted by him, and … hath since endeavoured to restore the said Town Clerke to his place, but the said Martin hath & doeth by all wayes and meanes obstruct him.[23]

---

19 Raynham Hall MSS Box 70 State papers and miscellaneous correspondence.

20 Townshend NA, T/C2/6.

21 Petition bound into the front of NA, T/C2/6.

22 The borough of Thetford was partly in Norfolk (the parishes of St Peter and St Cuthbert) and partly in Suffolk (the parish of St Mary), which may be the reason for the taking of evidence at Bury St Edmunds.

23 Raynham Hall MSS Box 70.

The 'class of 1658–9' had imposed their will on the Corporation. Townshend, in his capacity as lord lieutenant and representative of the Privy Council, was actually on the same side, sharing their religious and political sympathies. His solution to the violent dispute between the town clerk and this unruly faction had been that the former should retract his views, apologise and submit to the will of the Corporation. But Burrage Martin, hasty-tempered and undiplomatic, was personally abusive and high-handed with Townshend and that, rather than their views or dealings with Cropley, was what so angered the lord lieutenant. Had Martin been more circumspect and cautious, and more appropriately deferential to his superior, he would surely have achieved his aims without any difficulty.

The group did not suffer from the events of the summer and autumn of 1664. Indeed, the humiliation of Thomas Cropley, the most important of their opponents, greatly strengthened their hand. In 1665 Robert Tyrrell was confirmed for a second term as mayor, this time by the usual procedures of the Corporation, and he was succeeded in 1666 by Burrage Martin himself. John Hunt, another of those who had marched into Edmund Hunt's house and threatened the old man in his bed, was chosen mayor in 1667. He died in office in March 1668 and Robert Tyrrell filled the remainder of that term, while in December 1668 Thomas White, yet another of the conspirators, succeeded him. Tyrrell served four full mayoralties and one part-year between 1665 and 1680, while during the period 1660–75 the mayoralty was occupied in no fewer than eleven out of seventeen terms by those who were arrested and imprisoned in 1664. Their dominance of the Corporation seemed complete and permanent.

The turmoil of 1681–2

This comfortable position was of comparatively short duration. The sequence of assembly books resumes in April 1682 in the midst of renewed and much more serious upheaval.[24] Other sources give substantial detail about events in 1681, making it possible to reconstruct what had happened in Thetford. It is clear that in the late 1670s the Anglican Tory faction faced challenges: the dissenters and Whigs were gradually infiltrating the Corporation. Twenty years after the repressive legislation of the Clarendon Code the latter were slowly gaining strength, which caused grave disquiet among their rivals. The dominant figure in the political life of Thetford at the beginning of the 1680s was John Mendham, a formidable Anglican Tory. Because of the loss of the assembly book we cannot establish when he first became a member of the Corporation, but he was sufficiently senior to serve as mayor in 1674 and again in 1681. Mendham was not only very active within the Corporation but was also an agent for the Privy Council, reporting on the behaviour, beliefs and conversations of his colleagues and opponents. That provides us with intriguing insights.

An anonymous document among the Kings Lynn borough records gives an account of what happened in Thetford at the mayoral election of 1681.[25] Written a few

---

24   The Assembly Book covering April 1682–October 1718 is NA, T/C 2/6.
25   This document is uncatalogued: it is in the Kings Lynn borough archives, town clerk's papers. I am especially grateful to Susan Maddock for alerting me to this source thirty years ago, and for rechecking the reference in 2019.

years later, perhaps in 1689 or 1690, it is hostile to Mendham, but tallies with several other sources. It describes Mendham as 'an indigent person … endeavouring to Raise his fortunes (though by the ruine of the Corporacion)' by cultivating the acquaintance and patronage of Sir Leoline Jenkins, secretary of state to Charles II. The aim of both men, from their very different backgrounds, was to ensure the election of pliant MPs for the borough, 'as might be serviceable to the designes then on foot'. These 'designes' were the possible altering of the succession to exclude James, duke of York (because he was a devout Catholic), and the corollary of packing parliament with loyal supporters of the crown. Crucial to their success was the surrender of borough charters and the issuing of replacements, couched in such a way – by naming the members of the successor Corporation – that loyalty to the crown could be guaranteed.

According to the document, in the summer of 1681 Mendham tried to persuade the Corporation that the charter should be surrendered, but could not achieve his 'sinister designs … haveing but 14 who were Villaines enough to betray their trusts'. The end of his mayoralty was fast approaching, after which time he 'could not have soe great Intrest or Influence on the Corporacion'. However, as mayor he was required to supervise the election of his successor and swear him into office, and allegedly he deliberately absented himself from the morning's business on the crucial day, hoping thereby to render the election null and void and perpetuate himself in place. In reality, there was adequate precedent for the election of a new mayor in the absence of the incumbent. The Corporation followed those procedures and chose Wormley Hethersett for the ensuing year. Mendham, it was said, had previously told the borough officers to lock the door of the guildhall to prevent an election, but when this manoeuvre failed he appeared and pretended to approve of what had transpired, making excuses about not being present.

On the following day Hethersett went to Mendham's house and asked to be sworn as his successor. Mendham procrastinated, promising to perform the ceremony the next day at the guildhall during a special meeting of the Corporation. He failed to turn up. On 6 October 1681, a week after the election, Hethersett wrote to Mendham requiring him to come on 10 October, when a meeting of the borough court of record was scheduled, to carry out the ceremony. Mendham again failed to appear, but on 17 October wrote an urgent letter to Sir Leoline Jenkins, explaining his version of what had happened and arguing that his opponents tricked him:

> 11 or 12 of the Commoners, headed by one of the principal burgesses, with 3 or 4 not concerned went to an election without me by 10 and, I coming to the hall half an hour before 11, one of the Commons told me I had neglected my duty, but they had done it for me … I thought it illegal.[26]

Hethersett, 'perceiving that [his] designs were only Tricks & Roguery', sought a writ against Mendham to order him to swear him into office, a move confirmed by Mendham's letter to Jenkins, which states that 'they threaten to procure a Mandamus to force me to swear their person illegally elected'. But Mendham also argued that

---

26   *CSPD, Charles II,* vol. 22, pp. 518–19.

Hethersett was personally incapacitated because when made a principal burgess he had not sworn the necessary oaths under 13 Charles II (in other words, the Corporation Act 1661).[27] Jenkins, demonstrating confidence in the manipulation of the legal progress under the influence of the crown, replied in early November that the Privy Council could not assist directly but that

> his Majesty is well satisfied that you make the law your rule, and particularly that you proceed in matters relating to ... the statute of the 13th of the king ... I doubt not you'll have all the fairness ... and that those who would proceed by methods contrary to it will find their disappointment.[28]

Mendham, though, returned an inadequate response and a second writ was issued, a delaying tactic which meant that the Michaelmas law term expired and Mendham remained *de facto* mayor. In early January he wrote to Sir Henry Heveningham, one of Thetford's MPs, that his opponents 'still threaten a revenge to myself and friends but, though I be ruined, I will never yield to them'. He asked for authority from the Privy Council to purge the Corporation by applying the strict interpretation of the 1661 legislation, boastfully claiming that 'I can have the major part of the body to make any act here' – meaning that he held sway over the majority of the Corporation.[29] At the beginning of Hilary term he was arrested and on 28 January 1682 taken to London, but the following day was released by court officials 'who its presumed durst not suffer such a thing, unless by comand or intimation from some great Person'.[30] He took post-horses and rode furiously overnight to Thetford, arriving before 9 a.m. on 30 January.

Now he set about achieving his primary goal – the surrender of the borough charter. On the day of his return, 30 January 1682, he took decisive action, using the conformity clauses of the Corporation Act to eject suspect colleagues: 'he resolved to turne out two of the Members who were of a contrary opinion to himselfe & his Companions & put in two others who would comply with his treacherous designes'.[31] The vicar of St Peter's, Thetford, was persuaded to administer the sacrament to the two intended by Mendham as new members, even though neither was eligible:

> in order to make them capable according to the Corporation Act. One of which Persons was a professed Atheist and stood then actually excommunicated for not receiving the Sacrament (who upon this Extraordinary Occasion) gave him the Sacrament and was at that time Mace Bearer or some such like Inferior Officer ... and the other Person was the son of Mendham who was then but 16 Years of Age And had never before received the Sacrament.[32]

---

27   *Ibid.*, p. 552.

28   *CSPD, Entry Books Charles II*, vol. 62, p. 353.

29   *CSPD, Charles II*, vol. 23, p. 15.

30   The anonymous document, referred to above: Kings Lynn borough archives (town clerk's papers).

31   *Ibid.*

32   *Ibid.* and also the quotations in the remainder of this section.

While this 'Grand Piece of Impiety' was in progress, the mayor's officers were sent to summon a meeting of the Corporation at the Guildhall, but were instructed only to inform those who Mendham 'knew were of his owne stamp ... but not any of the rest of the Members'. These men met and promptly voted for the expulsion of two colleagues 'who were not present & who had no notice of this Assembly'. The two replacements were immediately admitted as common councillors, and 'they with the rest Instantly vote a Surrender of their Charter, & therein of their Liberties which they had but then just before sworne to maintaine'.

Mendham, no mean strategist, then rode post haste 'with his Stolen Charter' to London and delivered it to the Privy Council for cancellation, 'with mighty satisfaction that he had carried this Important point both in respect to his Adversaries in the Corporation which he was advised by this Strategem he had most assuredly baffled' and also that he had established a precedent whereby other charters could be forcibly surrendered if a Corporation was unwilling to do so. He was 'the lucky Instrument for effecting it'.

The Court of King's Bench, taking orders from the Privy Council, took Mendham back into custody 'after haveing permitted him this swing of Roguery', but this was window-dressing to conceal the murky proceedings with a veneer of legality, for they gave him generous liberty and comforts. Indeed, honourable confinement was seemingly part of the grand plan, for Hilary term ended with Mendham in nominal detention, and *still* mayor of Thetford, as he had not yet sworn his successor. In March 1682 the borough charter was formally surrendered (by Mendham in his ongoing capacity as mayor) and that meant that in the Easter term he was able to petition that, since the charter was no longer operative, he was no longer mayor, could not swear Hethersett into office, and should be released.

Aftermath

Mendham was set free and immediately, according to the anonymous chronicler of these events, he

> solicites & obtaines a New charter, wherein himselfe is made Mayor de Novo and such others added to him as should serve the Intent ... since which time he has been Mayor for 5 Years And of those 3 Years successively so that ever since he has been Gouvernor of the Corporation.[33]

The charter of 1682 was broadly the same as its predecessor, but a crucial clause entitled the king to name the mayor, recorder and ten principal burgesses of the 'new' Corporation, stating that these twelve had formal authority over the commonalty. The reissued charter, paid for by mortgaging some Corporation property and the rents of the town hall,[34] names John Mendham as mayor, while Burrage Martin, the battle-scarred veteran of thirty years of conflict, was a principal burgess and deputy mayor.

---

33   *Ibid.*
34   NA, T/C 2/6: 29 April 1682.

Wormley Hethersett was not content to accept the situation. With others he instituted legal proceedings against Mendham. In January 1683 the Corporation, presided over by Burrage Martin while Mendham was in London discussing matters of politics, agreed to make personal contributions of 40s for each burgess and 20s for each common councillor 'to defend John Mendham from all that shall oppose or disturbe him in any sute or busines relateing to the Corporation'. All signed their consent and the list was forwarded to Mendham in February.[35] With his invaluable connections to the Privy Council, *via* Sir Leoline Jenkins, Mendham took every opportunity to denounce his opponents, among them William Harbord, a leading Whig and dissenter who was one of the two MPs for Thetford. In June 1684, for example, he alleged that during October 1681, when parliament met at Oxford, Harbord said 'that he and others were wanting to go well armed to Oxford & skirmish with the King to find out his purpose, and if forced to buy liberties & religion from him would better have his security than word, as this is broken so often that not worth a groat'.

The allegiance of Thetford Corporation to the Anglican Tory fold and the crown was highlighted by its fervent response in June 1683 to the Rye House Plot, an alleged conspiracy to assassinate Charles II and his brother and heir, James, duke of York. At its meeting on 7 July the Corporation approved a lengthy and fulsome loyal address to the king, congratulating him on his escape – 'we … adore the Providence of Almighty God for the repeated wonders of his Care over your Majestie & most particularly for the happy discovery of this Horred Conspiracy' – and beseeching the Lord to defend him and his heirs 'against this and all other antimonarchicall Conspiracyes or Phannaticall Attempts'.[36]

But, following the accession of the Catholic James in February 1685, matters were turned on their head. The new king sought to gain the support of the Whigs and dissenters by reversing the changes of the latter part of his brother's reign and lifting the restrictions imposed by the Act of 1661. Thetford Corporation, recognising new realities and by now tilting away from Anglican Tory dominance, immediately declared that the surrender of the charter in 1682 had been an illegal act, and in the spring of 1686 abolished the customary oath of loyalty to the Church of England.

Mendham, leading the Anglican Tory faction, fought hard to maintain its – and his – status and power. For two and a half years control of the Corporation swung wildly as the rival factions sought to gain the upper hand. In May 1684 he had presented his accounts for the cost of the 1682 charter and his suit with Hethersett, and the Corporation had agreed to mortgage its own profits to pay for this,[37] but in February 1687 he was arrested for debt brought about by having been 'so long kept out of his monyes laid out by him for the service of this Corporation'. They had evidently failed to pay, despite several reminders that are recorded in the Assembly Book. Now, in 1687, they confirmed their liability, telling Alderman Garneham to go to Mendham 'to signifie to him the sence we have of what have befallen him; and that we looke upon our selves to have bin unfortunatly the occasion of it by not havein bin heitherto able to

---

35 NA, T/C 2/6: 8 January 1683; 2 February 1683.
36 NA, T/C 2/6: 7 July 1683.
37 NA, T/C 2/6: 5 May 1684.

pay him those considerable summes of money due to him'.[38] Whether Mendham ever received his long-delayed recompense is not known.

In April 1688, when a general election was promised by an increasingly desperate king, the Corporation sent a loyal address to James, emphasising their support for his now fading policy of liberty of conscience and concluding: 'Pardon us therefore dread Sir if we doe againe presume to assure your Majestie that we will doe our utmost Endeavours to chuse such members to represent us in the Insueing parliament as shall concur with your Majestie in such your Royall purposes'.[39]

Political tensions were in sharp focus. Mendham was mayor in 1686 and 1687, but in late September 1688 he sought a third successive term. The Corporation minutes record that he had 'showne & caused to be read unto us, A mandit signed and sealed (as he pretends) with the privie seale, desireing us to elect and continue with him ... to be Mayor for this next ensueinge yeare'. The common councilmen, 'not being well satisfied of the realitie thereof', proposed two candidates as usual, Mendham and John Seabrooke, a local gentleman. The latter 'hath the majority of votes and is declared to be fairly elected'.[40] This clumsy attempt by Mendham to use royal authority was bound to fail – why would James and his Privy Council favour a man who had been their opponent for so long – but it also contributed to the breakdown and collapse of the Corporation. With a single exception, there are no entries in the assembly book between 7 February 1690 and 23 September 1696. The exception records an unconstitutional gathering in early January 1693, attended by Edmund Russell as mayor, Wormley Hethersett as mayor-elect, one other burgess, six common councilmen and seven 'Cheife Inhabitants' of the town. Its sole purpose was to seek recovery of the 1574 charter, obtain the cancellation of that issued in 1682, and petition William III and Mary II to grant a new one. Their hopes were crowned with success: in the autumn of 1693 the king and queen issued a new charter, which reaffirmed that of 1574.

When he considered the gap of over six years in the entries George Burrell, the antiquarian who in the late eighteenth century saved many Thetford Corporation records from destruction, was puzzled. He annotated the assembly book at the foot of the minute dated 23 September 1696: 'I have no account nor can I discover how this could possibly happen, there must have ensued much disorder, which must have been the cause'.[41] The truth was that from the end of 1688 until a final resolution of the quarrels in 1707 Thetford had two rival Corporations – the Tory version, which claimed its authority under the 1682 charter, and the Whig one, validated under that of 1574 and bolstered by the 1693 reissue. Each appointed mayors and burgesses, held elections and claimed the assets and fruits of office. That was the culmination of half a century of upheaval, infighting, bitter acrimony and litigation. In all of this, as far as we know, the views of the ordinary inhabitants were of no concern or interest whatsoever.

The events in Thetford during the period under discussion exemplify the way in which the local dimension to national politics was of major significance, but they

---

38   NA, T/C 2/6: 4 February 1687.

39   NA, T/C 2/6: 30 April 1688.

40   NA, T/C 2/6: 28 September 1688.

41   NA, T/C 2/6: 23 September 1696.

also highlight how, at the local level in smaller boroughs, personal feuds and rivalries were a key factor. By virtue of their right to choose two MPs, the members of Thetford Corporation exercised a modest but nonetheless important power on the national stage. Here, as in many other small boroughs with a tightly restricted franchise, it was inevitable that forceful and aggressive personalities sought to manipulate the proceedings and collaborate with more powerful figures on, or controlled by, the Privy Council. Thetford in the later Stuart period was a microcosm of the turbulent and divisive politics that followed the Civil War and the Commonwealth.

Chapter 11

A local elite: a study of office holding in Long Melford, Suffolk

Lyn Boothman

In *The business of the Suffolk parish 1558–1625* David Dymond identifies the ecclesiastical and civil hierarchies of medieval and early modern England, and says 'the bottom level of the hierarchy, by far the biggest, consisted of thousands of parishes run by lay officers … '.[1] David has excelled at using the records produced by local office holders to illuminate the social, economic and political life of parishes.

Who were the people who gave their time to help administer their localities, to plan changes and developments at their local church, to attempt to control disruptive or illegal activities, to levy tax on their neighbours, to attempt to maintain quality among local food producers, to oversee the transmission of property or to distribute funds to the poor? This article provides evidence about married couples from Long Melford where the husband served as an office holder in one of three periods between 1661 and 1861. It considers stability within the parish, social status, occupation, the number of different offices held and continuity of office holding within families over time.[2]

Melford is a large village or small town in south-west Suffolk; Map 11.1 shows its location. Agriculture was always important, but the textile industry was a major part of the economy from the fourteenth until the later eighteenth centuries; other industries developed later and the road traffic and a strong gentry presence promoted work in the service sector.[3] The population grew from around 800 in the 1520s to some 1,500 in 1680; by 1811 it was about 2,100 and 2,870 in 1861.[4] The author's interest in Melford's population history has prompted the development of a population reconstitution which

---

1 D. Dymond, *The business of the Suffolk parish 1558–1625* (Ipswich, 2018), p. 2.
2 Long Melford is normally called Melford by its inhabitants and this article uses that shorter version of the parish name. In this period there were three women who served as office holders; all were widows of farmers and were continuing to run their family farms and served as overseer of the poor, probably when it was their farm's 'turn' to provide an overseer and their sons were not old enough. This article sometimes uses 'men' and 'he', which applies to 99.5 per cent of the individuals referred to. Almost all male office holders were married men or widowers.
3 N.R. Amor, *From wool to cloth, The triumph of the Suffolk clothier* (Bungay, 2016), pp. 1–3 for a brief introduction to the area; pp. 91–218 provide detailed information about the industry. The nineteenth-century industries included horsehair manufacture and weaving, coconut matting and a foundry: E. Wigmore, 'The nineteenth century industries', in E. Wigmore (ed.), *Long Melford, the last 2000 years* (Long Melford, 2000), pp. 75–8.
4 L. Boothman, 'Immobility and the immobile: a case study of Long Melford, Suffolk 1661–1861', PhD thesis (University of Cambridge, 2013), pp. 31–3.

Map 11.1. Location of Long Melford, Suffolk (courtesy Max Satchell).

uses the techniques of family reconstitution pioneered in the UK by the Cambridge Group for the History of Population and Social Structure (CAMPOP).[5] Most early reconstitutions used only parish register evidence of baptisms, marriages and burials, but some researchers have gathered information from a wider range of sources and this paper does likewise.[6] The more sources used, the wider the picture that can be gained about individuals and families and the better chance there is of identifying social status and of linking generations among the 'stable' families, enabling studies of kinship.

What we can know about individual lives depends on the survival of records: parish registers, rate books, wills, manorial records, maps and surveys, court and tax

---

5   E.A. Wrigley, 'Family reconstitution', in D.E.C. Eversley, P. Laslett and E.A. Wrigley (eds), *An introduction to English historical demography: from the sixteenth to the nineteenth century* (London, 1966), pp. 96–159. CAMPOP: <www.campop.geog.cam.ac.uk/about/history>, accessed 25 January 2019.

6   P. Sharpe, *Population and society in an East Devon parish. Reproducing Colyton, 1540–1840* (Exeter, 2002), pp. 11–12. S. King, 'Historical demography, life cycle reconstruction and family reconstitution, new perspectives', *History and Computing*, 8 (1996), pp. 62–77; F. Newall, 'Social and economic influences in the demography of Aldenham – an exploration of the application of family reconstitution', PhD thesis (University of Cambridge, 1985); W. Newman Brown, 'Wider reconstitution', *Local Population Studies*, 7 (1977), p. 44.

records both local and national, and many more. The author's PhD thesis focused on couples present in three periods with particularly good records: 1661–91, 1753–83 and 1831–61; for continuity with earlier articles, these periods are called A, B and C.[7] The thesis examined stability and mobility among couples resident in Melford and their relationship to social status, kinship and other factors. As far as the author is aware, there is no other published analysis of this type about office holders, so unfortunately this cannot be a comparative study.

Parish offices

In this study 'office holders' includes both posts to which people were appointed for a year or more, such as churchwarden, overseer of the poor, constable or ale-taster, and positions to which they were appointed on one particular occasion, or a series of such occasions, such as foreman (or deputy) of the manorial court baron jury (here called 'the homage') or member of the court leet jury.[8] For Melford, these are the six offices for which there is information over all three time periods, and they have been individually analysed. The latter two are not 'offices' in the usual sense but are roles that involved an individual with some type of formal responsibility towards their fellow citizens. The numbers for 'all office holders' include holders of other offices or appointments, such as being a highway surveyor or trustee of a local charity, about which there is occasional information.[9] There is not room here to give information about the history or responsibilities of individual offices, but some sources and studies are listed below.[10]

---

7   L. Boothman, 'Studying the stayers, the stable population of Long Melford, Suffolk over two hundred years', *Local Population Studies*, 95 (2015), pp. 9–28; L. Boothman, 'Studying the stayers, kinship and social status in Long Melford, Suffolk, 1661–1861', *Local Population Studies*, 101 (2018), pp. 4–25. There are records of some churchwardens, overseers and constables in an earlier period, 1585–1615, but fewer record sources makes comparison difficult.

8   Court leet jurors were known as 'capital pledges' in period A. The court leet was associated with the manor of Melford Hall, the largest of the four main manors, but had authority over the whole parish. Overseers of the poor are hereafter called 'overseers'. Information on homage foremen comes from the two largest manors, Melford Hall and Rectory.

9   There were twenty men in period A and twenty-two in period B who only held such offices, so are not included in the analysis when the main six roles are discussed.

10 M. Goldie, 'The unacknowledged republic: office holding in early modern England', in T. Harris (ed.), *The politics of the excluded c. 1500–1850* (Basingstoke, 2001), pp. 153–94; J. Pitman, 'Tradition and exclusion: parochial office holding in early modern England. A case study from North Norfolk, 1580–1640', *Rural History*, 15 (2004), pp. 27–45; H.R. French, 'Social status, localism and the middling sort of people', *Past and Present*, 166 (2000), pp. 66–99; H.R. French, '"Ancient inhabitants": mobility, lineage and identity in English rural communities 1600–1750', in C. Dyer (ed.), *The self-contained village? The social history of rural communities, 1250–1900* (Hatfield, 2007), pp. 72–95; J.R. Kent, *The English village constable 1580–1642: a social and administrative study* (Oxford, 1986); E. Lord, 'The petty constable in Cambridgeshire, c1640–1770', *Cambridgeshire Association for Local History*, Review (2017), pp. 3–14.

Table 11.1
Stability indicators among all known Melford couples, and among office holders.

		No. of couples	3GEN %	2GEN %	30YRONLY %	OTHER %
	Melford overall					
1	A: 1661–91	908	40.5	14.8	17.4	27.2
2	B: 1753–83	1008	49.9	10.7	19.3	20.1
3	C: 1831–61	1380	54.4	8.5	11.4	25.7
	All office holders					
4	A: 1661–91	204	51	13.2	21.6	14.7
5	B: 1753–83	262	55	3.4	27.1	14.4
6	C: 1831–61	151	50.3	9.9	17.9	21.9

Sources: all data in tables is extracted from the author's population reconstruction, which includes some eighty types of record. Sources include parish registers: SROB, FL509/4/1–9, 12, 15, and, for the Independent church, TNA, RG4/1853–4, 2883; office holders' accounts and records: SROB, FL509/1/15, FL509/5/1, FL509/7/1–9, FL509/7/12–15, Melford Hall, Hyde Parker Papers (HPP), Q7, 14, 19–25, TNA, SP46/135/104; the Hearth Tax returns: TNA, E179/257/12, E179/367/19, E179/183/15; rectory terriers: SROB, FL509/31,2, HA505/3/67, Melford Hall, HPP E143/21, M2, Q13; Easter Offering lists: SROB, FL509/3/15; rector's accounts: SROB, FL509/3/15, FL509/3/16; manorial records: SROB, FL509/13/3a, HA505/1, and FL509/13/3a, Melford Hall, HPP M1,3, 5–37, 39–49; the tithe apportionment map: SROB, FL509/4/3 and the censuses: 1841 – TNA, HO 107/1012/1 fos 2–44, HO107/1012/2 fos 89–168; 1851 – TNA, HO 107/1789, fos 359–444; 1861 – TNA, RG9/1131 fos 83–114, 130–48.

Note: A widower who remarried within his lifetime in Melford and was an office holder during both/ all marriages is counted only once.

Stability and mobility

This research considered longer-term stability among adults who were or had been part of a couple who had lived in Melford.[11] Indicators of stability relate to *family* links and to minimum *time* spent in the parish:

> *3GEN* means couples where at least one partner had at least one grandparent present in the parish, so were at least third generation;
> *2GEN* means couples where at least one partner had a parent present in Melford;
> *30YRONLY* means couples who moved into the parish as adults and at least one of whom stayed for thirty years or more;
> *OTHER* means couples who met neither family nor time indicators.[12]

Table 11.1 shows the stability status of all known Melford couples, alongside the figures for all office holders. The proportion of all couples with previous family links in Melford (3GEN plus 2GEN) was always over 50 per cent and it increased over time.

---

11   Boothman, 'Immobility and the immobile', pp. 1–11.
12   These four categories are mutually exclusive.

Among incomers, there were always fewer 30YRONLY couples than OTHER couples.[13] The nature of the responsibilities involved means that the majority of office holders were likely to come from the more stable part of the population, unless an office was dependent on a factor such as being owner or tenant of a particular property. Office holders made up 22 per cent of all couples in period A and 26 per cent in period B, but only 11 per cent in period C. In periods A and B office holders were more likely than all couples to be 3GEN, but in period C this was reversed. The proportion of office holder couples who had moved into Melford as adults (30YRONLY plus OTHER) varied a little across time, but the balance between the two groups altered. In periods A and B a significant majority of the office-holding incomers were 30YRONLY but in period C there were larger numbers of OTHER office holders. The changing nature of offices in period C, with the coming of the New Poor Law, the introduction of the police service, the declining importance of manorial courts baron and the end of the court leet, must be important here.

When offices were analysed individually, there were differences in relation to stability between offices and across time. Among churchwardens, constables, ale-tasters and homage foremen over two-thirds of couples in each period had a family background in Melford, so were 3GEN or 2GEN. The proportions ranged from 66 per cent of the homage in period A to 95 per cent of ale-tasters in period C. Among holders of these four posts in period C, around 70 per cent of couples were 3GEN, compared to 48 per cent of overseers and 51 per cent of court leet jurors. Many of the major local farmers were tenants who moved into the parish to lease a farm for relatively short periods; these men were likely to serve as overseers and as court leet jurors.[14] Among all the incomers who held a local office the 30YRONLY dominated, but among overseers and court leet jurors more OTHER men served.

Social status

The social groups used here are:

> *Social group 1* means gentry, higher professionals and the largest farmers, clothiers or manufacturers;
> *Social group 2* means substantial farmers and tradesmen, other larger employers, plus lower professionals;
> *Social group 3* means skilled workers, less substantial tradesmen and shopkeepers, husbandmen and small-scale landowners;
> *Social group 4* means semi-skilled and unskilled workers, including agricultural labourers and paupers.[15]

---

13 All figures used in this article, except those for the period 1585–1615 and those in Table 11.3, are taken from my PhD thesis, which gives more information about the processes by which results were calculated and their statistical significance.

14 The major landowners in Melford were the owners of Melford Hall and Kentwell Hall; most farmers leased land from one of these estates.

15 Indicators of status in the pre-Census period are often 'broad brush' because of a lack of data. The definitions of social groups are very similar to those used in K. Wrightson and D. Levine,

Table 11.2
Social status among all known Melford couples, and among office holders.

		No. of couples	Social group 1 %	Social group 2 %	Social group 3 %	Social group 4 %	Not known %
	Melford overall						
1	A: 1661–91	908	6.7	15.6	31.2	26.5	19.9
2	B: 1753–83	1008	4.1	15.4	39.1	33.2	8.2
3	C: 1831–61	1380	2.9	10.1	36.3	48.7	2
	Office holders						
4	A: 1661–91	204	15.2	40.2	40.7	2.9	1
5	B: 1753–83	262	8.4	47.3	42.4	1.1	0.8
6	C: 1831–61	151	9.9	31.8	50.3	6.6	1.3

Sources: see Table 11.1.

A wide variety of sources were used to ascribe status but they vary between the periods, so that the extent and precision of these status attributions must also vary; the exercise is possible because Melford has so many surviving records. However, even here it was not possible to ascribe a social status to all couples, particularly in period A, for which there is less information about the poor (who are less likely to be named in surviving records).[16] Table 11.2 compares, for each period, the social structure of all known Melford couples with that among office holders.

Among all couples the proportion in the two highest social groups declined between periods A and C, the proportion in social group 3 stayed relatively stable and the proportion in social group 4 rose. The majority of those whose status is not known are likely to have been in social groups 3 or 4, so the figures suggest a similar social structure in periods A and B, with a higher concentration in the lower social groups by period C. The decline in couples from social group 1 relates partly to lower population turnover and partly to a reduction in gentry households.[17] The proportion of couples in social group 2 declined between periods B and C; this can be attributed partly to the increasing size of farms (so fewer individual farmers) and partly to a similar rise in the numbers employed by individual employers in manufacturing. Farmers may also have had longer leases in this period, meaning lower turnover among this group.

Office holders were the 'working elite' of a parish, taking responsibilities that often demanded local knowledge, literacy and numeracy, so it is not surprising that many were from the higher social groups. The proportion from social groups 1 and 2 was similar in periods A and B, around 55 per cent; almost all the remainder were from

---

Population and piety in an English village; Terling, 1525–1700, 2nd edn (Oxford, 1995), pp. 31–6.

16 Sources include the 1841, 1851 and 1861 censuses, hearth tax and Easter offering returns, inventories, manorial records, parish apprenticeship, removal and settlement records, poor rate assessments and listings, poor relief records, other valuations and tax returns, tithe records and wills.

17 There were three large gentry houses in Melford, but in period A there were more relations of their owners living elsewhere in the parish.

social group 3. Period C showed a decline in the proportion from social group 2 and a considerable increase in the proportion from social group 3. All known churchwardens were from social groups 1 or 2, while there were always a small proportion of overseers from social group 3. Among constables and ale-tasters over 60 per cent were from social group 3, while homage foremen or deputies and court leet jurors were more evenly divided between social groups 2 and 3.

The relationship between stability and social status among all Melford couples changed over time. In period A, for example, 17 per cent of all 3GEN couples were in social group 2 but by period C just 6 per cent; in contrast, around a third of 3GEN couples were in social group 4 in the first two periods and by period C this had risen to nearly 57 per cent. Among incomers, couples in social group 4 made up a growing proportion of 30YRONLY couples, those who moved in and then stayed, but among OTHER couples the proportion in social groups 1 and 2 rose over time.

Occupation

It is rare before the census to have evidence of occupation for the majority of any population, but for men of higher social status in Melford it is often possible to deduce whether they worked in the primary, secondary or tertiary sectors.[18] Locally the primary sector was largely farming; the secondary sector covered manufacturing of all types, including textiles, and the tertiary included services, transport and servants alongside the status definitions of gentleman and pauper. Surviving records provide an idea of occupation for 85 per cent of office holders in period A, 84 per cent in period B and 94 per cent in period C.

In this textile town the secondary sector provided around 48 per cent of office holders of known occupation in all three periods. Over time the proportion from the primary sector fell as that from the tertiary sector increased: in period A 31 per cent were from the primary sector and 21 per cent from the tertiary; by period C only 17 per cent came from the primary sector and 35 per cent were from the tertiary. However, the six offices analysed separately showed very differing patterns. Constables and ale-tasters always showed the highest proportions in the secondary sector (70 per cent or over in periods B and C), churchwardens the lowest (27 per cent in period A, falling to 20 per cent in period C). At all periods overseers provided the largest proportion from the primary sector; the lowest proportions were almost always among constables and ale-tasters. In periods A and B churchwardens were the most likely to be from the tertiary sector but in period C this was true of homage foremen and their deputies.[19]

---

18   Wills, manorial records and tax returns are just some of the documents that make this possible. Occupations were classified using the PST: Primary, Secondary, Tertiary system devised at CAMPOP: <www.campop.geog.cam.ac.uk/research/projects/occupations/categorisation>, accessed 27 January 2019.

19   The percentages relate to those of known industrial sector. Kent suggested that in towns constables were most often middle-ranking tradespeople, in rural areas yeomen or husbandmen: Kent, *The English village constable*, pp. 80–130.

Table 11.3
Melford office holders serving in multiple offices.

	Only held one office %	Also served as Churchwarden %	Also served as Overseer %	Also served as Constable %	Also served as Ale-taster %
Period A: 1661–91					
1 Churchwardens	18	n/a	53	37	3
2 Overseers	58	30	n/a	18	5
3 Constables	57	19	16	n/a	17
4 Ale-tasters	72	3	9	29	n/a
N = 146					
Period B: 1753–83					
5 Churchwardens	17	n/a	78	5	5
6 Overseers	65	13	n/a	19	7
7 Constables	48	1	24	n/a	34
8 Ale-tasters	34	2	17	60	n/a
N=203					

Sources: see Table 11.1.

Notes:

1. As some men served in more than two offices the rows in Table 11.3 do not sum to 100 per cent.

2. Among 'all office holders' twenty men in period A and twenty-two in period B served in none of the six roles individually analysed in this study; another thirty-eight men in period A and thirty-seven in period B served only on the homage or leet; none of these are included in this table.

Patterns of office holding

Did churchwardens always also serve in another office? Were constables also likely to serve as ale-tasters? The patterns of office holding among churchwardens, overseers, constables and ale-tasters in periods A and B have been examined and Table 11.3 shows the proportion of men in each office who also held another of these offices. As mentioned earlier, period C saw substantial change in office holding and some offices existed for only a few years of this period so are not analysed here.

Of the 349 men who served in these offices only one held all four positions, while 241 held only one, ninety-six held two and eleven held three. In period A 71 per cent of men held one office (although they may have held it for several years or on several occasions) and 25 per cent held two; in period B the figures were 67 per cent and 30 per cent. In both periods churchwardens were most likely to hold more than one office; there was a decline in the proportion of constables and ale-tasters who held two or more offices in period B. Isaac Nevill, who lived from 1651 to 1712 and held all four posts, was a maltster who lived in the centre of the parish, on Melford Green. He was among the third generation of his father's family to live in that area, while his mother, Rebecca Nevill neè Payne, had had at least the four previous generations

Table 11.4
3GEN office holders: depth of ancestral links within Melford.

	All office holders N=	All 3GEN office holders N=	Office holders 3GEN via husband N=	3GEN	4GEN	5GEN	6GEN	7GEN	8GEN +
1 A: 1661–91	204	104	76	24	24	19	6	3	0
2 B: 1753–83	262	144	107	32	21	18	15	15	6
3 C: 1831–61	151	76	64	17	14	6	5	7	15

Sources: see Table 11.1.

Note: all of the office holders in period A whose ancestry can be traced back four or more generations had early sixteenth-century ancestors who left wills. See fn. 20, p.137.

of her family in Melford. Isaac was appointed an ale-taster when he was thirty, a constable at forty-two, a churchwarden when he was fifty-five and an overseer in the year of his death.

Continuity among office holders

To consider continuity among office holders, ancestors and descendants of all 3GEN office holders are first traced and then continuities of office holding within families are analysed. Table 11.4 shows the ancestral links of 3GEN office holders (where 3GEN status came through the husband), who made up around 40 per cent of office holders in each period.[20] The proportion of these men with deeper ancestral links, men who might have traced their families beyond their grandparents, was near 70 per cent in each period, slightly higher in period C.[21]

It is unlikely that anyone could have had in-depth knowledge about all the families in a parish of Melford's size. However, Table 11.4 suggests that there were office holders in Melford who had the potential to know many local families well. But were there 'office holding families', with a tradition of office holding and membership of the local elite? Table 11.5 shows the proportions of office holders who had direct ancestors or descendants who also held office.

A man could, of course, have had more than one direct ancestor or descendant who had also held office; for example, ten office holders in period A each had four

---

20 Table 11.4 was originally constructed to enable comparison with the ancestry of Richard Gough, of the parish of Myddle in Cheshire. D.G. Hey (ed.), *The history of Myddle* (London, 1981). For this reason the ancestry of only the office holder, not his wife, was considered. Table 11.5 includes the ancestry of both husband and wife.

21 The number of generations that were possible to trace increased, of course, with time.

Table 11.5
Continuities in Melford office holding.

Group and period	1 N=	2 Office holding ancestors in B, %	3 Office holding ancestors in A, %	4 Office holding descendants in B, %	5 Office holding descendants in C, %
1 Office holders in A	204			24	8
2 Office holders in B	262		31		19
3 Office holders in C	151	33	14		

Sources: see Table 11.1.
Note: The figures here relate to the existence of any ancestor or descendant, not the number of them. The gap between the end of period A and the beginning of period B is fourteen years longer than that between periods B and C.

or more office holding descendants in period B. Among office holders in period B, 9 per cent had both direct ancestors who were office holders in period A and direct descendants who held office in period C. Just over 36 per cent of office holders in period C had one or more direct ancestors who were office holders in period A, period B or both. There were six men who had ancestral links that could be traced back to the sixteenth century, who were themselves office holders in period A and had office-holding descendants in both periods B and C. There were continuities in office holding, but we do not know whether local knowledge was passed on from one generation to the next or, if so, whether it was used within the community as a source of information about local policies or customs.

If Melford had a family that passed on such information across the generations it may well have been the Kings. John King, who served as either ale-taster or constable in the 1830s, was the last in a direct line of thirteen fathers and sons who were office holders, the earliest being a William King who served as churchwarden in 1541. All these generations of the King family owned or rented land, but until the end of the seventeenth century they were particularly important in the textile industry; many were nonconformist.[22]

Conclusion

This study may provide additional context to other studies of the work of local office holders. Throughout the period of this study Melford offered a wider range of employment than many small towns and continued to offer work to incomers of varying social status even as the textile industry declined. Its landholding pattern guaranteed that the local elite changed in the same way as the remainder, the majority, of the population, so that elite always included newcomers.

---

22 That William King was tenth great grandfather to the John King who held office in the 1830s. There were another three related King men who were also office holders during that period.

Patterns of office holding must have varied considerably; there are underlying differences and changes over time in parish circumstance that must influence local office holding. Where farmers owned their own land they were more likely to stay put. The relative importance of the primary, secondary and tertiary sectors varied widely. The power of local lordship, variations between open and closed parishes and differences in social and occupational structures and in the strength and structure of the local economy over time were probably crucial. Attitudes to incomers taking local office could well have varied from place to place and 'rotas' of service would have been important where they existed. Some changes, such as the increase in average farm size or the decline of a local industry, will have occurred in many places, but not necessarily at the same time. Other developments, such as changes in the social status of incomers, may only have happened in some communities, and may have had very varying impacts.

Chapter 12

Suffolk cheese and Scottish whaling

Evelyn Lord

Introduction

In *Researching and writing history: a guide for local historians* David Dymond gives advice on how to choose a subject for research. He acknowledges that this choice 'is influenced by several factors, such as our existing knowledge, our family and educational background, the aspects of life which influence us most, and of course the availability of sources'.[1] The choice of subject for this short essay is unashamedly influenced by family background and a family tragedy that united the two distant places of Suffolk and Scotland, while the final factor in David's making a choice, 'the availability of sources', had already emerged in the Anstruther Port Books, which documented a link between Scotland and Suffolk in the mid-eighteenth century. Thus two of David's criteria for local history research, time and place, were satisfied. The third, which David places first, theme, is more difficult, but the theme of this essay falls loosely into his category of 'economic history' and contains broadly distinct yet overlapping areas of interest that 'shade imperceptibly into many other forms of history'.[2]

The story starts in Scotland. On 31 March 1757, in the port of Anstruther on the north of the Firth of Forth in Fife, Scotland, a 345-ton ship, the *Rising Sun*, bound for the 'whale fishing in the Greenland Seas', presented its victual loading list to the Customs. There were to be forty-three men aboard the ship: thirty-nine British and four foreign (Dutch harpooners). It was taking eighteen different commodities, including thirteen Suffolk cheeses.[3] How, why and where had a relatively small port in Scotland learnt about and sourced cheese from an English county hundreds of miles away? This essay discusses the production and marketing of Suffolk cheese and considers how the connections between Scotland and Suffolk might have been made.

Suffolk cheese

Although Suffolk cheese was famous for its keeping qualities, in the seventeenth and eighteenth centuries it had a bad reputation for its taste. 'Suffolk Cheese is proverbially

---

1   D. Dymond, *Researching and writing history: a guide for local historians* (Lancaster, 2009), p. 30.
2   *Ibid.*, pp. 31–2.
3   NAS, E 504/3/3 Customs Accounts Anstruther, 1754–1763.

execrable.'[4] Sometimes known as Suffolk Bang or Suffolk Thump, this was a cheese so hard that rhymes were written about its intractability to bite or knife.

> Those that made me were uncivil,
> For they made me harder than the devil:
> Knives won't cut me, fire won't sweat me,
> Dogs bark at me, but can't eat me.[5]

Its ability to repel the knives of hungry men and the teeth of vermin made it a popular cheese with the Navy Victualling Board. However, when Samuel Pepys, a member of the Navy Board, took some home it did not meet with approval. On 4 October 1661 he wrote in his diary that he returned home after a day on Navy business and a visit to the theatre, 'where I find my wife vexed at her people for grumbling to eat Suffolk cheese – which I am vexed at'.[6] Pepys wife's people were probably her servants, as Suffolk cheese was considered a food fit for servants, labourers and the poor.[7] Evidence for its use as a staple food for the poor comes from Mendlesham's churchwardens accounts. In 1610 Francis Cocke was paid 20d 'for a chamber to lay the Cheese in, for selling it out [to the poor], and his wif for tendinge it with rubbinge [salting] and turning'. In the same year the parish paid £10 6s 0d for ninety-eight cheeses, which were subsequently weighed to determine the wastage caused by shrinkage when stored.[8]

By the eighteenth century the cheese had made the county of Suffolk a laughing stock in the rest of the country, as described by the Suffolk rural poet Robert Bloomfield in his poem *The Farmer's Boy*:

> Unrivall'd stands thy country cheese, O! Giles,
> Whose very name alone engenders smiles;
> Whose fame abroad by every tongue is spoke,
> The well-known butt of many a flinty joke![9]

The importance of the Navy victualler to Suffolk cheese-makers can be seen in a decision made in 1708 that Suffolk dairies should change from butter to cheese-

---

4   A. Suckling, *The history and antiquities of Suffolk,* vol. 1 (London, 1846), p. x.
5   Considerable effort has been made to trace the origin and antiquity of this rhyme, used in many secondary sources as referring to Suffolk or Essex cheese. It does not appear in the original edition of Thomas Tusser's *Five Hundred Pointes of Good Husbandrie* of 1557, but only in Payne and Heritage's notes to the 1878 edition, p. 281, which reference 'Bloomfield'. It was probably current in the eighteenth century, but so far no documentary source has been found.
6   R.G. Latham and W. Matthews (eds), *The diary of Samuel Pepys,* vol. II, 1661 (London, 1995), p. 191. Suffolk cheese has been compared to Parmesan, which was considerably more expensive – so much more valuable, in fact, that Samuel Pepys buried his Parmesan to protect it during the Great Fire of London.
7   V. Cheke, *The story of cheese* (London, 1959), p. 90.
8   D. Dymond, *The business of the Suffolk parish, 1558–1625,* SIAH (Needham Market, 2018), p. 66.
9   R. Bloomfield, *The Farmer's Boy,* printed in *The Annual Register,* 42 (1800), pp. 460, 461.

making.[10] But by 1758 the Navy Victualling Board had received so many complaints about the cheese that the decision was made to provision the ships with Cheshire or Gloucester cheese instead.[11] As the Navy usually purchased 22,200 tons of cheese a year,[12] its discontinuation of Suffolk cheese threw a large amount of Suffolk cheese onto the open market.

The production of Suffolk cheese

Why was Suffolk cheese so durable and hard? The answer to this is that it was a by-product of Suffolk butter, which was in great demand in the London market. The cheese was made with the 'flet', or the milk left after the cream for butter had been skimmed off. 'Skim-milk remains little better than water, so it is no wonder that the cheese made of it is not good'.[13]

Rennet was added to the skimmed milk to stop it going sour and to create curds and whey. Rennet comes from enzymes found in the stomach of ruminants, in particular the stomachs of unweaned calves, which enable them to process milk. Now available in a commercial form, in the eighteenth century it was made in each dairy by removing the stomach (bag) from a dead new-born calf, washing and scouring it, and hanging it up to ferment: a smelly process described in graphic detail by Richard Bradley, who was of the opinion 'that one reason that Suffolk cheese is so noted for its hardness, is on account of the badness of the rennet'.[14]

Once the curd was thickened, the whey was drained off and either fed to livestock or given to the poor, and the curd was cut with knives into mounds, salted and hard pressed, wrapped in muslin and placed on shelves to mature. In Suffolk the maturing process was about two weeks, so this was a cheese that could be made and sold in a short time and at a low cost. That the main component was the waste from the process of butter-making throws some doubt on the hearsay evidence cited by Thirsk of a switch from butter- to cheese-making in 1708, as there is no indication that this switch, which should have resulted in a better cheese, did so, and sixteen years after this alleged switch Daniel Defoe described Suffolk cheese as 'the worst cheese in England'.[15]

There was a strong tradition of dairying in parts of Suffolk from the early sixteenth century. Between 1507 and 1513 the Sibton Abbey estate kept between 66 and

---

10 J. Thirsk, *Food in early modern England* (London, 2006), p. 281. There are problems with this statement as its only source is a letter in the Cheshire Record Office family papers of the Ardenes of Bredbury: DAR A/65/2.

11 M. Knox, *Suffolk cheese* (Beccles, 2002), p. 9. N.A.M. Rodgers, *The wooden world. An anatomy of the Georgian Navy* (London, 1986), p. 85; J. Macdonald, *Feeding Nelson's Navy* (London, 2014), p. 31. TNA, ADM 112.

12 Rodgers, *The wooden world*, p. 84.

13 R. Bradley, *The country housewife and ladies' directory* [1736]. Facsimile edition, ed. C. Davison (London, 1980), pp. 74, 75.

14 *Ibid.*, p. 74.

15 D. Defoe, *A tour through the whole island of Great Britain*, vol. 1 1724–1726, facsimile edition (London, 1968), p. 53.

140 cows producing milk for thirty-eight to eighty-six 'wey' of cheese a year (a 'wey' was 256lb, a Suffolk weight for cheese, probably a wagon- or wain-load).[16] Sibton also featured in Defoe's eighteenth-century account of the dairy industry in Suffolk, which he described as an area called 'High Suffolk with rich soil, and a long tract of ground wholey employed in dairying' stretching from Stowmarket to Needham Market and on to Woodbridge and Orford, with Woodbridge the main market and port for the export of butter and cheese to London. This can be compared to Arthur Young's later eighteenth-century description of the 'great dairying region covering much of north east Suffolk, where the enclosed clay land has been put down to grass'.[17] The 1811 County Report to the Board of Agriculture listed twenty-three parishes dedicated to dairying on a tract twenty miles by twelve. These parishes were in an arc with a group of parishes around Coddenham, another group around Framlingham, including Sibton, and another area around Wingfield. The report states that butter was the main product of these dairies, with some cheese.[18] This indicates that the area around Sibton had a very long history of dairying and cheese-making.

Evidence from the county itself should shed more light on cheese-making: for example, probate inventories and wills list cheese-making implements, and litigation was conducted over weights and measures, the selling of bad cheese, bad credit and failure either to supply a contracted weight of cheese or defaulting middlemen. All of these sources have to be used with caution, especially as, traditionally, the main producers and sellers of cheese were women – the farmers' wives and daughters who were often absent from the records. Just occasionally they are glimpsed, such as Widow Sarah Perse of Benacre, whose will in 1628 left her son Thomas a cheese board and six cheese vats, and in the early nineteenth century it was a 'Mrs C' who supplied the information about dairying in Suffolk to the Board of Agriculture in 1811.[19]

Scottish whaling

The Scottish whaling industry was the direct result of government intervention, when in 1733 it started to offer bounties to any British vessel of between 200 and 400 tons equipped for whaling in the Arctic seas. In 1733 the bounty was 20s per shipping ton, regardless of whether any whales were caught, and as the price of whale oil increased in 1750 the bounty was increased to 40s a ton.[20] As well as the bounty, if the ship caught any whales then it could sell the oil (boiled down from blubber) and

---

16   A. Denny (ed.), *The Sibton Abbey estate*, SRS II (Ipswich, 1960), pp. 38, 39.

17   J. Theobald, 'Changing agriculture in High Suffolk 1650–1850', in D. Dymond and E. Martin (eds), *A historical atlas of Suffolk* (Ipswich, 1988; repr. 1989 and 1999), pp. 134, 135.

18   W. Marshall, *The review and abstract of the county reports to the board of agriculture*, vol. 3; first published in 1811, reprinted in 1818, facsimile edition of 1818 reprint (New York, 1968), pp. 460–2.

19   M. Allen (ed.), *Wills of the archdeaconry of Suffolk 1627–1628*, SRS LVIII (Ipswich, 2015), p. 94; Marshall, *Review and abstract*, pp. 461–5.

20   G. Jackson, 'Government bounties and the establishment of the Scottish whaling trade 1750–1800', in J. Butt and J. T Ward (eds), *Scottish themes in honour of Professor S. Lythe* (Edinburgh, 1976), pp. 46–50; G. Jackson, *The British whaling trade* (London, 1978), pp. 54, 55.

the whalebone, which increased the profit on what was a long and perilous voyage into the northern seas.

The Anstruther Whale Fishing Company was founded in 1756. The twin burghs of Anstruther Easter and Wester were trading and fishing ports with a long history of strong trading links with Scandinavia and the Baltic. The registers of ships paying tolls to Denmark to pass through the Grand Belt into the Skagerat, which list the ships' ports of embarkation and their home ports on the return voyage, show a continual stream of ships sailing into the Baltic from Anstruther throughout the eighteenth century.[21] Outfitting its first whaling ship was a natural progression of the town's maritime economy.

The scheme for the company was promoted by Baillie Waddell (a shipbuilder) and James Anderson (a shipmaster), with Sir John, Sir Philip and David Anstruther (local gentry), and Robert Fall (a member of a Dunbar shipping family). It was to be modelled on the already existing Dunbar whaling company.[22] To promote the company the burghs of Anstruther gave it a waste corner on the Forth for a boiling house, which became known as Greenland Close.[23] First a ship had to be procured and fitted out. At this time few ships were built as whalers – usually a redundant collier was purchased and its keel strengthened to deal with the ice, at a cost of about £2000 sterling.[24] The partners of the Anstruther whaling company had to finance this and also had to pay for the ship's provisions, at a rate of £10 sterling upon every share, which had to be paid by May 1757.[25] The total cost of the provisions came to £216 sterling.[26]

Fully equipped, and supplied with Suffolk cheese, the *Rising Sun* sailed for the Greenland fisheries. On this voyage it was successful, returning on 25 October 1757 with one whale.[27] It made six further voyages, catching one whale in 1759 and two in 1760, but none in 1758, 1761 and 1762, when it was decommissioned. A smaller ship of 216 tons, the *Hawke* was purchased by the Anstruther Company in 1758. Its victualling list included twenty-five Suffolk cheeses.[28] It worked on the Greenland fishing grounds until 1762, when it was crushed in the ice.[29] During that time it caught

---

21 N.E. Bang and K. Korst (eds), *Tabeller over Skibsfart og Varentransport gennem Orersund, 1661–1783*, vol. 1, Lists of home ports of ships passing east and west through the sound 1700–1760 (Copenhagen, 1930).

22 A rare eighteenth-century copy of the Dunbar partnership exists in the British Library: the *Contract of copartnery of the East-Lothian and Merse whale-fishing company*. A facsimile has been reproduced by Eighteenth Century Print Editions.

23 NAS, GD 86/13/648 Letter from Sir John Anstruther to David, earl of Leven; Scottish Fishing Museum, Anstruther; G. Gourlay, *Anstruther illustrations of Scottish burgh life* (Cupar, 1888), p. 53.

24 N. Watson, *The Dundee whalers 1750–1914* (East Linton, 2003), pp. 14, 15.

25 NAS, GD26/13/648.

26 NAS, E 504/3/3.

27 NAS, E 504/3/3.

28 NAS, E 504/3/3.

29 C.W. Sanger 'Scottish northern whaling and sealing', in R. Coull, A. Fenton and A. Veitch (eds), *Scottish life and society, boats, fishing and the sea* (Edinburgh, 2008), pp. 396, 397.

no whales so, apart from its bounty, it produced no profit, and after its loss the company ceased trading and Anstruther was no longer involved in the whaling trade.

Connections

There is good evidence from before the 1707 Act of Union between Scotland and England of Anstruther ships in East Anglian ports, and of a flourishing coastal trade between East Anglia and the north-east of Scotland as far as Aberdeen in the sixteenth century. Small boats hugged the coast, laden with herrings, cod and salmon and, most importantly, Scottish white salt from the salt pans on both sides of the Forth, heading southwards and returning with beer and hops.[30] Between 1610 and 1614 at least six different Anstruther ships were trading in King's Lynn: *le Margery*, *The Angel*, *The Blessing*, *The Joye*, *The Katherine*, *The Andrew*, *The Paul* and *The Margaret*.[31] This shows that mariners from Anstruther were familiar in East Anglian waters, but it is not evidence that they ventured into Suffolk, although N.G. Williams traces a voyage that went from Dunwich to Aberdeen, from there to Calais and back to Dunwich. He also states that the Yarmouth fish curers did not like Scottish salt, and this was distributed further south.[32] Between the seventeenth and nineteenth centuries there is a gap in evidence for Anstruther ships in Suffolk waters: Article IV of the Act of Union gave Scotland free trade with England and so removed Scottish ships from English customs records and English ships from Scottish tariffs.[33] Interaction between the two areas must have continued, but it is not until the mid-nineteenth century that there is any further documentary record of this. In 1863 there is a newspaper report of what appears to have been an annual event, with Scottish fishing boats gathering at Cellardyke in Anstruther for a voyage south to Lowestoft.[34] The procession of boats 'was usually led by the Montrose boats' and included 'fifty first class sea boats from Cellardyke/Anstruther'.[35]

Evidence also shows that Suffolk cheese was being carried overseas from at least the fourteenth century onwards, and by the sixteenth century it had an international reputation, with cheese shipped from Woodbridge, Walberswick, Dunwich and Southwold to the English garrison in Calais, and from Ipswich to Flanders; but from the medieval period onwards London was the most important consumer of Suffolk

---

30   N.G. Williams, *The maritime trade of East Anglian ports 1550–1590* (Oxford, 1988), pp. 80, 81; G.A. Metters, *The King's Lynn Port Books 1610–1614*, NRS LXXIII (Norwich, 2009), pp. 50, 53, 58–60, 89, 102, 111, 116, 143, 147, 156, 157, 187.

31   *Ibid.*, pp. 50, 53, 58, 89, 111, 156.

32   Williams, *Maritime trade*, pp. 83, 209.

33   T.M. Devine, C.H. Lee and C.C. Peden (eds), *The transformation of the Scottish economy since 1700* (Edinburgh, 2005), p. 22.

34   Possibly for the annual Great Yarmouth herring fishery and fair.

35   Quoted in P.F. Anson, *Fishing boats and fishing folk on the east coast of Scotland* (London, 1930; reprint 1971), p. 99. In the Scottish Fisheries Museum in Anstruther there is a quotation from an Anstruther fisherman about his visits to Lowestoft in the nineteenth century.

cheese.[36] Suffolk cheese was sent from Ipswich to Scotland to support Henry IV.[37] Two and a half centuries later Oliver Cromwell shipped at least 645 tons of Suffolk cheese, supplied by Denis Gauden, merchant and navy victualler, to feed his troops in Scotland.[38] Although it can be shown that there were physical links between Anstruther and Suffolk in the more distant past, this does not explain how the whaling fleet came to be carrying Suffolk cheese and how the connections between Suffolk and Scotland were made in the eighteenth century when sources for this connection are rare.

Marketing Suffolk cheese

The successful marketing of cheese was essential to the economy of the producer and the local area. By the eighteenth century there were several methods by which Suffolk cheese was sold. The first two methods involved direct selling, to the consumer at the farmhouse door or at local markets and fairs, while the third involved selling to institutions such as the overseers of the poor to sell on or distribute to the needy.[39] In order to access larger regional fairs Suffolk dairies combined and arranged for one dairyman to take their cheeses to these fairs, including Stourbridge Fair in Cambridge.[40] However, the increasing commercialisation of trade and the growing population of London led to a more sophisticated system of marketing dairy produce. Cheese was purchased in bulk by middlemen working for either the Navy victualling board or London cheesemongers. These were local men with responsibility for purchasing the cheese from the farm, packing it and shipping it onwards to London or elsewhere. At its destination it could be divided, repackaged and sold on to other retailers. Thus, the producer and the consumer were separated by a chain of at least four processes, and by the mid-eighteenth century middlemen had tight control over Suffolk cheesemakers.[41]

This was a system that could go badly wrong; although Fussell suggests that it depended on the honesty of the farmers, Chartres argues that it disadvantaged the farmer, as the middlemen could purchase the cheese in bulk from the farmer on six months' credit, holding on to the cheese to see how prices rose and fell, and if the price never reached the required standard the out-of-date cheese was returned to the farmer. As early as 1609 a Suffolk farmer, Robert Cooper, took Beccles cheese factor

---

36 Williams, *Maritime trade*, pp. 45, 85, 161–3.

37 N. Amor, *Late medieval Ipswich: trade and industry* (Woodbridge, 2011), p. 236.

38 *CSPD, 1650*, pp. 121, 590, 603. Sir Denis Gauden was never paid for these shipments and died a bankrupt.

39 G.E. Fussell, *The English countryman* (London, 1953), pp. 66, 127: Dymond, *Business of the Suffolk parish*, p. 66.

40 G.E. Fussell, *The English dairy farmer* (London, 1966), p. 25.

41 J. Thirsk (ed.), *The agrarian history of England and Wales, 1640–1750*, vol. V, part II (Cambridge, 1987), p. 362.

Thomas Horth to court over failure to honour his credit.[42] Chartres claims that a clique of cheese factors at Woodbridge manipulated prices, while Knox mentions factors at Beccles and Westerfield places them at Woodbridge and Dunwich.[43] The factors were averse to taking financial risks themselves, as their function was to build networks of supply and connect these to the main market; in the case of Suffolk this was London.

Do any of these marketing systems suggest a source for Suffolk cheese in Scotland? Over a four-year period a total of 80–100 cheeses were consumed in victualling the Anstruther whaling ships, whereas the amounts shipped by factors came to thousands of tons of cheese a year.[44] Shipping such small amounts north would not have been economically viable for the factors, but the cheese could have been purchased from London cheesemongers. Anstruther's MPs, Sir John Anstruther II and Sir Henry Erskine, were naturally regular visitors to the capital.[45] However, there is no evidence to suggest that they facilitated the supply of Suffolk cheese to Scotland.

Another way that the Anstruther whaling company might have come to know about the special keeping quality of Suffolk cheese was through Captain James Fall of Dunbar, the father of Robert Fall, one of the promoters of the Anstruther whaling project and the son-in-law of Sir John Anstruther. As well as being an MP, James Fall was the captain of the *Happy Janet*, a privateer leased and victualled by the Royal Navy in 1745.[46] Was the Navy's supply of Suffolk cheese part of the link between Anstruther and Suffolk? Again, there is no evidence to support this.

Even though not recorded after 1707, coastal shipping between Anstruther and East Anglian ports must have continued, and Scottish port books show that Baltic traders often made circular voyages from the Baltic or Scandinavia to ports such as Dunkirk, Rotterdam or Amsterdam, and could have crossed the North Sea to East Anglia and then continued coastwise. There is one small piece of circumstantial evidence that might suggest that an Anstruther ship had called in and taken on cargo in East Anglia before returning home. On 29 September 1743 *The Friendship of Anstruther* arrived in Anstruther from Bergen. Its cargo was wheat, beer and malt, the traditional cargo taken back to Anstruther from East Anglia in the seventeenth century. These commodities

---

42   Fussell, *The English dairy farmer*, p. 289; J. Chartres, 'The marketing of agricultural produce', in Thirsk, *Agrarian history*, p. 486; Thirsk, *Agrarian history*, p. 513. In 1638 Thomas Horth was listed as one of the most important shippers from Great Yarmouth, T.S. Willan, *The English coastal trade 1600–1750* (Manchester, 1938), p. 46.

43   Chartres, 'The marketing of agricultural produce', p. 488; Knox, *Suffolk cheese*, pp. 30, 31; R. Westerfield, *Middlemen in English business*, Transactions of the Connecticut Academy of Arts and Science 19 (New Haven, 1915), pp. 152, 202. Wherever there was cheese to be marketed there were middlemen in operation: see, for example, C. Hallas, 'Supply responsiveness in dairy farming', *Agricultural History Review*, 39/1 (1991), pp. 1–16 on Wensleydale and Swaledale cheese.

44   NAS, 504/4/4; Westerfield, *Middlemen*, p. 204.

45   L. Namier and R. Brooks (eds), *The history of Parliament House of Commons 1755–1790* (London, 1985), pp. 24, 402.

46   R. Sedgewick (ed.), *The history of Parliament House of Commons, 1715–1754*, vol. 1 (London, 1970), p. 32; *The Falls of Dunbar*, John Gray Centre Dunbar, <https://www.johngraycentre.org/people/movers_shaker/the-falls-of-dunbar-1692-1796/>, accessed 19 November 2019.

could have come from Bergen, but this is unlikely, and written in the margin of the entry in the customs record is the word 'Free', showing that no duty had to be paid, suggesting that this was indeed produce from England. The *Friendship* was owned by Andrew Waddell. The Waddell family were not only baillies of Anstruther but owners of at least four ships and promoters of the whaling project the Anstruther Whale Fishing Company, and it is possible that it was through their coasting trade that Suffolk cheese was sourced. There is some evidence that shows how this might have been done.[47]

There was a custom that ships on the coastal or Baltic and Scandinavian routes carried not only mixed cargoes for a number of merchants but instructions on what the ship's master was to buy for the return voyage: for example, David Wedderburne, a Dundee merchant, sent out his ships with complicated instructions on selling his merchandise and what was to be purchased in England or France, and T.C. Smout includes the text of two commissioning letters for Baltic voyages in his book on the pre-Union economy of Scotland.[48] It is probable that coasting ships taking coal, salt and, by the eighteenth century, lead from the duke of Queensbury's works south were commissioned to bring back the cheeses for the whalers. The documentary sources have not been traced to prove such a connection, but instructions could have been given to the ships' masters verbally and so never recorded.[49]

There is one last unifying factor to be considered that connected Suffolk and north-east Scotland – the North Sea. The North Sea was an avenue for trade, a crossroads for people and for culture. The eighteenth-century sailors and fishermen whose livelihood depended on the sea shared its dangers and its advantages. Shoals of herring attracted fishing boats from all communities, ships from all of the nations on its shores stopped to pay the Sound tolls, and sharing the icy Greenland waters chasing the whale and cod fishing around Iceland meant shared experiences. The sea was the link between Scotland and Suffolk, and it has been argued that common factors created a North Sea cultural, economic and social region until around 1800.[50] Price writes of the North Sea gluing regions together, and this author describes the North Sea as a unifying arch that united the peoples bordering it in hard work, capital and common endeavour.[51]

---

47 NAS, 504/4/4; their other ships included the *Janet of Anstruther*, the *Andrew*, the *Alexander* and, in 1749, the *Cumberland*. Given that the duke of Cumberland was the victor of Culloden the Waddells were nailing their loyalty firmly to the mast.

48 Willan, *English coastal trade*, p. 52 from the Compt. Book of David Wedderburne; T.C. Smout, *Scottish trade on the eve of the union, 1660–1707* (London, 1963), pp. 204, 205.

49 Willan mentions *transires* and bonds attached in bundles to English port books, which might have contained some of the missing information about coastal trade with Scotland. Willan, *English coastal trade*, pp. 4–8; nothing similar is attached to the Scottish port books and Willan has only a few references to English trade with Scotland, these mostly referring to the ambiguous Berwick-upon-Tweed.

50 This is discussed in detail in J. Roding and L. Heerma Van Voss (eds), *The North Sea and culture (1500–1800)* (Hilversum, 1996).

51 J. Price, 'Regional identity and European culture', in Roding and Van Voss, *The North Sea*, p. 82; E. Lord, 'Reading the landscape: the moral, political and cultural construction of the North Sea landscape', in Roding and Van Voss, *The North Sea*, pp. 64–77.

Conclusion

In *Researching and writing history: a guide for local historians* David writes, 'indeed themes may be chosen for which evidence is relatively meagre or difficult to interpret, but even if questions remain unanswered or only partially answered they are worth raising as a contribution to historical debate'.[52] Hopefully, the best use of the sources available has been made in this essay, but the question of how the link between Anstruther and Suffolk was made in the eighteenth century remains unanswered. Some theories on this have been discussed, and eventually the missing pieces from the jigsaw that connects Suffolk and Scotland may be found, marking the connection between the eighteenth-century seamen risking their lives on the North Sea and Suffolk dairy farmers.

---

52   D. Dymond, *Researching and writing history*, p. 33.

Part IV: Modern

Chapter 13

Workhouse disorder in Suffolk, 1835–55

Harvey Osborne

This chapter is informed by several pioneering contributions by David Dymond to our understanding of poverty and the operation of the poor law in Suffolk, including 'Parish and hundred workhouses before 1834'.[1] The Poor Law Amendment Act of 1834 ostensibly heralded an immediate and radical break with the past. The New Poor Law introduced centralisation and uniformity in the management and organisation of poor relief, grouping separate parishes into unions under the supervision of a central authority. It sought to eliminate the sundry systems of wage subsidy and allowances routinely provided in former times to the working poor and to restrict all outdoor relief for the able-bodied. Concomitant with the assault on outdoor relief, the New Poor Law also initiated the creation of union workhouses, whose external appearance and internal regimes embodied the principles of deterrence and discipline inherent in the reformed system. The new workhouses quickly assumed totemic significance for both reformers and critics of the new system as well as within the imagination and culture of the labouring poor themselves. Poor Law Commissioners approvingly noted that their 'prison-like appearance … inspires a salutary dread of them'.[2] The labouring poor highlighted their own understanding of the internal regime of the new institutions with a simple, but expressive, sobriquet, 'the bastilles'.[3]

Recent historiography has acted to modify some aspects of our understanding of the New Poor Law, often in response to the findings of detailed local studies of the post-1834 system in operation.[4] Historians have also begun to question 'early

---

1   Published in D. Dymond and E. Martin (eds), *An historical atlas of Suffolk* (Ipswich, 1988; repr. 1989 and 1999), pp. 120–1.

2   E.C. Tufnell, quoted in M.A. Crowther, *The workhouse system 1834–1929: the history of an English social institution* (London, 1981), p. 41.

3   BPP, 1846, IX (602), Select Committee into the Game Laws, Part I (see evidence of Frederick Gowing of Snape, Suffolk, for a determined defence of the application of the term 'bastille'), pp. 629–30.

4   S. King, 'Thinking and re-thinking the New Poor Law', *Local Population Studies*, 99 (2017), pp. 5–18; S. Shave, *Pauper policies: Poor Law practice in England 1780–1850* (Manchester, 2017); Crowther, *The workhouse system*; L. Hollen-Lees, *The solidarities of strangers: the English poor laws and the people 1700–1949* (Cambridge, 1998); F. Driver, *Power and pauperism: The workhouse system 1834–1884* (Cambridge, 1993); S. Gallaher, 'Children and families in the workhouse populations of the Antrim, Ballymena, and Ballymoney Poor Law Unions in the mid-nineteenth century', *Local Population Studies*, 99 (2017), pp. 81–92; J. Purser, 'The workhouse population of

historiographical notions of the depth and reach of the power of union staff and the guardians to whom they reported'.[5] Although it has traditionally been assumed that 'the disciplinary regime of the "bastille" simply crushed its unfortunate inmates under a huge apparatus of rules and regulations', it is clear that the internal regime of the workhouse was frequently challenged by those confined within its walls.[6] Inmates did not always submit passively to workhouse discipline. Workhouses were frequently disorderly spaces and the threat of rebellion was often present. Resistance and misconduct took many forms. Paupers routinely refused to work, assaulted workhouse staff, damaged property, absconded and occasionally rioted. While the poor law authorities usually blamed such transgressions on the most dissolute and criminal, these actions more often represented attempts by a broad range of inmates, including the temporarily resident poor, to defend widely held notions of customary and moral rights and to uphold concepts of individual self-respect.

Despite this, limited attention has been paid to the problems that the workhouse often experienced in maintaining order and the extent to which paupers actively resisted and defied its disciplinary regime.[7] Although popular opposition to the implementation of the New Poor Law has been relatively well documented, few historians have followed David Green in highlighting how workhouse inmates often challenged internal discipline and sought to negotiate conditions.[8] In early nineteenth-century London, the context for Green's research, a large number of urban workhouses served a varied pauper population, among whom the causal poor, particularly vagrants, proved the 'most troublesome'.[9] However, despite the reputation of the capital's workhouses for unrest, the statistical evidence suggests that a more significant problem existed in certain rural counties in the south and east of England, notably Sussex, Surrey, Kent, Wiltshire, Essex and Suffolk. Suffolk, for example, had a relatively small population and few workhouses compared to London, yet accounted for 6 per cent of all those sent to prison for offences in workhouses in England between 1835 and 1842.[10] This examination of workhouse disorder in Suffolk will suggest that collective and individual acts of

---

the Nottingham Union, 1881–1882', *Local Population Studies*, 99 (2017), pp. 66–80; N. Goose, 'Workhouse populations in the mid-nineteenth century: the case of Hertfordshire', *Local Population Studies*, 62 (1999), pp. 52–69.

5   King, 'Thinking and re-thinking', p. 16.

6   Driver, *Power and pauperism*, p. 1.

7   King, 'Thinking and re-thinking', p. 5.

8   D. Green, 'Pauper protests: power and resistance in early nineteenth-century London workhouses', *Social History*, 31/2 (2006), pp. 137–59 and *Pauper capital: London and the Poor Law, 1790–1870* (Farnham, 2010); N. Edsall, *The anti-Poor Law movement, 1834–44* (Manchester, 1971); J. Knott, *Popular opposition to the 1834 Poor Law* (London, 1986).

9   Green, 'Pauper protests', p. 146.

10 BPP, 1843, XLV (63), Abstract returns of persons committed to prisons in England and Wales, for offences in union workhouses under Poor Law Act. Of 9,225 such cases in England, 547 were in Suffolk.

dissent were commonplace in the county's workhouses in the twenty or so years following poor law reform. It will also demonstrate that the problem of workhouse disorder in rural areas often had a strong cyclical dimension connected to the temporary residence of the able-bodied poor during seasonal troughs in demand for labour.

Suffolk was considered 'more deeply pauperised than any other county in England' prior to the 1834 Poor Law Amendment Act.[11] As David Dymond and Peter Northeast have identified, annual expenditure on poor relief in the county was among the highest per capita in England – typically four times the level recorded in some northern counties. In the years immediately following the end of the Napoleonic Wars spending on poor relief in Suffolk reached £1 per head of population.[12] By the early 1830s the expense of maintaining the poor had fallen back marginally, although, as contemporaries such as John Glyde later revealed, average annual costs often concealed enormous variations between Suffolk parishes, ranging from '5s 5d per head in one parish to £3 16s 0d per head in another'.[13] On the eve of poor law reform 'over half the population of Suffolk was considered to be receiving some form of relief'.[14] Reformers believed that such dependency only served to corroborate their critique of the 'old demoralizing ruinous system of poor law management'.[15] Following the Amendment Act, James Phillips Kay, the energetic Assistant Commissioner for Poor Laws in Suffolk and Norfolk, moved quickly to create new poor law unions in the region. The results in Suffolk were influenced by the presence of numerous existing incorporations created between 1756 and 1779 under local acts of parliament. Many of these already possessed large workhouses, often former houses of industry such as that at Nacton (Figure 13.1). Between June and December 1835 nine of the eleven existing Suffolk incorporations were dissolved and converted into poor law unions,[16] and an additional seven new unions were established in areas where incorporations had formerly been absent. By 1837 six new workhouses had been constructed in those Suffolk unions without existing, convertible, buildings; the twelve remaining unions adapted existing accommodation to conform to the requirements of the 1834

---

11 J. Glyde, *Suffolk in the nineteenth-century: physical, social, moral, religious and industrial* (London, 1855), p. 164.

12 D. Dymond and P. Northeast, *A history of Suffolk* (Frome, 1995), p. 97. See also S.G. and E.O.A. Checkland (eds), *The Poor Law report of 1834* (London, 1979), p. 440.

13 Glyde, *Suffolk in the nineteenth-century*, p. 165.

14 Dymond and Northeast, *History of Suffolk*, p. 97.

15 BPP, 1835, XXXV (500), First Annual Report of the Poor Law Commissioners for England and Wales, Appendix B, Report of Charles Mott, p. 113.

16 Mutford and Lothingland and Bury St Edmunds retained their incorporated status after 1834. The former converted to Union status in 1894 and the latter joined with the Thingoe Union in 1907. Two Suffolk unions, Risbridge and Newmarket, included parishes from adjoining parts of Essex and Cambridgeshire. The Thetford Union included fourteen Suffolk parishes, but was predominantly a Norfolk entity.

Figure 13.1. West view of the main building of the Woodbridge Union workhouse at Nacton in 1899 – a former house of industry built in the mid-eighteenth century (© Suffolk Record Office, reference SROI FSC 242/29/39).

Amendment Act.[17] One of those new workhouses was at Wickham Market and served the Plomesgate Union (Plate 13.1).

Wherever new workhouses were built or existing accommodation was converted, central tenets of the reformed system were observed. On entry to the workhouse paupers were compelled to bathe, submit to a medical examination and surrender their clothes and possessions in exchange for a workhouse uniform. They were forbidden to leave without permission from the workhouse master, which would be granted only if adequate notice was given. Segregation was strictly enforced according to a sevenfold classification system devised by the Poor Law Commission, based on distinctions of sex, age and whether a pauper was deemed infirm, aged or able-bodied. Children within the workhouse were to be educated. Diet was plain, frugal and monotonous. Meal times were to be taken in silence.[18] Tobacco and spirits were forbidden. The able-bodied were set to work. Pauper labour sometimes supported the functioning of the institution itself; women were frequently engaged in domestic labour

---

17 New workhouses were required in the newly created Hoxne, Ipswich, Plomesgate, Sudbury, Thingoe and Newmarket Unions. The Risbridge Union constructed a new workhouse in 1856 after initially adapting the former Halesworth workhouse in 1836. The former Loes and Wilford Hundred house of industry became the county asylum for pauper lunatics in 1829.

18 D. Englander, *Poverty and poor law reform in nineteenth-century Britain, 1834–1914* (London, 1998), p. 39.

within the workhouse, but it usually involved repetitive, laborious and punitive tasks such as oakum picking, stone breaking, pumping water or corn grinding. All elements of daily routine were conducted within a strict timetable, whose configuration, along with a raft of other petty regulations, was laid out in regulations issued by the Poor Law Commission.[19] Reformers believed that this regime would inculcate industrious and moral habits in the poor. They also understood that, rather than the material conditions of institutional life, it was the 'strict discipline of well-regulated workhouses, and in particular the restrictions to which the inmates are subject … [that] are intolerable to the indolent and disorderly'.[20] Rule-breakers faced a range of punishments. Minor infractions, disobedience, absconding, refusing to work, swearing and creating noise were categorised as disorderly behaviour and punished by reductions in diet for up to forty-eight hours. Paupers who repeated these offences within a week were deemed to be refractory, a category that also encompassed more serious breaches of discipline including drunkenness, indecency, theft, damage to property, assaults and abuse of workhouse staff. Refractory paupers faced additional levels of punishment, including confinement for up to twenty-four hours. Most workhouses contained lock-ups or refractory wards to confine the recalcitrant and administer punishment internally, but persistent and serious offenders could be taken before magistrates and, if convicted, imprisoned for up to twenty-one days with hard labour.

In the months after the creation of unions in Suffolk the most palpable signs of opposition to the workhouse system came in the form of protests outside the new institutions, but these collective expressions of popular antipathy toward the New Poor Law had largely evaporated by the spring of 1836.[21] By June, Assistant Commissioner Kay was able to report that the workhouse test had been successfully applied across Suffolk, leading to dramatic reductions in expenditure on outdoor relief and also in the number of able-bodied paupers willing to tolerate life within the reformed workhouses. As Kay asserted, 'the reformation of the discipline of these houses, introduced under the authority of the Poor Law Commissioners, has occasioned the dispersion of their able-bodied inmates'. Furthermore, he continued, 'the number of able-bodied males and females who have accepted relief within the walls of the Union Workhouses (excepting for very limited periods) has been … small'.[22] Kay's reports to the Poor Law Commission were often self-congratulatory and his statements should not always be accepted as fact, but his assertions about the combined impact of a deterrent workhouse regime and a more parsimonious approach to outdoor relief were not unfounded. Henry Owen, chairman of the Hoxne Union, reported that before 'the adoption of the workhouse system' upwards of 800 unemployed labourers from local parishes were granted outdoor poor relief during the winter season, but during the winter of 1837 only fifty-two such labourers had been willing to accept 'temporary relief

---

19   TNA, MH 10/2, Circulars to union officers, 1836.
20   Checkland and Checkland, *The Poor Law report*, p. 338.
21   Edsall, *The anti-Poor Law movement*, pp. 35–6. TNA, HO 41/12, Home Office Disturbance Entry Book, February 1834–June 1837.
22   BPP, 1836, I (595), Second annual report of the Poor Law Commissioners for England and Wales, Appendix B, report of James Kay, pp. 161–2.

within the Hoxne Union workhouse'.[23] The guardians of the Cosford Union similarly reported that, even though 'the population of the Union is more than double that of the old Incorporation … the average number of inmates in the workhouse is reduced from 190 to 140'.[24]

Those who emphasise continuity in poor relief policy after 1834 are required to consider the dramatic financial savings realised in the wake of reform. In Suffolk the annual cost of poor relief, calculated at £245,509 in 1834, had fallen to £136,870 by 1837.[25] However, although most unions in the county made a determined attempt to eradicate outdoor relief payments to able-bodied men in the immediate aftermath of reform, in some circumstances the working poor continued to be supported outside 'the house'. Indeed, despite the Assistant Commissioner's presence at the first meeting of the Plomesgate Union in December 1837, the guardians proposed and agreed a motion 'that it is advisable to continue the present system (of out-relief)'.[26] Like most other Suffolk unions, Plomesgate continued to relieve outdoor paupers 'in-kind' and with cash payments throughout the 1830s and 1840s and in most months supported between 1,200 and 1,500 outdoor paupers, while its 'indoor' population rarely exceeded 200.[27] Other East Anglian unions also continued to support the able-bodied outside the workhouse, allowing tasks normally conducted within the institution, such as oakum picking, to be completed within the home, or by adopting adaptations of the labour-rate system that employed paupers in useful work while again otherwise allowing them to live independently.[28] Kay himself expressed frustration at the continuance of outdoor relief in Suffolk, although he conceded that the 'gradual disallowance of out-door medical relief may require the exercise of greater prudence than the removal of other forms of out-door relief'.[29] Anne Digby and John Archer have claimed that provisions to allow for outdoor relief in extraordinary circumstances, such as sickness or injury, afforded a loophole which was used extensively in Norfolk and Suffolk to continue outdoor payments to the able-bodied. Through such practices 'outdoor relief reasserted itself' in some unions as the 'predominant method of payment to the able-bodied'.[30] However, the perpetuation

---

23 BPP, 1837, XXXI (546), Third annual report of the Poor Law Commissioners, Appendix B, addresses from boards of guardians, relative to the operation and effects of the Poor Law Amendment Act, Cosford Union, p. 101.

24 BPP, 1837, XXXI (546), Third annual report of the Poor Law Commissioners, Appendix B, addresses, Hoxne Union, p. 102.

25 BPP, 1837, XXXI (546), Third annual report of the Poor Law Commissioners, Appendix D, List of unions formed, parishes included, population, average poor-rates and number of guardians, p. 259.

26 SROI, ADA 6/AB1/1, Plomesgate Union Minute Book, 5 December 1837.

27 SROI, ADA 6/AB1/1–4, Plomesgate Union Minute Books, 1837–1844.

28 E. Mann, 'Shipmeadow Union Workhouse: Diary of an inmate, 1837–52', *PSIA*, XXIII/1 (1937), p. 48.

29 BPP, 1836, I (595), Second annual report of the Poor Law Commissioners for England and Wales, Appendix B, report of James Kay, p. 181.

30 A. Digby, *Pauper palaces* (London, 1978), pp. 144–5; John E. Archer, *'By a flash and a scare': incendiarism, animal maiming, and poaching in East Anglia, 1815–1870* (Oxford, New York, 1990), p. 51.

of outdoor relief to the able-bodied through the exploitation of legitimate exemption clauses was subject to significant fluctuation often connected to attempts by the central poor law authorities to enforce greater stringency in local policies or to the impact of worsening economic conditions.[31] Digby and Archer have argued that both factors contributed to a subsequent tightening in relief policy in East Anglia at points, particularly during the 1840s and 1850s, with the concomitant effect that able-bodied paupers were periodically 'more prone to see the inside of the Union House'.[32]

Contemporary reports certainly suggest an upsurge in workhouse disorder in Suffolk during the 1840s and 1850s. In 1843 111 paupers were gaoled for refractory conduct in East Suffolk alone.[33] In 1852 8 per cent of all those committed to prison for offences in workhouses in England had been gaoled in Suffolk; only two significantly more populous counties, Middlesex and Lancashire, sent more paupers to prison.[34] An examination of these offences within a local context can help to highlight why some Suffolk workhouses came to rely so heavily on the courts during this period. Surviving judicial evidence from the late 1840s and the 1850s allows an analysis of prosecutions connected to disorder in the Plomesgate and Woodbridge Union workhouses in East Suffolk, where 266 judicial proceedings were instigated against paupers for disorderly and refractory conduct between January 1847 and March 1855.[35] These institutions were largely representative of the two types of workhouse found across Suffolk after 1834. The Woodbridge Union Workhouse was a former house of industry, adapted to conform to the terms of the Amendment Act. The Plomesgate Union Workhouse was a new purpose-built redbrick building constructed in 1836. The Woodbridge Workhouse was adapted to hold 350 people in 1836, although its capacity was later increased to 456, whereas Plomesgate had a nominal capacity of 411.[36] Both Unions served similar rural and agricultural hinterlands, with populations of just over 20,000.[37]

Although both workhouses attempted to discipline unruly paupers internally, serious and repeat offenders were tried at Woodbridge Petty Sessions and, if found guilty, conveyed onward to the county gaol in Ipswich. Of the 266 prosecutions for disorderly and refractory behaviour that came before this court between 1847 and 1855 the majority related to offences by male paupers (203), although a significant number of cases concerned females (63). Most male offenders were identified as agricultural labourers, although other rural crafts and trades were represented, including shoemakers, bakers, gardeners, bricklayers, sailors, whitesmiths, drovers, millers and blacksmiths. The occupations of female offenders were not routinely identified by the workhouse authorities and the courts. Women tended to be defined

---

31   Digby, *Pauper palaces*, p. 144.

32   *Ibid.*, p. 144.

33   Archer, *'By a flash and a scare'*, p. 55.

34   BPP, 1852–53, LXXXIV (973), Number of inmates of workhouses who were committed to prison during the year 1852 for offences committed while they were inmates.

35   SROI, BB 11/1/2/1–3, Woodbridge Petty Session minute books, 1/1/1847 to 13/3/1855 and J465, Ipswich gaol receiving book, 1840–1870.

36   R. Whitehand, *Facts about Suffolk workhouses* (Felixstowe, 2013), pp. 41–9.

37   W. White, *History, gazetteer and directory of Suffolk* (London, 1855), p. 28.

only in terms of marital status, the majority of those prosecuted for disorder being single. All of those prosecuted of both sexes were, without exception, able-bodied. The ages of those committed ranged from thirteen to fifty-four years, although the average age of offenders was twenty-three, with the majority aged between seventeen and twenty-five. The exact kind of misbehaviour for which these paupers were typically prosecuted varied slightly according to gender. Over half of females committed were charged with wilful and malicious damage, which frequently related to the breaking of windows. Sarah Williams (seventeen), Esther Gilbert (twenty-one) and Eleanor Smith (twenty), for example, were found guilty of committing this offence at the Plomesgate Workhouse on 31 May 1848 and were subsequently gaoled for between ten and fourteen days. Other common offences by female paupers included insubordination, refusal to work, damaging doors and furniture, desertion, theft of cloths and linen and other forms of often unspecified misbehaviour. Some female offenders were repeatedly brought before the magistrates for such offences and oscillated between workhouse and prison as a result. The previously mentioned Eleanor Smith committed eight separate offences, all relating to the destruction of property in Plomesgate Workhouse, between March 1847 and April 1850, and spent the equivalent of eight and a half months in prison as a result.

The kind of infractions commonly associated with female inmates were also committed by men, including, chiefly, the destruction of various forms of workhouse property: windows, doors and furniture. However, intransigent male paupers often displayed a greater tendency to engage in more serious forms of insubordination, principally refusal to work. They were also more likely to abscond and to be charged with violence toward workhouse staff and other inmates. Henry Osborne (nineteen) received fourteen days' hard labour for absconding from the Woodbridge Workhouse in late July 1849, only to repeat the offence on his return to the institution at the end of his prison sentence. Osborne served further prison terms for inciting other paupers to insubordination in early February 1850, breaking windows on his return later that month, and for absconding again the following January. Robert Mills (twenty-seven), William Cattermole (twenty-one), Amos Ringe (sixteen) and Frederick Simpson (thirty-one) were all gaoled for separate assaults on the porter of the Plomesgate Workhouse across successive winters in 1850–52. William Cattermole repeated the offence on his return to the workhouse in January 1852. Jesse Pooley (thirty-four) also received a twenty-one-day sentence for attacking Jonathan Moore, the master of the Plomesgate Workhouse, in June 1852. Sometimes violence was directed at other paupers. Emma Newson (nineteen) and John Garrod (forty) were both gaoled in June 1847 for separate assaults on fellow inmates in Plomesgate Workhouse.[38]

Those paupers brought before the courts have left little evidence of the precise motivations behind these offences, which, as Green has highlighted, 'were part of a wider pattern of transgression and misbehaviour in the workhouse'.[39] Many misdemeanours undoubtedly reflected the personal frustration and misery of those

---

38   SROI, BB 11/1/2/2, Woodbridge Petty Session minute book, 1/1/1847 to 17/6/1852 and J465, Ipswich gaol receiving book, 1840–1870.

39   Green, 'Pauper protests', p. 138.

who found themselves both destitute and confined. Some malcontents also probably threatened the peace and safety of fellow inmates as much as they challenged the authority of the workhouse authorities. Nonetheless, it would be wrong to dismiss all individual and collective forms of misbehaviour as merely impulsive and aimless expressions of anger. Misconduct often reflected not only individual attempts to exert independence and self-respect but a wider pattern of quotidian resistance to the workhouse system. These included overt attempts to challenge discipline and authority and to negotiate and influence conditions, often involving collective solidarities and networks of paupers. Decisions to refuse to work were often taken collectively by small groups of able-bodied paupers, as at Plomesgate in January and November 1847 and at Woodbridge in August 1848 and January 1852. Two other male paupers joined William Rainbird (twenty-five) in refusing to attend morning divine service at Woodbridge Workhouse in February 1850, an offence that earned each man fourteen days' hard labour. David Parker (eighteen) and Henry Osborne (nineteen) acted together on several occasions between February 1850 and January 1851 when damaging property and absconding from Woodbridge Workhouse. Between July 1849 and January 1851 Osborne was also prosecuted several times for similar offences in the company of Mark Gladden (seventeen). Mary Ann Fitch (nineteen), Hannah Cooper (seventeen) and Sarah Cattermole (eighteen) frequently attended Woodbridge magistrates court together in 1852 for transgressions ranging from refusal to obey orders to breaking windows. These young women were also part of an overlapping group of co-offenders that included Eleanor Smith (twenty-one), Esther Gilbert (twenty-two), Sarah Coates (eighteen), Elizabeth Enemy (twenty-one) and Sarah Fitch (nineteen), whose misdemeanours encompassed absconding, breaking windows and insubordination.[40]

The profiles of those prosecuted for offences committed within the Woodbridge and Plomesgate Workhouses support the impression that the young able-bodied unemployed were the least compliant and the most challenging of inmates. However, as census and workhouse records reveal, for much of the year these categories of pauper were not usually present within Suffolk's workhouses in significant numbers. During most months, more than 60 per cent of the population of the Plomesgate and Woodbridge Workhouses were typically either children aged fifteen and under or older and infirm residents aged sixty and above. At the end of March 1851, for example, over 40 per cent (95) of the Plomesgate Workhouse's total population of 224 was aged fifteen or under, with a further 26 per cent (59) aged over fifty. A similar balance prevailed in the Woodbridge Workhouse, where those aged fifteen or under (141) and fifty-one and over (50) were by far the largest cohorts in an overall population of 297.[41] The typical rural workhouse had a similarly constituted population during the late spring, summer and autumn months, with a preponderance of very young and aged paupers. However, just as the level of outdoor pauperism fluctuated in response to seasonally acute unemployment and hardship, so too did the

---

40 SROI, BB 11/1/2/1–3, Woodbridge Petty Session minute books, 1/1/1847 to 13/3/1855.

41 TNA, HO 107/1802, 1851 Census, Plomesgate Union House, ff. 279r–288r and HO 107/1801, 1851 Census Woodbridge Union House, ff. 249r–256v.

number of inmates in Suffolk's workhouses.[42] Throughout the 1840s the Plomesgate Workhouse, for example, typically contained fewer than 150 inmates between April to October, but its population swelled between November and March, when up to 250 paupers could be resident. The population of the Woodbridge Workhouse also grew significantly during the winter, when 50 to 100 additional paupers were present throughout January and February. This annual influx of temporary inmates was almost entirely comprised of the adult able-bodied poor. Within this category the young and single were often prominent, as those most likely to be laid off during winter lulls in agricultural production and the least likely to profit from loopholes that provided for some families to be relieved outdoors. They were also among the least amenable to workhouse discipline.

Predictably, there was a strong relationship between seasonal changes in workhouse populations and the incidence of disorder. Of the 266 cases prosecuted at the Woodbridge sessions between 1847 and 1855 over half (136) related to offences committed between December and March, with most disturbances consistently occurring in January and February. Further demonstration of the correlation between the seasonal admission of greater numbers of the able-bodied poor and the increased risk of internal disorder occurred during the early 1850s, when several Suffolk workhouses experienced serious and sustained rioting. The Newmarket Union Workhouse was one of those affected and the challenges of coping with large numbers of able-bodied paupers are highlighted in correspondence sent by the workhouse master to the Lord Lieutenant of Suffolk, Earl Stradbroke, in February 1850. Charles Clarke reported that:

> During the present winter ... the male paupers maintained have been on repeated occasions vicious and disorderly ... the number of male paupers, now maintained, is one hundred and twenty-five and the only officers of the establishment are myself, a schoolmaster, a porter and a superintendent of labour.[43]

In other Suffolk workhouses that experienced winter riots during the early 1850s disturbances were initiated by able-bodied inmates often unhappy about the separation of husbands and wives. Married men instigated riots at Woodbridge in 1850 and within the Bosmere Union House for three consecutive winters up to 1853.[44] The Bosmere Workhouse endured a week of disturbances in February 1850 following entreaties from male paupers that 'they wanted to see their wives'. Some 500 paupers were maintained in the workhouse at the time, including 100 able-bodied

---

42 K.D.M. Snell, *Annals of the labouring poor: social change and agrarian England, 1660–1990* (Cambridge, 1987), pp. 20–1; G. Boyer, *An economic history of the English Poor Law, 1750–1850* (Cambridge, 1990), pp. 86–8.

43 SROI, HA 11/B/1/24, Rous family archives, 1846–1879.

44 TNA, HO 41/19, Home Office disturbance entry books, 1848–1852; MH 12/12081, Poor law union papers (Woodbridge Union 1848–1850), Letters to Sir John Walsham, Asst. Poor Law Commissioner, from G.W. Jones on behalf of board of guardians, 8 February 1850; *Ipswich Journal*, 21 February 1852

men. Once the trouble subsided, the apartments of the male paupers were searched, revealing 'a number of files, small iron bars and knives'.[45] Rioting at the Woodbridge Workhouse in January 1850 also began after male paupers demanded to see their wives and 'not be parted again'. The master's refusal to acquiesce won the respect of the guardians, although, revealingly, they later reflected that perhaps he 'should have given way, there being 70 able bodied men in the house'. During the trouble that followed able-bodied inmates demonstrated little deference for the disciplinary regime of the workhouse or its internal architecture. Rioting subsided only after the 'partial destruction of some parts of the building', which had involved 'pulling down the walls, doors, windows … the ignitable parts of which were then piled up by the male paupers and set on fire'.[46] These disturbances, led by married men seeking to assert natural marital rights underpinned by Christian morality, were more widely marked by gender and gender-based assumptions, not least those concerning patriarchal authority within the domestic family household, which the workhouse system disrupted. Nor were women passive bystanders in major workhouse riots. William Simpson, in a rare example of pauper testimony, observed that, although rioting in the Wangford Union Workhouse in January 1844 was initiated by able-bodied men, 'the conduct of the women was equally violent and more destructive. They broke every pane of glass in the room, destroyed and burnt chairs, forms and all they could lay their hands on'.[47]

Attempts were naturally made to severely punish those who led and participated in major workhouse riots, although the numbers prosecuted for their part in such disorder could be surprisingly low. Even after a major disturbance at Newmarket Workhouse in 1850 the master reported that, although 'four were convicted of riot and assault … many other inmates who took part in the said riot and disturbances could not be individually identified'.[48] Oftentimes, as Anne Crowther has observed, the central poor law authorities regarded 'reliance on the magistrates … (as) … a sign of failure in local administration'.[49] Following rioting at the Wangford Union Workhouse, the master, Thomas Balls, was forced to resign after Sir John Walsham, the Assistant Poor Law Commissioner, concluded that he was 'unequal to the task of maintaining order and strict discipline in a Workhouse containing so many able-bodied Paupers at one time'.[50]

Workhouse masters such as Thomas Balls or Charles Clarke, who were responsible for supervising large numbers of resentful paupers, possibly deserve some sympathy. As Crowther has argued, the ideal of the reformative and disciplinary regime 'was unworkable without powers of enforcement which did not exist'.[51] Aside

45   *Ipswich Journal*, 21 February 1850.
46   TNA, MH 12/12081, Poor law union papers (Woodbridge Union 1848–1850), Letters to Sir John Walsham, Asst. Poor Law Commissioner, from G.W. Jones on behalf of board of guardians, 8 February 1850.
47   Mann, 'Shipmeadow Union Workhouse', p. 46.
48   SROI, HA 11/B/1/24, Rous family archives, 1846–1879.
49   Crowther, *The workhouse system*, p. 211.
50   D. Smith, 'The 1844 Riots at Shipmeadow Workhouse', *Suffolk Review* (1987), p. 4.
51   Crowther, *The workhouse system*, p. 44.

from the disadvantages that flowed from the fact that 'workhouse populations changed continually, making discipline more difficult than in asylums or prisons', staff numbers were often insufficient to maintain order.[52] According to returns collected by the poor law authorities in 1849, the 'average' workhouse, containing around 225 inmates, had a staff of six, of which the medical officer and chaplain were part-time.[53] These official figures overstate staff capacity at some workhouses, as at Woodbridge during the winter of 1849, when the master, Mr Truelove, the porter, William Hudson, and the schoolmaster, Jacob Myson, who was seventy-nine, were responsible for supervising over 400 paupers.[54] The Plomesgate Workhouse operated with a full-time staff of similar dimensions. In these circumstances it is unsurprising that local workhouse officials often required the support of magistrates, police and, on occasions, local military forces to maintain or restore order. Such was the intensity of rioting within the Bosmere Workhouse in February 1851 that magistrates summoned the 11th Hussars from Ipswich to pacify the institution.[55] Things were little better twelve months later, when it took the best part of a week to fully recover the building after sustained rioting and then only through the efforts of '25 policemen and 12 parish constables'.[56] Police armed with cutlasses were also deployed within the Woodbridge Workhouse in the aftermath of rioting in 1850.[57] The Woodbridge Board of Guardians had by this time adopted a policy of routinely stationing policemen within the workhouse during wintertime to deter trouble. Other Suffolk workhouses did likewise, notably those of the Bosmere and Wangford Unions.[58] Given the physical and social isolation of many rural workhouses, this was prudent.[59] In an appeal for the recruitment of additional special constables to help quell workhouse disturbances, Charles Clarke of the Newmarket Workhouse drew attention to the fact that, 'being situate out of the town of Newmarket, we cannot at a short notice command the services of a constable'.[60]

The Victorian workhouse could not always control inmates in the way that the architects of the workhouse system envisaged and as historians have sometimes assumed. Maintaining order and enforcing compliance, even at the best of times, required workhouse staff to possess both considerable talent and luck.[61] Inmates

---

52   *Ibid.*, p. 208.

53   BPP, 1849, XLVII (306), Return of officers employed in unions under poor law board in England and Wales. Crowther, *The workhouse system*, p. 127.

54   TNA, HO 107/1802, 1851 Census, Plomesgate Union House, ff. 279r–288r and HO 107/1801, 1851 Census Woodbridge Union House, ff. 249r–256v. SROI, ADA 12/AB1/7, Minutes of the board of guardians of the Woodbridge Union, 1848–50.

55   TNA, HO 41/19, Home Office Disturbance Entry Books, 1848–1852.

56   *Ipswich Journal*, 21 February 1852.

57   TNA, MH 12/12081, Poor law union papers (Woodbridge Union 1848–1850), Letters to Sir John Walsham, Asst. Poor Law Commissioner, from G.W. Jones on behalf of board of guardians, 8 February 1850.

58   Smith,'The 1844 riots at Shipmeadow workhouse', p. 2. *Ipswich Journal*, 21 February 1852.

59   Crowther, *The workhouse system*, p. 133.

60   SROI, HA 11/B/1/24, Rous family archives, 1846–1879.

61   Englander, *Poverty and poor law reform*, p. 41.

were frequently difficult and often truculent. Expressions of insubordination were routine and persistent, but workhouse disorder in counties such as Suffolk in the decades immediately following reform also had a strong cyclical dimension connected to seasonal underemployment in an agricultural economy weighted toward arable farming. The impact of structural poverty and seasonal unemployment was felt most severely during the late winter months and often brought more of the able-bodied poor into the workhouse. Those temporarily resident were the least responsive to workhouse discipline and, although able-bodied and unemployed adults were, even during the worst of winters, a minority of the inmate population, their seasonal presence underscored the consequences of 'congregating masses of paupers' in the workhouses.[62] Moreover, although the provision of outdoor relief continued long after 1834, significantly more able-bodied applicants appear to have been subject to the workhouse test during the 1840s and 1850s. This included married couples, alongside the young and single who were always the most likely to be denied outdoor relief in any circumstances. Archer has observed that 'after 1853 when agriculture picked up and the rural work-force either began to leave the land or else were employed more steadily throughout the year, we see a rapid decline in both anti-poor law protest and indoor relief'.[63] Crowther and David Englander also argue that large-scale workhouse disorder became less common after mid-century, and that later outbreaks of indiscipline tended to be 'individual rather than collective'.[64] Despite contemporary anxiety about the major workhouse riots that punctuated many Suffolk winters during the early Victorian period, individual, prosaic and often surreptitious forms of resistance to the workhouse regime were probably always the most common expressions of pauper discontent. James Scott's notion of 'everyday resistance' – foot-dragging, false compliance, pilfering, feigned ignorance and sabotage – is apposite in this context.[65] Like inmates in other types of disciplinary institution, paupers within Suffolk's early Victorian workhouses did not always passively conform to the regulations and disciplinary regime of the institution, and on frequent occasions 'exerted independence, influenced treatment and questioned authority'.[66]

---

62 BPP, 1836, I (595), *Second annual report of the Poor Law Commissioners for England and Wales*, Appendix B, report of James Kay, p. 161.

63 Archer, *'By a flash and a scare'*, p. 55.

64 Englander, *Poverty and poor law reform*, p. 43; Crowther, *The workhouse system*, p. 211.

65 J.C. Scott, *Weapons of the weak: everyday forms of peasant resistance* (New Haven, 1985), p. xvi.

66 Green, 'Pauper protests', p. 138; A. Clark, 'Wild workhouse girls and the Liberal Imperial State in mid-nineteenth century Ireland', *Journal of Social History*, 39/2 (2005), pp. 389–409; T. Myers and J. Sangster, 'Retorts, runaways and riots: patterns of resistance in Canadian reform schools for girls, 1930–60', *Journal of Social History*, 34/3 (2001), pp. 669–97.

Chapter 14

The suburbanisation of Sutton, Surrey

David Woodward[1]

Introduction

In *Researching and writing history: a guide for local historians*, David Dymond writes that local historians should pay more attention to 'the relentless march of suburbanisation'. He suggests that this should involve more 'than just mapping the growth', but should also consider 'the suburban way of life which stands for personal, family and social ambitions which have deeply influenced national life'.[2] This paper aims to examine the 'relentless march' in the context of one Surrey settlement and to discuss how life in old villages such as Sutton was transformed beneath rows of Victorian villas and the expectations of the households who moved into them.

Sutton, Surrey

Situated twelve miles from central London and now a London borough, in the early nineteenth century Sutton, in the ancient county of Surrey, was a one-street village on the London to Brighton road. Its houses spread from The Green at the north of the village to The Cock on the North Downs in the south. Sheep grazed on the chalk downland, while at the foot of the hill, on London Clay, arable crops dominated. Despite the enclosure of the South common in 1809 and the North common in 1816, until the mid-nineteenth century the village was still rustic in character.[3] Between 1851 and 1861 its population increased by 129 per cent, from 1,387 to 3,186, and further rapid development meant that between 1861 and 1891 it increased still further, by 338 per cent, to 13,977.[4] Its agricultural land had been built on, and it had become a suburb of greater London. This essay is concerned with the process of suburbanisation and its effects on the village.

---

1   David Woodward died in 2012. His nearest relatives have given permission for the publication of this compilation from his University of Kingston PhD thesis. Previously, he was a student with David Dymond on the University of Cambridge Masters in Local History course. The title of the thesis was 'Suburban development in five neighbouring South London parishes in the middle decades of the 19th century'.

2   D. Dymond, *Resarching and writing history: a guide for local historians* (Lancaster, 2009), p. 36.

3   *VCH Surrey*, vol. 4, pp. 243, 244.

4   *VCH Surrey*, vol. 4, p. 451.

Suburbanisation

The chronic over-crowding of Britain's industrial towns and cities in the late eighteenth and early nineteenth centuries meant that these began to spread outwards into the surrounding hinterland. In the ancient county of Surrey the villages closest to London (Vauxhall, Battersea and Lambeth, for example) were colonised by industry and workers. These unplanned industrial sprawls were part of the concentrated growth of the centre and cannot be described as suburbs in the traditional sense, as nineteenth-century suburbs had distinctive characteristics. Life in the outer suburbs was seen as enabling households to reside in tranquillity and privacy as part of an exclusive society.[5] Sutton provided not only tranquillity but beauty as well. John Ruskin described the area around the village 'as no lovelier piece of lowland scenery can be seen in lowland England', and Holt's 1890 *Directory* described it as 'a place eminently suited for the promotion of health'.[6]

Theories on how and why Victorian suburbs and suburban life developed have been explored in detail by urban historians. The emphasis of many of the theoretical discussions has been on changes in transport, in particular the opening of the railway and railway links from the periphery to the centre. It has also been argued that demographic growth drove the expansion of some areas. Christopher French suggested that population growth, migration and improved transport provided the impetus behind the creation of London's suburbs, such as Sutton. Alternatively, David Reeder argued that population growth and improved transport could not account for the suburban development alone, as land had to be available to build on, as well as capital to finance the building.[7] In the case of Sutton it was also the provision of gas and piped water which helped to attract the middle classes into the more salubrious outskirts of the town, such as the Benhill estate and, by 1870, the chalk downs to the south of the town.

If population growth, improved transport, building land and capital were in place what else was needed to make people move? Here the class element comes into play. In the traditional town the wealthy preferred to live in the centre of things, while the poorer folk often lived outside the walls.[8] The West End of Victorian London was and is still where the aristocracy have their town houses, but it was the burgeoning middle classes who wanted to move out to more spacious and exclusive areas to live

---

5   R.G. Morris, 'Structure, culture and society in British towns', in M. Daunton (ed.), *The Cambridge urban history of Britain*, vol. 4 (Cambridge, 2000), p. 414; G.P. Bevan, *Tourists guide to the county of Surrey* (London, 1882), p. 8; P. Fitzgerald, *London city suburbs: as they are today* (London, 1893), p. 90.

6   J. Ruskin, *The crown of wild olive* (London, 1904), p. 5; Holt's *Directory of Sutton* (London, 1896), p. 1.

7   C. French, 'Who lived in suburbia? Surbiton in the second half of the nineteenth century', *Family and Community History*, 10/2 (2007), p. 95; D. Reeder, 'H.J. Dyos and the urban process', in D. Cannadine and D. Reeder (eds), *Exploring the urban past: essays in urban history by H.J. Dyos* (Cambridge, 1982), p. xviii.

8   Amsterdam in the Golden Age is a good example of this.

beside like-minded people.[9] How far middle-class demand pushed the creation of a suburb is the final element in suburbanisation.[10]

Transport

The availability of good, reliable and fast transport connections was one of the key elements in the formation of suburbs. Sutton had benefited from the railway since 1847, when the London, Brighton and South Coast Railway opened a line from Epsom to London Bridge, and by 1868 Sutton was also linked to Victoria via Mitcham Junction.[11] Sutton had trains every twenty to twenty-five minutes to the London terminus at Victoria for the West End and entertainment and to London Bridge for the City.[12] Sutton was 'a place for the City man'.[13] The proportion of first- and second-class tickets sold in Sutton – 56 per cent in 1869 – reinforces the idea that the suburban incomers were white-collar professionals seeking more spacious living.[14] A first-class return into London from Sutton cost 2s 6d, a second-class 2s and a third-class 1s 9d: these were not fares that the labouring classes could afford.[15]

The birthplace column of the 1881 census shows that 80 per cent of the inhabitants of Sutton by that time were born elsewhere; 48 per cent came from the rest of Surrey, but the remainder were from more distant parts, including Devon and Ireland. Many of the newcomers were domestic servants attracted by employment in the new suburban households. Others were households moving out from central London. Some 1,442 persons were born in Middlesex, across the river from Surrey, including in parishes in the City of London and the west of the city. The census for 1861 shows that 30 per cent of employed adults were in domestic service, a proportion that had risen to 39 per cent by 1881. Most of these were female: 53 per cent of the population was female in 1851 and 59 per cent in 1881.[16]

---

9   F.M.L. Thompson, *The rise of respectable society 1830–1900* (London, 1988), p. 73; P. Willmott and M. Young, *Family and class in a London suburb* (London, 1960), pp. 6–7; N. Hayes, 'Calculating class: housing, life-style and status in the English provincial city', *Urban History*, 1 (2009), pp. 113–40.

10 F.M.L. Thompson 'The rise of suburbia', in R.J. Morris and R. Rodger (eds), *The Victorian city: a reader in British urban history, 1820–1914* (London, 1993), pp. 162, 171; A.A. Jackson, *Semi-detached London: suburban development, life and transport 1900–1939* (London, 1973), p. 23.

11 H.P. White, *Greater London: the regional history of the railways of Great Britain*, vol. 3 (Newton Abbott, 1963), p. 58.

12 TNA, RAIL 414/560 Passenger and Fare Statistics 1860–69.

13 Morgan's *Family and Advertising Almanac* (1869), p. 7.

14 TNA, RAIL 425/560 Passenger Traffic Between London and Stations within fifteen miles, in the Metropolitan District, Year Ending 31 October 1869.

15 TNA, RAIL 414/560 Passenger and Fare Statistics 1860–69.

16 *VCH Surrey*, p. 451. TNA, RG 418 1861 census return for Sutton; TNA, RG/758 and 759 1881 census returns for Sutton.

The availability of building land

This movement of population into Sutton would not have been possible without land being made available for building: landowners' role in suburbanisation was crucial. The largest landowner in Sutton was Thomas Alcock, lord of the manors of Sutton, Banstead and Kingswood. Even before the opening of the railway, with an eye to the main chance and knowledge of profitable changes that had followed the railway elsewhere, he had consolidated his agricultural estates in Sutton. He laid out new roads and sold large strips of land to the National Freehold, the Perpetual, the Government Clerks and other investment societies, who in turn subdivided their holdings and sold these for housing, thereby 'enabling many persons to become owners and freeholders'.[17] The result of the subdivisions and the sale to speculative builders was piecemeal unplanned developments and poor quality control.

Two contrasting large estates were built in the mid-nineteenth century: the Newtown estate, to the east of the High Street, and the Benhill estate, north-east of the High Street. The Newtown estate, closer to the railway, was laid out as terraced housing, interspersed with a few detached and semi-detached houses, with no unifying architectural style.[18] Newtown quickly became over-crowded and unhygienic because of a lack of clean water[19] and was, by the 1880s, experiencing recurring outbreaks of disease such as typhoid and diphtheria; Dr Cox, the town doctor, noted cesspits running into wells in the Newton Lanes. Newtown was seen as socially deteriorating, with disease linked to moral conduct. The larger houses built for the managerial class in the 1850s had become multi-occupancy pauper dwellings.[20]

The Benhill estate was built after 1865, when piped water and gas were added to the village. It contained some detached and semi-detached villas, some with large gardens and as many as eight bedrooms, and it included some smaller terraced houses, but its main drawback was its distance from the railway station.

The difference in the size of houses and the layout of the estates, together with the occupation column in the census, shows that the Newtown estate was attractive to the lower-paid clerks and artisans, Benhill to white-collar workers. Thus in Sutton two types of suburb existed in the 1840s–60s. However, in 1865, with the coming of piped water, more agricultural land was released, newer housing was built to the south of Newtown and the commuting class living in Newtown moved into this more exclusive development. This was also the case with another later development on the chalk 'green-field' site on Sutton Hill. Being in a well-drained premium position, plots there attracted wealthier and socially mobile residents, who could afford a

---

17   G. Rookledge and A. Skelton, *Rookledge's Architectural Identifier of Conservation Areas* (London, 1999), p. 18; Sutton Town Council, *Official Guide to Sutton* (1906), p. 21.

18   D. Reeder, 'A theatre of suburbs: some patterns of development in West London, 1801–1911', in H.J. Dyos (ed.), *The study of urban history* (Leicester, 1968), p. 269.

19   L. Charlesworth, D. Evers, R. Mitchell and C. Reid, *100 years of public health in Sutton, 1883–1983* (Sutton, 1983), p. 30; R.P. Smith, *A history of Sutton, AD 675–1900* (Carshalton, 1970), p. 70.

20   Letter by Dr John Cox to *The Sutton and Epsom Advertiser and Surrey Reporter*, 2 November 1881; *The Sutton and Epsom Advertiser and Surrey Reporter*, 1 April 1882.

premium that became mirrored in the worth and rateable value of the residences and the social prestige of the residents. These semi-detached and detached houses were acceptable to the incoming middle classes on both health and aesthetic grounds.[21]

In the space of fifty years the whole character of Sutton had changed. It was no longer a rustic village but a town. Where once cattle and sheep had grazed and crops had grown there were now houses, and where there had been agricultural labourers' cottages and rural tradesmen, there were now retail shops. Once a homogeneous settlement, Sutton now had separate neighbourhoods for labourers, artisans and the 'middle class' – divided into lower- and upper-middle classes – all recognisable as such from the position and standard of the housing.

Sutton had become suburbanised principally because of the railway, which allowed daily commuting to London, but also because a speculative landlord had released agricultural land for building. None of this would have been possible if there had not been a perceived demand for housing of a specific type and because of the attractiveness of homes away from the centre, with its pollution and hustle and bustle. The result was a mass migration out of the city, which in turn changed the social mix of Sutton and brought in not only the household head and his family but domestic servants and the service industry. Demography and the growth of cities might have pushed people out of the centre, but it was the perception of a demand that made this possible.

Living in the suburb

Nineteenth-century suburbia was essentially a middle-class enclave in which the male world of work outside the home and the female domestic domain were separated and new bourgeois expectations of life and leisure were formed. This was the world of the Grossmiths' *Diary of a Nobody* and H.G. Wells' *Ann Veronica*.[22]

Thus, a distinctive feature of Sutton's suburbs was the gender and age gap during the day, as the males of the household departed for the City, leaving wives, children, sisters, the elderly and servants behind. This separation and the daily commute to the workplace were essential features of suburban life, as a household's standard of living depended on a steady income and the household head was often the sole financial support of a household of as many as eight dependants. It meant that the males could escape and find not only employment but leisure activity outside the home, while the females of the family were sequestered in the home. The male sphere of amusement was the private club or billiard room, the female's sphere was the drawing room. The physical character of the suburban middle-class houses, set behind hedges, guarded by porches, and inside 'stuffed with warm brightly coloured goods, everything padded or covered, created a womb-like haven for the middle-class women'.[23] This could result in a desire to escape into charity work, amateur dramatics or reading circles, or into lassitude. In 1884 the anonymous author of *Girls, wives and mothers: a word to*

---

21   B. Robson, *Urban social areas* (Oxford, 1975), p. 28.

22   G. and W. Grossmith, *The diary of a nobody* (London, 1892); H.G. Wells, *Ann Veronica* (London, 1909).

23   R. Parker, *The subversive stitch* (London, 1984), p. 157.

the middle classes decried the lack of practical skills among middle-class girls who could not sew a hem or put on a button.[24]

Not only did the suburbs separate the sexes, but 'suburban life was the ultimate experience of the separation of the classes ... the very rich and the very poor were excluded, and the middle class pattern could develop unmolested'.[25] The middle class lived in socially exclusive areas, and Roy Lewis and Angus Maude suggest that living in a middle-class area made residents feel middle class and subscribe to middle-class values.[26] There are examples of the character of the middle-class houses in Sutton, and the way in which these were graded by class, in the 1881 census. Glenhurst, a large detached house on The Common, occupied in 1881 by William Flack, a broker aged thirty-nine, his wife, three children and a governess, cook, lady's maid and a housemaid, was an upper-middle-class household. A semi-detached house in Grange Crescent, occupied by John Barry, a Bank of England clerk also aged thirty-nine, his wife, two daughters and a cook and housemaid, was a middle-middle-class household. Finally, in Gander Green Lane a terraced house lived in by Robert Gabb, a clerk aged forty-eight, his wife, one daughter and one general servant, was a lower-middle-class household.[27]

The middle class moved to suburban Sutton with expectations of an ideal village community, healthful air and a life among people of their own kind. They left behind the inner-city organs of sophisticated entertainment, and as a result local cultural societies and clubs were established.[28] By 1874 Sutton was an Urban District Council and had a library, tennis courts, a horticultural society and a cricket team. A public hall opened in 1877 where concerts and amateur dramatics were performed, and at the same time leisure facilities at home were increased, with the larger houses having billiard rooms, music rooms and conservatories, where neighbours could gather.[29] By 1880 Sutton and its suburbs had matured.

Conclusion

Suburban Sutton had forged a new society, but was it part of a community? In the nineteenth century there appeared to be little intermixing socially or occupationally between the different social strata in the town. The bourgeois newcomers to the suburbs had values more significant to them than those of the existing community. The newcomers' lifestyle was shaped by these shared values and their stage in the life cycle: it is no coincidence that the ages of two of the three 1881 heads of households cited above were the same.

By the beginning of the twentieth century Sutton had become one of the most

---

24 *Ibid.*, p. 156.

25 L. Davidoff, *Worlds between: historical perspectives on gender and class* (Oxford, 1999), pp. 58, 59.

26 R. Lewis and A. Maude, *The English middle class* (London, 1950), p. 18.

27 TNA, RG/758 f. 51 and 759 f. 49.

28 A. Saint, 'The quality of London's suburbs', in J. Hewer (ed.), *London suburbs* (London, 1999), p. 21.

29 Church's *Directory of Sutton* (1880); S. Goodwins, *Sutton past and present* (Stroud, 2004).

desirable localities for suburban living: 'Its situation is perfect'.[30] 'The Sutton of old speedily threw off its lethargy and its tranquil village aspect' and became, in a few years, a town.[31] But a community it was not: the physical and social barriers between the working and the middle classes continued to exist. The middle-class suburbs had 'a vitality which came from meeting the needs of its own inhabitants, and which, in an architectural sense invented itself as it went along'.[32] The working-class areas were packed with small decaying terraced cottages. Sutton's suburbs, on the other hand, continued to grow, and the extension of the railway encouraged suburban development over the North Downs to Banstead, Epsom and Leatherhead.

In conclusion, this case study of the suburbanising process in the second half of the nineteenth century indicates that a number of factors influenced the timing, nature, extent and impact of suburban growth. Improved transport and available land and capital for building were clearly fundamental, but also crucial in the growth of suburbia were the aspirations of the expanding middle classes to leave behind the problems associated with inner-city living and to find space, fresh air and a comfortable lifestyle in the suburbs.

30   Holt's *Directory of Sutton, Carshalton, Wallington and District* (1904), p. 3.
31   Holt's *Directory of Sutton* (1905), p. 3.
32   D.A. Reeder, *Suburbanity and the Victorian city* (Leicester, 1980), p. 2.

Chapter 15

Godmanchester and the census

Ken Sneath

David Dymond's love of local history shone through his lectures, and he always emphasised the importance of placing local history in a wider and comparative context. This paper focuses on Godmanchester, but aims to follow David's emphasis. The census is one of the most important sources for uncovering the history of a community. However, published studies of local communities in the nineteenth century using census data are still limited.[1] One example, by Mark Brayshay, studied one primary industry, the mining communities of west Cornwall, an area of depopulation and changing household structure.[2] In this paper I am going to explore what census data reveals about an agricultural area, agriculture being by far the largest activity in the primary economic sector.[3] To what extent did 'the great agricultural depression' impact upon Godmanchester, a small town in the Ouse Valley in the predominantly agricultural county of Huntingdonshire?[4] Analysis of the two censuses for 1851 and 1891 sheds light upon the social and economic changes of the second half of the nineteenth century.

Nineteenth-century English census records were compiled not by householders but by enumerators. They were based on information supplied by householders and these original schedules were transcribed into the enumerators' books. While the process of transcription created the potential for errors to occur, the original schedules were more problematic. Many householders were illiterate and recorded ages and birthplaces were sometimes inaccurate. The extent of inaccuracy has been measured in certain locations. Audrey Perkyns' study of age-recording in six Kent parishes concluded that ages were mainly accurately recorded even by the elderly,[5] while a

---

1   D. Mills and K. Schurer, *Local communities in the Victorian census enumerators books* (Oxford, 1996), p. 3.

2   M. Brayshay, 'Depopulation and changing household structure in the mining communities of west Cornwall, 1851–1871', in D. Mills and K. Schurer (eds), *Local communities in the Victorian census enumerators books* (Oxford, 1996), pp. 326–45.

3   Agriculture employment represented 23.7 per cent of male and female employment in 1851 in England and Wales, whereas mining represented 3.6 per cent: L. Shaw Taylor and E.A. Wrigley, 'Occupational structure and population change', in R. Floud, J. Humphries and P. Johnson (eds), *The Cambridge economic history of modern Britain vol. 1 1700–1870* (Cambridge, 2014), p. 71.

4   R. Perren, *Agriculture in depression 1870–1940* (Cambridge, 1995), pp. 7ff; S.A. Royle, 'The development of small towns in Britain', in M. Daunton (ed.), *The Cambridge urban history of Britain, vol. III* (Cambridge, 2000), pp. 151ff.

5   A. Perkyns, 'Age checkability and accuracy', in D. Mills and K. Schurer (eds), *Local communities in the Victorian census enumerators books* (Oxford, 1996), p. 134.

study of Preston found that 14 per cent of 475 people in two successive censuses (1851 and 1861) gave discrepant birthplaces for the same individuals.[6]

Although supplying false information was a criminal offence, many people did not know their precise age or place of birth and sometimes just guessed. One problem was age-rounding – the tendency of people to report their age as a round figure such as fifty instead of their precise age of, say, fifty-one or fifty-two. There was also a prevalence of rounding downwards rather than upwards. While the 1841 census did not require precise ages for people 'aged 15 and upwards', in 1851 household schedules required 'age last birthday' to be recorded. Despite the change in the instructions, rounding of ages continued in practice in 1851 and subsequent censuses and was still visibly present in census data collected towards the end of the century. Analysis of national census data showed pronounced age spikes particularly at decadal age points thirty, forty, fifty and so on. The extent to which age spikes are present in a data set can be measured by the Whipple Index.[7] Any index number in excess of 100 shows that rounding is present. The higher the index number above 100, the greater the incidence of age rounding. An index above 125, found in many parts of East Anglia, is considered a poor level of accuracy. The Whipple Index for Godmanchester was calculated to be 115 in 1851 (an acceptable result) and 98 in 1891 (very accurate). The data reveals that rounding of ages had therefore disappeared in Godmanchester by 1891.

The census was not a continuous record but a snapshot of the population on one day. The 1851 census was chosen as the earlier benchmark for this study because it was the first that aimed to record precise ages and birthplaces.[8] The census recorded those present in each dwelling on census night. Those absent from their homes were not recorded, but visitors were. For example, on census night 1851, twenty visitors to the town were recorded in Godmanchester. There were twenty-five visitors in 1891. Lodgers and visitors were rather problematic categories and Armstrong suggested that the term 'visitor' might sometimes be a more genteel term for a lodger or a paying guest.[9] Lodgers decreased sharply between the two census dates, from 104 in 1851 (4.4 per cent) to 48 (2.3 per cent) in 1891. There were definitional problems about

---

6   E. Higgs, *Making sense of the census revisited* (London, 2005), p. 89.

7   The Whipple Index is calculated as follows:
     A) Count the number of individuals with ages recorded as either 25, 30, 35, 40, 45, 50, 55, 60;
     B) Multiply this total by 5;
     C) Count the number of individuals (inclusive) from 23 to 62;
     D) Divide the total of A by the total of C and multiply the answer by 100.
     D. Mills and K. Schurer, 'Population and demography', in D. Mills and K. Schurer (eds), *Local communities in the Victorian census enumerators books* (Oxford, 1996), p. 76.

8   The 1841 census required the age only to the nearest five years for those 'aged 15 and upwards' and no precise place of birth. The 1851 census also introduced the relationship of recorded individuals to the head of the household.

9   A. Armstrong, *Stability and change in an English country town: a social study of York* (Cambridge, 1972), p. 184.

what constituted a household that impacted upon the use of the term 'lodger'.[10] Further research is required to determine how the fall in the number of lodgers should be interpreted. Problems also arose in recording occupational data. At best, census records recorded only main occupations and did not reflect seasonal or part-time work or much of the work carried out by women and children.

Despite the problems, there is much that is positive about the census as a source. It sought to record everyone, which many other historical records do not. What does the census data tell us about Godmanchester? First of all, it enables us to calculate the population: 2,337 in 1851 but only 2,095 in 1891. The fall in population may come as a surprise to some, as the population was rising by more than 10 per cent per decade in England and Wales throughout the second half of the nineteenth century.[11] Indeed, Godmanchester's population was only slightly higher in 1951 (2,499) than in 1851.[12] If Godmanchester had followed national trends it would have increased its population by 153 per cent between 1851 and 1951 to over 6,300.[13]

To put that in a still wider perspective, Godmanchester's population at the end of the nineteenth century was not greatly different from what it was at the end of the thirteenth century. In the fourteenth century the population of England roughly halved as a result of the Black Death, successive plagues and harvest failure.[14] It took nearly 500 years for the population to recover to its former level at the end of the thirteenth century. In Godmanchester the population was around 2,000 in 1279 – little different from the 1891 figure.[15] F.W. Bird provided anecdotal evidence for Godmanchester's falling population in the second half of the nineteenth century:

> The young men go to various situations or enter the army;
> The girls go out as household servants.[16]

Examination of Godmanchester's Anglican parish registers strongly suggests that migration led to the falling population. There was a large excess of baptisms over burials, which, without migration, should have resulted in a rising population (Table 15.1). The second half of the nineteenth century was a period of demographic transition. It was a widespread phenomenon involving a change from high birth rates and high infant death rates to lower birth and infant death rates as societies industrialised. This can be seen in Godmanchester, where, over a thirty-five-year period, age at death increased dramatically and those who died at age five or less fell from 42 per cent to 15 per cent of deaths. Conversely, two-thirds of deaths were

---

10   Higgs, *Making sense of the census*, p. 74.

11   E. Wrigley and R. Schofield, *The population history of England 1541–1871* (Cambridge, 1989); R. Woods, *The demography of Victorian England and Wales* (Cambridge, 2000).

12   M. Green, *Godmanchester* (Cambridge, 1977), p. 42.

13   TNA, *Census returns of England and Wales, 1851*, <http://www.visionofbritain.org.uk/unit/10061325/cube/TOT_POP>, accessed 19 November 2019.

14   K. and P. Sneath, *Godmanchester: a celebration of 800 years* (Cambridge, 2011), pp. 46–7.

15   *Ibid.*, pp. 45ff.

16   F.W. Bird, *Memorials of Godmanchester; reminiscences of F W Bird* (Peterborough, 1911).

Table 15.1
Parish register data in Godmanchester.

| | 1851–6 | | 1886–91 | |
	Total	Mean	Total	Mean
Baptisms	348	58	295	49
Marriages	80	13	74	12
Burials	230	38	144	24

Table 15.2
Age at death in Godmanchester.

| | 1853 | | 1888 | | Total | |
Years	No.	%	No.	%	No.	%
5 or less	15	42	3	15	18	32
6–64	15	42	4	20	19	34
65+	6	16	13	65	19	34
Totals	36	100	20	100	56	100

Table 15.3
Household size in Godmanchester.

Community	Mean household size 1851
Padstow parish	4.37
Godmanchester	4.40
Mitford (arable)	4.75
York	4.80
Atcham (pastoral)	4.90
Ladywood (manufacturing)	5.21
Camborne	5.30
Preston	5.40
Rural Lancashire	5.50
St Just	5.50
Edgbaston (high proportion of business and professional)	7.92
Rural England	4.70

aged sixty-five or over by 1888 (Table 15.2). Outward migration was no doubt caused by the push of agricultural depression and the pull of more attractive employment possibilities elsewhere. Nationally the number of full-time farmworkers fell from 891,000 in 1871 to 688,000 in 1911.[17] Rising demand for food was met from a rapid growth in imports, imported wheat doubling between 1872 and 1892.[18]

Household size provides information about housing density of occupation and its link to mortality levels. It also reflects the demographic transition and reduction in family size that occurred over the later nineteenth century and into the twentieth century. Garrett *et al.* concluded that this transition was highly complex and more gradual and developmental than is often believed.[19] Census data will play a major part in uncovering the nature of this demographic transition, but published data is still very limited. In 1851 the mean household size in Godmanchester was 4.4 people, including children (Table 15.3) – relatively low compared with limited published data for other communities.[20] However, the decline in household size in Godmanchester over the last 150 years is striking. By 1891 it had fallen to 4.0, but by the 2011 census household size in the town was 2.3 and it is still falling. Further research to pinpoint the evolutionary or revolutionary nature of the change is required as data becomes available. There has been only a tiny change in the balance between the sexes. In both 1851 and 1891 there were fifty-two females to forty-eight males in Godmanchester's population, whereas today the relationship is fifty-one females to forty-nine males. This ratio increases with age as a result of the longer life expectancy of females. For those aged over sixty-five, the sex ratio was fifty-five females to forty-five males in both 1891 and 1851.

The age structure of the population has changed dramatically (Table 15.4).[21] The population is much older, now as life expectancy has increased. The average age of a person living in Godmanchester today is thirty-nine (both mean and median), whereas in 1891 it was only twenty-nine (mean) and just twenty-four (median) and in 1851 twenty-six (mean) and twenty-one (median). We have a higher proportion of people over sixty-five (15 per cent in 2011, compared with 8 per cent in 1891 and 5 per cent in 1851). There are always exceptions to the rule, and the oldest residents in the town in 1851 were a pauper shepherd named Fisher, who was 97, and Barley, a carpenter, who was 95. The oldest in 1891 was a farm labourer in Cambridge Street by the name of Riseley. He was 88 and living with his wife, who was 84.

What about the living arrangements of older people? Did they live with their children in extended families, or in separate households? Analysis of the 1891 returns show that the majority continued to live in separate households. Only just over a quarter (26 per cent) of those aged sixty-five and over lived with their sons or daughters.

---

17   Perren, *Agriculture in depression*, p. 22.

18   *Ibid.*, p. 8.

19   E. Garrett, A. Reid, K. Schurer and S. Szreter, *Changing family size in England and Wales 1891–1911* (Cambridge, 2001), p. 437.

20   D. Mills and K. Schurer, *Local communities in the Victorian census enumerators books* (Oxford, 1996), pp. 311, 333.

21   <https://www.statista.com/statistics/281174/uk-population-by-age/>, accessed 16 July 2019.

Table 15.4
Age structure in Godmanchester.

Age group	Godmanchester 1851 (%)	Godmanchester 1891 (%)	Godmanchester 2011 (%)	UK 2016 (%)
0–14	38	33	18	17
15–24	17	18	12	12
25–54	32	33	55	41
55–64	8	8		12
65+	5	8	15	18

There was a small difference by sex, with males over sixty-five (28 per cent) more likely to live with offspring than females (24 per cent). One cannot assume that older people living with a son or daughter always meant that the offspring were caring for elderly parents. Mr Allen, a gardener living in West Street, was sixty-six but had two sons aged eight years and three years living with him and his much younger wife of forty-six. Another gardener in West Street, Mr Brickstock, was seventy-one years old and his wife sixty-six and they shared a house with their thirty-year-old daughter, who was recorded as an 'imbecile'. Census returns recorded the disabilities of residents using what are now regarded as politically incorrect terms. There were several other examples in Godmanchester of such disabilities, including a forty-year-old man recorded as an 'imbecile from birth'.

The census returns recorded where people were born. We discover that, in 1851, no less than 83 per cent of Godmanchester's population were born in Huntingdonshire and a further 7 per cent were born in the neighbouring counties of Cambridgeshire, Essex, Northamptonshire and Bedfordshire. Nearly two-thirds (64 per cent) were born in Godmanchester itself. Just five people were born overseas, the furthest coming from the West Indies. By 1891 the movement of population within the country was starting to accelerate. Those born in the county had fallen to three-quarters of people resident in Godmanchester on census night and 54 per cent were born in Godmanchester. The remainder came from various parts of the country, including Wales and Scotland. Immigration was still negligible, for only six people were born overseas, including in India, the Bahamas and the USA. The contrast with today is stark, when one in eight (12.5 per cent) of the UK population was born abroad.[22]

Birthplace data also opens a window on where marriage partners were born. Most wives resident in the town were born not far away. Although only 38 per cent (1851; 30 per cent in 1891) of wives were born in Godmanchester itself, the majority (75 per cent in 1851; 65 per cent in 1891) came from within Huntingdonshire. The Anglican

22   Population of the UK by country of birth and nationality: 2015 ONS <https://www.ons.gov.uk/peoplepopulationandcommunity/populationandmigration/internationalmigration/bulletins/ukpopulationbycountryofbirthandnationality/2018>, accessed 16 July 2019.

Marriage Register also reveals where spouses were born. Brides were almost always married in their home parish. In the five-year period 1851–5 there were sixty-five recorded marriages in the parish church (St Mary's). All brides were 'of this parish', as were fifty grooms (77 per cent). The remaining grooms either came from other parts of the county (8 per cent) or from other parts of the country, including two from Yorkshire. In the five-year period 1891–5, 65 per cent of grooms came from Godmanchester. The results suggest a trend for marriage partners to be found from further afield as the century progressed. A brief review of the marriage register for the 1990s revealed that, a century later, only just over a quarter of grooms came from the town and not all the brides did either.

Further research can be carried out to compare census records of birthplace with Anglican parish registers. This would give an indication of accuracy of birthplace and age information. As the majority of Godmanchester's population was born in the town, the task is limited to the one parish register. However, not all children were baptised in the parish church and by 1851 nonconformity (mainly strict and particular Baptist and thus strongly opposed to infant baptism) had reached very high levels in the town.[23]

Recent research has suggested that the greater the age difference from the husband, the lower the wife's life expectancy.[24] The 1891 census recorded that in Godmanchester around 29 per cent of wives had younger husbands, 56 per cent had older husbands and 15 per cent were exactly the same age as their husband. There were some substantial age differences in marital relationships. Mr Wright, a carpenter in Duck End, was married to a woman 15 years older than himself and Mr Pettit, a bricklayer who lived in St Anne's Lane, was married to a woman 13 years older than himself.

On the other hand, General Baumgartner of Island Hall was twenty-one years older than his wife, who was born in Ireland, the furthest distance from Godmanchester of any of the wives' birthplaces. Mr Suter from West Street was eighteen years older than his wife. In 11 per cent of marriages the age difference was ten years or more, but the average (median) age difference between marriage partners was three years.

Surnames of residents included many names still represented in Godmanchester today. In 1851 the most common surnames were Mason (fifty-four cases), Chandler (forty-eight), Wright (forty-two), Maile (forty-one), Dighton (forty), James (thirty-seven) and Flint (thirty-three). One in eight of Godmanchester's population had one of these seven surnames. In 1891 the most common seven accounted for only a slightly lower percentage (11.5 per cent) of the town's population. The rank order had changed and now the commonest surname by far was Dighton (fifty-one), followed by James (thirty-seven), Clifton (thirty-four), Green (thirty-three), Wright (thirty), Reeve (thirty) and Foster (twenty-eight). There were now only seventeen Masons and fourteen Chandlers, the most common in 1851.

---

23 D.M. Thompson (ed.), *Religious life in mid-19th century Cambridgeshire and Huntingdonshire: The returns for the 1851 census of religious worship* (Cambridge, 2014), pp. 104–5.

24 'Downside of marriage for women: The greater a wife's age gap from her husband, the lower her life expectancy', *Science Daily*, 12 May 2010, <https://www.sciencedaily.com/releases/2010/05/100512062631.htm>, accessed 16 July 2019.

One way of tracking the intercensal movements of families is to analyse where their children were born. For example, an innkeeper in Post Street (Page) was born in Stevenage, but his wife hailed from Ashcott in Somerset. Their first child, a daughter (aged five in 1891), was born in Ashcott, where they must have set up home after their marriage. But when their second child was born two years later they were living in Great Barford, Bedfordshire. A year later they had arrived in Godmanchester and two further sons were quickly added to the family.

In terms of male employment it would appear that census returns were reasonably robust, although in practice many men were not confined to one employment. More than 95 per cent of males in Godmanchester aged sixteen to seventy in both 1851 and 1891 had recorded occupations. The most common occupations of males in this age group related to agriculture (37 per cent in 1851 but falling to under 30 per cent of recorded male occupations by 1891). The next most frequently recorded occupations were in manufacturing (23 per cent in 1851 and 16 per cent in 1891) and the building trades (11 per cent in 1851 and 14 per cent in 1891). By 1891 several occupations related to the railway, including porters, platelayers, signalmen, engine drivers, guards and the station master. The birthplaces of these railway workers showed that most had migrated to Godmanchester for their employment. Many of those aged over seventy recorded in the census were designated as having retired or living on their own means.

Investigating the category of males aged ten to fifteen reveals something about when male children began employment. The official school leaving age in 1891 was thirteen and nearly all ten- to twelve-year-olds in Godmanchester that were categorised were recorded as scholars. However, there was a ten-year-old grocer's assistant, an eleven-year-old errand boy and a newspaper-seller and a milk boy both aged twelve years. In 1851 there were still younger children with recorded occupations: a chimney sweep aged eight, a labourer aged seven and – surely an error – a butcher aged four! At age thirteen, about half were still scholars and half in low-level employment such as domestic service, errand-running and agricultural labour. In reality, it is likely that many children would have run errands and helped in shops or family businesses and the census returns provide only brief glimpses of this practice. Further information can be gleaned from the Queen Elizabeth School log book. The entry for 26 June 1882 recorded: 'miserable attendance – great number of boys away haymaking, many unqualified to go to work' and, on 29 April 1884: 'a few boys are away to gather cowslips'.

It was very rare for wives to have a recorded occupation (only 4 per cent). This failure to record the work of women was a common feature of census returns. The domestic work of women in the family home was rightly excluded, but the work of 'women who are regularly employed in any but domestic duties' should have been noted. In fact, women often worked for pay on a casual or part-time basis.[25] The family that comprised just a male breadwinner with dependent wife and children was not as common as in the popular imagination. Females aged sixteen to seventy not categorised as wives with recorded occupations were mainly employed as domestic servants, dressmakers and laundresses. The youngest recorded female with employment was a twelve-year-old dressmaker.

---

25   Higgs, *Making sense of the census*, p. 101.

Table 15.5
Age and sex of servants in Godmanchester.

	1851	*1891*
Age <35 years	93%	91%
Mean age	22	23
Median age	19	21
Sex: female	93%	94%

Domestic servants were largely young and female (Table 15.5).[26] There was virtually no change in the number, age and sex of servants during the second half of the nineteenth century. Most domestic servants (73 per cent in 1851, 67 per cent in 1891) were born in Huntingdonshire; the rest mainly came from Cambridgeshire or Suffolk. Those born in Godmanchester increased from 25 per cent of the total in 1851 to 45 per cent in 1891.

Godmanchester had a small elite group of just seven households in the highest social class I of public and professional people in 1891.[27] With the exception of the two independent ministers, Strict Baptist and Salvation Army Captain, who had no servants, the remaining five households had at least three domestic servants and in two cases four. A fifth of all the servants in the town were employed in just these five households.

The census document does not give precise addresses, only streets, but some buildings, such as pubs, farms and the vicarage, were identified. Using the census record in conjunction with a contemporary street map of Godmanchester (1886), it is possible to track most houses that were standing in 1891 and identify their occupants. The census of the town starts with the vicarage, where the vicar, Rev. Chamberlain, was resident in 1891. On census night a niece from the USA was staying in the vicarage. The vicar had a cook and two female maids in the household. The census progresses northwards along Post Street until it comes to the photographer Hendry's household, which comprised Hendry, his wife, his six children and a domestic servant. Along the Causeway it is possible to track the businesses operating in 1891. They included Matson the butcher, Okins the fishmonger and Beck, a watch jobber and jeweller.

This glimpse of census record data in the second half of the nineteenth century reveals how much Godmanchester changed. Contrary to national trends, the population of the town fell sharply as a result of outward migration, triggered by the push of agricultural depression and the pull of more attractive employment possibilities elsewhere. This paper shows how demographic changes that began in the later nineteenth century and continued into the twentieth played out in one community. In Godmanchester, the percentage of the population employed in

---

26 Farm servants are excluded.

27 E.A. Wrigley, *Nineteenth-century society: essays in the use of quantitative methods for the study of social data* (Cambridge, 1972), pp. 215ff.

agriculture was falling and the expansion of the tertiary economic sector was beginning. The movement of population was increasing, and this impacted on the choice of marriage partners. This paper adds to the limited published evidence of the demographic transition, the reduction in family size of households and the increasing lifespan of the local population. Census records are not only a mine of information for historians reconstructing the social and economic histories of their communities but also invaluable for those seeking to trace their family tree or the history of their house.

Chapter 16

Canon Arthur Pertwee's
Brightlingsea, 1872–1912

Sean O'Dell

Introduction[1]

Over the last few decades British academic history has seen a growth in the number of studies that have sought to explore and analyse the lives and experience of 'ordinary' people within wider historical contexts. As a former student of David Dymond, a key figure in such developments, the author continues to be inspired by the commitment in his work to 'reconstruct human lives as completely as possible' and to draw meaning from the 'fascinating particulars' that are to be found when one begins to research in a local historical context.[2] There is so much to be gained from this approach, not least in that we may further understand the experience of a much broader spectrum of the population in all its fascinating diversity. In this spirit, the following contribution focuses upon the vicar and people of a small Essex port during the late nineteenth and early twentieth centuries.

The relationship between vicar and parish is often recorded to have been routine, dutiful and mindful of pastoral care. Occasionally it has been somewhat more than this. The Reverend Canon Arthur Pertwee, vicar of the parish of Brightlingsea, Essex, from 1872 to 1912, was, like so many in his care, one of the 'great submerged majority of humbler "ordinary" people who generally turn out to have had "extraordinary" lives'.[3] During his incumbency Arthur Pertwee made an extraordinary contribution to his parish in a number of ways. In his ministry he regularly went beyond what would be reasonably expected of him, not least by becoming highly active and involved in the working lives of his parishioners, the majority of whom worked at sea. He did this knowing that he was in a place where such working lives were extremely difficult, often very dangerous and, as a result, had a high casualty rate. Pertwee's most tangible legacy is a frieze of commemorative tiles inside the parish church: a poignant and lasting physical monument to those of his parish who lost their lives at sea (Plates 16.1 and 16.2). Beyond this, he was instrumental in elevating the status of the civic

1   I would like to express my gratitude to the following for invaluable help with this paper and my wider researches at Brightlingsea: Dr David Dymond, Dr Evelyn Lord, Mrs Nicola O'Dell, Ms Janet Russell, Mrs Margaret Stone, Mr Peter Allen, Mr Alan Williams and Dr Chris Thornton.
2   D. Dymond, *Researching and writing history: a practical guide for historians* (Salisbury, 1999), p. 11.
3   D. Dymond (ed.), *Parson and people in a Suffolk village: Richard Cobbold's Wortham, 1824–77* (Wortham, 2007), p. 1.

community in the wider locality, reflecting its development as a busy and increasingly populous maritime port.

Brightlingsea

Brightlingsea is a small north Essex port situated in the estuary of the river Colne. It was mentioned in *Domesday* as 'Brictriceseia' and described as a manor of ten hides held by King Harold.[4] The town's location in the large, sheltered estuary is well suited to fishing and the cultivation of oysters. The maritime activities and trade of the small village that was later to become a town are detailed in a manuscript that describes ships that were provided for defence against the Spanish Armada.[5]

During the early nineteenth century, before the arrival of Pertwee, the port was still limited in size and population: just 807 persons were recorded as residing there in 1801.[6] The growth of the port was substantial over coming decades: by the early 1870s it is described as a parish of 3,560 acres on the estuary of the river Colne (eight miles south-east of Colchester) with a population of 2,585 and a large trade in the fishing of sprats and oysters.[7] By the middle of the century Brightlingsea was sending a large fleet of oyster-fishing smacks each year in February and March to Jersey and the south-west channel. Around 300 inhabitants of the port were licensed to dredge for oysters in the river Colne estuary and nearby creeks by the Corporation of Colchester, an activity that occupied some 160 inshore smacks and their crews.[8] By the second half of the nineteenth century the port was thriving as a result of the oyster trade, fuelled by demand for fresh oysters in London. The Board of Trade recorded in 1867 that Brightlingsea's sea-going oyster fleet was by now the largest on the north Essex coast, comprising some seventy-four vessels totalling 819 tons and crewed by 212 men and boys.[9] The small waterside craft community was rapidly transforming into an industrialised urban port.

Canon Arthur Pertwee

Arthur Pertwee arrived in Brightlingsea in 1872. The previous incumbent, the Reverend William Latten, had died in service.[10] Canon Arthur Pertwee, as he was formally known, gained his MA from Pembroke College, Oxford, in 1863 and subsequently served as a curate at Brancepeth, County Durham, until 1864. From there he moved to a parish

---

4   E. Dickin, *The history of Brightlingsea* (Brightlingsea, 1939), pp. 3, 10.

5   *Essex and the sea*, ERO Publications 30 (Chelmsford, 1970), Fig. 22.

6   1851 Census of Great Britain, Population Tables 2, Table [1], 'Population Abstract'.

7   J. Wilson, *The imperial gazetteer of England and Wales* (Edinburgh, 1874), pp. 1, 270.

8   *White's Directory of Essex* (1848), pp. 450–1. It is uncertain if the 160 smacks were all from Brightlingsea. Most of the town's mariners worked the common grounds near the harbour or went offshore; see H. Benham, *Essex gold* (Chelmsford, 1993), pp. 84–5.

9   Mr Pennel's report, in *House of Commons accounts and papers*, LXIV (Shipping) session (1867).

10   ERO, D/P 312/2/1: Certificates of ordination (1861–72).

in Leicester as vicar; this was his ministry before his move to Brightlingsea.[11] He came to the port at a time when the maritime trades were approaching their most active, demanding and treacherous years. Local GP Dr Dickin, in his history of the town (published in 1939), claimed that Pertwee quickly developed a strong relationship with the seafaring families of the parish. This relationship developed to such an extent that he would go to sea with the oyster crews to experience for himself the hardships they endured. Similarly, Dickin records that he often showed great courage in a practical sense: for example, he is noted as administering directly to the crew of a ship which lay off Brightlingsea who were suffering with an outbreak of smallpox. It is also recorded (and, indeed, spoken of in the community today) that during stormy weather Pertwee would climb the 100-foot tower of All Saints' church in the hours of darkness with a lantern to show and maintain a guiding light to the smacks at sea making for home. The tower, a local navigational landmark, is said to be visible some seventeen miles out to sea. Pertwee's guiding light would have become clearer as the smacks neared the estuary.[12]

Pertwee was, therefore, clearly a man given to acting in a practical manner to bring support to his parishioners, but this also seems to have been in concert with a keen desire to maintain an informed theological agenda. He was influenced by the Oxford Movement and he made it a priority to introduce a more ornate ritual to services.[13] But his was not the only ministry in the parish. After the Evangelical Revival, around the turn of the nineteenth century, numbers of dissenting congregations in England had increased dramatically. The 1851 national census of religious attendance shows that the various nonconformist denominations accounted for nearly half the country's worshipping population.[14] Dissent in rural areas of Essex during the nineteenth century was not uncommon and Brightlingsea was no exception in gaining a diverse nonconformist community at this time. The Wesleyans arrived in 1796, meeting at private rooms until they built a small wooden chapel in 1804 that was extended in 1822.[15] During 1842 a larger chapel was planned.[16] The foundation stone of the new chapel was laid on 18 July 1843 and in 1861 plans were drawn up for a Wesleyan School.[17] The New Jerusalem Church (Swedenborgian) arrived in the parish with the ordination in 1813 of Mr Arthur Munson as the New Church minister for the town. A chapel was built in 1814 and a much larger one in 1867.[18] Examination of registers indicates that membership of the New Church was generally from the poorer maritime

---

11   *Crockford's Clerical Directory* (1888).

12   *BPM*, July 1884; Dickin, *Brightlingsea*, pp. 97–8; D. Fairhall, *East Anglian shores* (London, 1995), p. 57.

13   Dickin, *Brightlingsea*, pp. 97–8.

14   D. Hey (ed.), *The Oxford companion to local and family history* (Oxford, 1996), pp. 328–9.

15   ERO, D/NM 1/2, Chapel book (1822).

16   J. Baker, *Introduction of Wesleyan Methodism into Brightlingsea* (1844), ERO, Transcript 295; Accounts (1822–57), ERO, D/NM 1/1, Accounts (1822–57).

17   ERO, D/NM 1/2, Plans for Wesleyan school (1861), ERO, E/P 15/1, Plans for Wesleyan school.

18   A. Wakeling, *Brightlingsea Society of the New Church: A history 1813–1968* (Brightlingsea, 1968), pp. 8, 11–25.

families, including oyster dredgers and sail-makers.[19] Further nonconformist groups were set up around this time, including the Congregational Church[20] and the Primitive Methodists.[21] A Salvation Army headquarters was established at nearby Hurst Green before moving to a permanent building near the centre of the town around 1908.[22] So, during the early decades of the nineteenth century, Brightlingsea's Anglican Church community were aware of the possible diminishing of their membership as a result of other religious organisations. In 1836 a new chapel-of-ease, Saint James's, was consecrated in the very centre of the town. The grand brick-built chapel in the High Street relieved the need for a journey of a mile and a half out of town on Sunday mornings to the more remote medieval parish church and placed the Anglican Church visibly at the heart of the community.[23]

However, despite there being such a diverse religious identity in Brightlingsea, Pertwee took to the task of ministering to the whole of the parish, not just those who worshipped in his church; there is no recorded evidence of any tension or dispute between his ministry and any of the other congregations. Nonconformist congregations were largely comprised of families who were moving to the town and working in the maritime trades (as cross-referencing of census surnames and chapel records strongly indicates), yet he embraced them all without hesitation. This is evidenced in no small part by his regular contributions to the *Brightlingsea Parish Magazine*, which was introduced shortly after his arrival in the parish and probably under his influence. The magazine began to feature a regular section each month entitled 'Gossip from the Hard': the Hard was the waterfront area near where the fishing smacks lay at their moorings. After the first edition was published in 1882, Pertwee eagerly took to reporting the fortunes of the oyster and sprat boats and their crews and families in the 'Gossip from the Hard' column. He was only able to do this as a result of his close working relationship with the families and crews (regardless of their denomination) and his keen understanding of their trade, based on his experience and time spent on the boats. At this time the offshore oyster trade was approaching its busiest (and most hazardous) years. The town's large first-class oyster-fishing smacks were heading for the Terschelling Banks, off the Dutch coast, during the winter months in search of new deep-sea oyster grounds.

Brightlingsea was home to a thriving boat-building industry, which had helped develop 'first class' deep-sea oyster-dredging smacks. These were equipped to deal with heavy seas, long voyages and the transportation of live catches. But the Terschelling (or 'Skilling' as the area was known locally) Banks proved to be a very dangerous place to dredge for oysters; from its inception the *Brightlingsea Parish Magazine* would contain reports and commentaries from the pen of Arthur Pertwee concerning the terrible disasters that local oyster smacks had suffered on their voyages there. But despite the dangers of this trade, and to the distress of the vicar,

---

19   D. Steel, *Sources for nonconformist genealogy and family history* (Chichester, 1973), p. 787.

20   ERO, D/NC 30/1, Church book (1846–94), cross-referenced with census data.

21   Dickin, *Brightlingsea*, p. 101.

22   ERO, D/UBR PB21/15, Plan for Salvation Army hall (1908).

23   ERO, D/P 8/1/16, Consecration, chapel-of-ease (1836).

Brightlingsea crews persisted. In 1883 nineteen parishioners were lost in a storm at sea. Writing in a cautionary tone in January 1884, Pertwee listed the twelve crew of the smacks *Pride* and *Walter and Henry* (from Dover) who had perished at the oyster grounds during the previous month. He appealed to Brightlingsea crews, noting that over the previous year no fewer than five Brightlingsea smacks and their crews had been lost at sea, and that by now the sea had claimed twice as many men and boys as were lying in the 'old churchyard at home'. He went on to urge that, despite their admirable bravery, it was madness for the oyster crews to try to take on the 'unequal struggle' of fighting against the winter storms of the North Sea.[24] At a service in the parish church during 1891 Pertwee described to his congregation how in his eighteen years at the parish of Brightlingsea 101 lives had been lost at sea.[25]

The Brightlingsea tiles

Sometime after the losses of 1883 Pertwee commenced the installation of his monument to Brightlingsea mariners lost at sea. He began to install six-inch-square ceramic memorial tiles, some retrospectively, which came to form a dado on the walls of the nave and south aisle of All Saints' church (Plate 16.1). The first tile is dated 1872: the year Pertwee arrived at Brightlingsea. The tradition of installing tiles has continued from that date and they have now reached 211 in number, the most recent dated 1988. The majority of the casualties were from the fishing and oyster-dredging communities at first, but, as the tradition of installing tiles was continued through into the twentieth century, wartime casualties were also included. Each tile was hand painted, with distinctive gothic letters on a white background recording the name, age, date and place of loss (Plate 16.2). They were originally supplied by the church-decorating firm Cox, Sons, Buckley & Co. The tiles are unusual, of course, but not unique. A small number of churches in Staffordshire have similar installations, yet the design of the Brightlingsea tiles differs somewhat from the usual lozenge shape of such memorials.[26] It is possible that Pertwee was influenced by Ernest Geldart, architect and rector of Little Braxted, in the decision to install this remarkable memorial frieze in Brightlingsea parish church. Geldart, who preached at Brightlingsea on an occasional basis, is said to have used commemorative tiles in 1882.[27]

The last three decades of the nineteenth century were highly significant for Brightlingsea in another respect. Pertwee was among a small number of key individuals who moved into the parish, embraced the community and actively sought to promote its status and journey to full, formal urbanisation as a borough with its own town corporation. Another newcomer who made a significant contribution in this

---

24 'Gossip from the hard', *BPM* (January 1884).

25 Benham, *Essex gold*, p. 92.

26 L. Pearson, 'Memorial and commemorative tiles in nineteenth and early twentieth century churches', *TACS Journal*, 9 (2003), pp. 13–23.

27 A. Wakeling and P. Moon, *Tiles of tragedy: Brightlingsea's unique maritime memorial*, 2nd edn (Stockton-on-Tees, 2003), passim; <https://tilesoc.org.uk/tile-gazetteer/essex.html>, accessed 19 November 2019.

regard at that time was John Bateman. A wealthy member of the gentry, in 1871 he purchased property at Moverons in Brightlingsea parish and the nearby Rectory Hall and Lodge Farm. He is recorded as a former deputy lieutenant for Staffordshire and justice of the peace for Essex. He went on to represent Brightlingsea division on Essex County Council and to serve as a member of Brightlingsea Urban District Council and the Kent and Essex Fisheries Committee.[28]

In 1885, as part of the drive towards enhanced civic status, Pertwee and Bateman were instrumental in re-establishing a historic link between Brightlingsea and the port of Sandwich in Kent by unilaterally declaring Brightlingsea a non-corporate member of the Cinque Ports. This term originated from the Norman-French term for the number five: during the eleventh century Edward the Confessor contracted five of the most strategic ports on the south coast to build ships and provide men for his service. After the Norman Conquest this became a means to keep the two halves of the expanded realm together. However, after the loss of Normandy in 1205 the ships became a vital part of England's defence. Brightlingsea had earlier become a 'Limb' of the head port of Sandwich by contributing to the town's ship-building requirements. The Essex port was also seen as a useful half-way stop on the voyage to the annual herring fair at Yarmouth (see chapter 12). The Cinque Ports were presided over by the Lord Warden, based at Dover, Kent. Brightlingsea conveniently extended his powers north of Sussex and Kent over the full width of the Thames estuary and had the additional benefit of providing oysters. The Lord Warden had his own oyster layings in Brightlingsea Creek until around the 1670s. Nowadays the Cinque Ports have only a ceremonial role; however, a base for the Lord Warden of the Ports is still maintained at Walmer Castle. All new Lords Warden are installed at Dover. Brightlingsea is still the only Essex 'Limb': all other members of the confederation, together with their Limbs, are situated in Kent and Sussex.[29]

In recognition of this ancient link, a 'Deputy of the Cinque Port Liberty of Brightlingsea' was now to be elected by the freemen of the town. John Bateman gifted the town chain of office, mounted with an opal jewel, the mount of the opal carrying the inscriptions *Urbs Brictriceseiae ex dono Johannis Bateman* 'The Town of Brightlingsea by the gift of John Bateman' and *Pulchra Matre Filia Pulchrior* 'From a Beautiful Mother, a More Beautiful Daughter'. The silver chain was made from alternating links of crossed sprats and oyster shells – an acknowledgement of the industry that allowed the town to flourish.[30] On election to office, each successive deputy would be presented with the 'Great Opal' and silver chain of office, to be worn until such time as they became mayor of the town.[31] The 'Great Opal' chain is still worn by the deputy.

The work of Pertwee, Bateman and the Brightlingsea townspeople was enhanced somewhat by further administrative changes after the Local Government Act of 1888. The town, now with its own parish council, became part of the Tendring Rural District

---

28   Dickin, *Brightlingsea*, p. 53.
29   <http://www.cinqueportliberty.co.uk/brightlingsea.htm>, accessed 19 November 2019.
30   C. Dove, *The liberty of Brightlingsea* (Brightlingsea, 1974), passim; Dickin, *Brightlingsea*, p. 117.
31   ERO, D/DCm/Z1A, Deed of gift, chain of office (1892).

in 1894. But the continued drive for a more representative urban status in local affairs, coupled with the revived Cinque Port Liberty, led two years later to the creation of the Brightlingsea Urban District.[32] The population of the town had grown considerably, yet that of the surrounding largely agricultural district had shrunk or remained static. Pertwee and Bateman's ultimate aim was, of course, for Brightlingsea to become a borough.[33]

Conclusion

In the latter years of the nineteenth century the oyster-fishing and dredging industry went into decline and demand for oysters seemed to be waning, despite government moves to protect the oyster grounds.[34] Overfishing and -dredging were seen to be part of the problem, as was the lack of a formal 'closed season'.[35] Bad weather during the winter of 1894–5 disrupted dredging offshore and was followed by a dramatic fall in the price of the catch. To make matters worse, the consumption of oysters had been linked to recent outbreaks of typhoid fever.[36] And so the demand for oysters slumped and Brightlingsea mariners were forced to move to stow-boating for sprats and dredging scallops during the winter months and crewing for the large pleasure and racing yachts that began to use the port on an annual basis during the summer.[37] The mariners and seafarers of the town and those whose trades supported them had lost a substantial and lucrative trade, and in the decade preceding the outbreak of the First World War the economy of Brightlingsea was no longer growing. Any aspirations of becoming a borough had faded completely by the time the Reverend Canon Arthur Pertwee left office in 1912. His legacy as one of Essex's most active and committed clergymen, however, remains visible and tangible in a remarkable frieze of memorial tiles at Brightlingsea All Saints' Church, the port's Cinque Port association and the recorded history of the area.

---

32 F. Youngs, *Guide to the local administrative units of England*, 1 Southern England (London, 1979), p. 132.

33 Dove, *Liberty*, passim.

34 Parliamentary Papers online: 1808 (296) Bill for more effectual protection of oyster fisheries; 1823 (461) Bill for protecting and regulating public oyster fisheries in England and Wales; 1876 (65) Bill for better protection of oyster fisheries.

35 J. Hore and E. Jex, *The deterioration of the oyster and trawl fisheries of England: its cause and remedy* (London, 1880), p. 50.

36 *BPM* (January 1895), see also R. Neild, *The English, the French and the oyster* (London, 1995), p. 105.

37 *BPM* (January–May 1900).

Chapter 17

The concept of place in local history and regional literature: the fictional England of Bernard Samuel Gilbert[1]

Andrew J.H. Jackson

Introduction

David Dymond evolved his conceptualisation of place through versions of his guide to researching and writing local history published between 1981 and 2009.[2] This chapter will discuss his suggestions on place, alongside other key themes. Dymond's thinking was systematic and dynamic, and can be applied to localities and regions existing in historical fact in particular periods in the past, as well as those located in fictional constructions. The discussion will take for consideration and contextualisation the investigation of a literary district, 'Bly'. Bly was constructed through the creative writings of Lincolnshire-born Bernard Samuel Gilbert, but can be recognised as corresponding with East Midlands and East Anglian landscapes and communities more broadly, as well as life in rural England in the years up to and through the First World War.

Dymond on place

Dymond's guide can be located within a broader body of work on practice in local and regional history.[3] The work passed through a number of editions and reprints. His *Writing local history* of 1981 set out to extend what was on offer by way of guides, and it was little

---

1 This chapter draws on papers presented at conferences of the Lincoln Record Society, the Social History Society and The National Archives, Kew, in April, June and October 2018, respectively; and public lectures for the Lincoln branches of the Geographical and Historical Associations in 2017 and 2018. The author is grateful for the comments and encouragement of audiences at these events, and in other conversations in Lincolnshire and elsewhere.

2 D. Dymond, *Writing local history: a practical guide* (Chichester, 1981); *Researching and writing history: a practical guide for local historians* (Salisbury, 1999); *Researching and writing history: a guide for local historians* (Lancaster, 2009), pp. 1–9.

3 See, for example: Andrew J.H. Jackson, 'Local history and local history education in the early twenty-first century: organisational and intellectual challenges', *The Local Historian*, 38/4 (2008), pp. 266–73; Andrew J.H. Jackson, 'Problematising and practising "community-focussed" local history: on the Ermine, a council estate in Lincoln in the 1950s and 1960s', *International Journal of Regional and Local Studies*, 6/2 (2010), pp. 48–71.

changed when it took the form of a second edition in 1988. The guide was subjected to greater reworking in preparation for its appearance as *Researching and writing local history* in 1999. A subsequent edition, a decade later, saw less rewriting. This chapter considers the 1981, 1999 and 2009 editions. The original 1981 publication would provide advice on achieving 'a personal reconstruction of the past'. Dymond produced his publication in the context of a changing field of practice. Local historical research was being shaped by the engagement with, and influence of, a broad range of disciplines other than history, such as geography and sociology, and the presence and impact of community-led and 'bottom-up' popular participation. At the same time, he expressed concerns that the ways in which local history was developing had left it 'seriously fractured and divided'.[4] Against this background Dymond prescribed a tripartite conceptual framework for exploring local and regional pasts: time, place and theme.

Place for Dymond, when writing in 1988, was expressed most evidently in terms of spatial scales. Individual places, groups of places, districts and regions lent themselves to exploration, with the study of single places clearly being an attractive and practical proposition for many local historians, typically resident therein. Essential, though, was the achievement of 'a clear sense of place', and that the historical writing conveys to the reader the reassurance that the author had actually 'visited the place'. Moreover, giving centrality to the concept of place in a study acts to check overly specialist and singular thematic treatment, which might detract from giving readers 'a coherent impression of the landscape or townscape which contained his [the local historian's] human story'.[5]

Dymond returned to place in his *Practical guide* of 1999. Its conceptualisation had evolved further. He gave place a more extended consideration. Local history, ten years on, continued to reflect major divides. Dymond gave emphasis to the splits between local and family historians and between the academic and amateur. The latter divide was mirrored in turn in the preferences shown towards single-place study or wider district and regional focus and attention. This said, local history in general 'resists fragmentation and over-specialisation' and 'remains wide-ranging, inclusive, integrating and interdisciplinary'. Furthermore, it should be considered possible to strike a balance between attempting 'broader judgements and generalisations' about places while also appreciating and recognising 'particularism' wherever it is found.[6]

In 1999 Dymond positions the concept of place alongside that of space. This is especially significant, for by locating place in the more dynamic notion of 'space', historians can better comprehend notions of 'distance', 'the outside world' and 'mental maps and horizons' in the past and through time. This reconceptualisation of place within space is critical, and is further elaborated in explanations of how to approach localities in their wider worlds, and the groups of means through which a place makes and experiences internal and external connections: administrative and legal, geographical and economic and personal and cultural. Moreover, situating places within shared universes also mitigates against a pulling away from one another of urban and rural history, a further and growing divide.[7]

---

4   Dymond, *Writing local history*, pp. ix, 1.
5   *Ibid.*, pp. 5–7.
6   Dymond, *Researching and writing history: a practical guide*, pp. 5–11.
7   *Ibid.*, pp. 23–8.

Dymond's sub-chapter on place in his guide of 2009 adds little to what he had set out a decade earlier. Reconceptualisation of place, where it is evident, is more striking where it features in the opening chapter. Here, for local historians, place is not set in space. Instead it is located within the central concern of the local historian, and most simply put, the study of 'people *in* their place'. In this edition of his guide, physical and environmental determinism is acknowledged, but is less prominent. Dymond recognises the strength of developments in biographical and family and population history, with which local history overlaps, as well as its merging with various other historical sub-disciplines. He also acknowledges the preference of some for micro-history as a term for describing localised approaches, with its interest in human relations and relationships, place-related or less so. Moreover, postmodernism had posed an additional challenge, drawing attention to the individuality, subjectivity and provisionality of any study attempted on a place. In the face of this Dymond urged that the inevitability of some exercise of the historical imagination in reconstructing place ought to be paralleled by an ever more vigilant recourse to the 'hard' evidence and transparent analysis and articulation. This said, despite the ongoing and new challenges, Dymond's faith in the appeal and power of a democratised local history, and how through engagement with their home environments local historians can 'inform and influence the future' of places, remained undiminished.[8]

Through Dymond's three guides, he gives various examples of the writings of local historians, including how they approached and expressed place. The discussion that follows here, however, turns to the construction of place in regional fiction. Authors in this genre were concerned to varying degrees with capturing and preserving local historical knowledge and understanding, sharing this motivation with historian contemporaries. Moreover, these writers of fiction to differing extents shaped places in ways that are and have been mirrored in historical writing. Moreover, some historians recognise the value of fictional writings as primary sources. They act as repositories for factual information on urban and rural localities and regions, and the contemporary sentiments towards them. Among the more sophisticated constructions is that found in Bernard Samuel Gilbert's 'Bly'.

Place in fiction and non-fiction

The development of regional fiction was a prominent strand within English literature through the second half of the nineteenth century and into the early twentieth.[9] For the later end of this timeframe, this output contributed to the construction of a particular interpretation and impression of the Great War. The conflict represented a major cultural discontinuity, most evident in the life of the countryside and rural society. Regional fiction lends an essential hand in understanding the ways in which contemporary impressions were produced and instilled into the popular imagination, and in particular

---

8   Dymond, *Researching and writing history: a guide*, pp. 1–9.

9   A.J.H. Jackson, 'The early twentieth-century countryside of Bernard Samuel Gilbert: Lincolnshire poet, novelist, playwright, pamphleteer and correspondent, 1911–14', *Midland History*, 41/2 (2016), pp. 228–9.

the manner in which the countryside and rural life in the years following the war became perceived to be tangibly and intangibly different from that which existed pre-war.

There are many authors who have contributed to forming this picture of the pre-1914 world, and how it was disrupted, destroyed even, by the impact of the First World War, for individuals, families, communities, structures, relationships, cultures and practices. L.P. Hartley's conceptualisation of the past being a foreign country, in *The Go-Between*, has something of an iconic status.[10] To this can be added, for example, Flora Thompson's *Lark Rise*.[11] Henry Williamson, author of *Tarka the Otter*, was also anxious to capture the life that was fading away in a north Devon being opened up and stirred by the intrusion of the modern world.[12] These works have collectively formed our associations with, and perceptions of, pre-war and post-war England, and the manner of the transition between the two.

The rural fiction of the Victorian, Edwardian, wartime and inter-war countryside and country life had various features that united it. The positive attributes ascribed to rural places and areas were many, while rural community life lent itself to romantic, sentimental and idealised constructions. The senses of change, of the countryside being 'opened up', and of 'improvement' were all viewed ambiguously, as both welcome and hostile. Meanwhile, the physical environment, comprising the soil and the climate, combined with the human, notably the distribution of people, land, wealth and power, to determine the form and well-being of localities and communities. In the hands of the regional authors, fictional districts aligned with the observable in fact, whether, for example, in and around Thomas Hardy's Dorset, Flora Thompson's Oxfordshire, D.H. Lawrence's Nottinghamshire, Henry Williamson's north Devon 'Ham' or Bernard Gilbert's Bly.[13]

There can, of course, be added to this fictional genre other non-fictional literatures. One of the founding inspirations of landscape and local history, W.G. Hoskins, and one of the inspirers of oral history, George Ewart Evans, both gave emphasis to what seemed like a world that was being lost over the first half of the twentieth century.[14] Evans, in Suffolk, was particularly attentive to capturing disappearing customs, wisdom and dialect. This is evident in Lincolnshire as well, for example, in the work of the folklore historian Maureen Sutton, and in the volumes produced by the Boston publisher Richard Kay on the county's dialects, including within the poetical works of Bernard Samuel Gilbert.[15] Sociologists and others in the 'communities studies' tradition have also observed a sense of change and an air of decline and demise. This is reflected in the likes of David Steel's examination of Corby Glen, in south Lincolnshire, and, in

---

10 L.P. Hartley, *The Go-between* (London, 1953).

11 F. Thompson, *Lark rise* (Oxford, 1939).

12 H. Williamson, *Life in a Devon village* (London, 1945).

13 Jackson, 'The early twentieth-century countryside', pp. 228–9.

14 G.E. Evans, *Ask the fellows who cut the hay* (London, 1956); W.G. Hoskins, *Local history in England*, 3rd edn (London, 1984).

15 G.E. Campion, *Lincolnshire dialects* (Boston, 1976); B. Gilbert, *Lincoln Fair and other dialect poems* (Boston, 1986); M. Sutton, *'We didn't know owt': a study of sexuality, superstition and death in women's lives in Lincolnshire during the 1930s, '40s and '50s'* (Donington, 2012).

Suffolk, Ronald Blythe's *Akenfield*.[16] These various authors of fiction and writers of non-fiction have observed or have commentated, in common, on that which had occurred during, or was set in train after, the First World War, including: the losses from all ranks in the trenches, the lessening of the presence and role of the big house, a struggling agrarian economy, the lure of opportunities to be found in the larger towns and cities, and the weakening of community structures and shared and collective identity.

Gilbert's place

Bernard Gilbert was born in Billinghay into a seed merchant's business. Billinghay is just over twenty miles south of Lincoln, and *Kelly's Directory* records a population for the settlement of 1,288 in 1922. At the age of thirty he turned to professional writing, moving briefly to Woodhall Spa and then Lincoln, and, for the war years up to his death, to London. Before the First World War he wrote in various genres and for different media: poetry, plays, novels, political commentary and local newspaper articles. His output slowed during the war, when he served in the ministry of munitions. His work, from a literary perspective, is diverse, creative, imaginative and rich; from a historical perspective it is astute, observant, prophetic, empathetic and radical.[17]

Gilbert's place in this genre of rural literature was established through his early publications from 1911. However, his engagement is more substantive and sophisticated from 1921. In that year he published *Old England: A God's-eye view of a village*.[18] *Old England* was the first of a projected set of ten volumes that would form a broader series, also entitled 'Old England'. He reached volume nine, however, which was published in the year of his death in 1927. *Old England*, as the opening volume, does not, at the time of its appearance, give a sense of the wider district that would follow later, 'Bly'. The first work seeks to capture a unit that will show 'the factors and problems of the land which are basic in rural England'. The unit that he chooses is the village. It is 'a self-contained cosmos, a large family, and has no beyond. Its soul is coherent and complete.' He continues:

> I have taken such a village at one moment during the war and endeavoured to give a camera-obscura presentment of the multitudinous intrigues, ambitions, desires, disputes, interests, and all the social, political, financial, sexual and religious factors which thread the fabric so closely.[19]

The volume is based around a place named Fletton. Gilbert writes of Fletton that it is 'essentially a type, its people are to be found in every village'.[20] The work, following its various sections of introduction, acknowledgement and disclaimer, opens with an extract from a fictional County Directory of 1914: 'Fletton is a parish and village on the

---

16   D.I.A. Steel, *A Lincolnshire village: the parish of Corby Glen in its historical context* (London, 1979); R. Blythe, *Akenfield* (Harmondsworth, 1978).

17   Jackson, 'The early twentieth-century countryside', pp. 226–8.

18   B. Gilbert, *Old England: a God's-eye view of a village* (London, 1921).

19   *Ibid.*, p. vii.

20   *Ibid.*, p. v.

road from Bly to Barkston, eight miles south-west of Bly (the nearest railway station) in the Western Division of the County.'[21] The extract thereafter follows the format of the entries typically associated with contemporary commercial directories, with references to the church, patronage, landownership, acreage, local services, private residents, inns, local officials and office holders. The greater part of the volume is then comprised of 192 poems and soliloquies in the voice of each of the 192 adult residents of Fletton. The work closes with a 'Who's Who', giving a brief listing for each of those characters, with name, marital status and, in many instances, political-party and religious-denominational affiliation. He also includes around fifty family trees of the principal families of all classes.[22]

In the second volume of the 'Old England' series, *King Lear at Hordle*, there appears for the first time a map of the whole fictional district of Bly. He also lays out a skeleton description for Bly, listing its places and population sizes and the area's principal seats. In this can be found Fletton and the places that are the setting for the twelve plays that make up *King Lear at Hordle*: Hordle, itself, but also, from various areas of Bly district, Tanvats, Carrington, Marshfellowton, Belton, Thorpe Tilney, Holt in the Marsh, Herries St James, Pantacks, South Winch, High Morton and Wong.[23]

In *King Lear* Gilbert sets out something of the physical and cultural character of the two zones of Bly – a familiar higher and lower land dichotomy:

> In the fens and marshes the soil is rich, and from five to ten times as high in price as the heath and the wold. There are few baronial seats; partly because, only having been recently reclaimed, they never came under feudal sway; partly because they were parcelled into small plots when drained; and finally, because the peasantry are fierce individualists who cling onto their holdings at all cost.[24]

This is to be found juxtaposed with, elsewhere:

> [On the] high-land labourers are more servile; they have no chance of starting small holdings on that thin soil, which can only be farmed successfully in large tracts. Their land is well wooded, with great stretches of grass, and lends itself to hunting and shooting and picturesque homes; and it is there that the feudal barons reign supreme.

Gilbert also seeks to tackle stereotyping in *King Lear at Hordle*:

> City writers generally view our villages as incredibly innocent 'Sweet Auburns': assemblages of thatched roofs, topped with a spire and flanked by a hall. They see work going on at a leisurely pace, poultry occupying the streets, red-cheeked children at play, and feel that here is the simple life. When they discover with what

---

21 *Ibid.*, p. ix.
22 *Ibid.*, pp. 257–97.
23 B. Gilbert, *King Lear at Hordle and other rural plays* (London, 1922).
24 *Ibid.*, p. xviii.

brutal plainness the two great impulses of human nature take effect – preservation and reproduction – they call the villages licentious: but their state is far healthier than that of our cities, which are – with regard to sex – cesspools scented to hide their smell.[25]

Gilbert's fictional district continues to unroll through the subsequent seven volumes. Volume three, *Tyler of Barnet*, includes a detailed construction of another village, the fen-edge Low Barnet. In *Tyler*, Gilbert elaborates at some length on Fen landscape and culture, his native environment: 'To many people the Fens are dull because there are no contours to break the view, but they have a calm dignity of their own that gradually steals over the senses. Their effects are not unlike the ocean, and their sunrises and sunsets can be wonderful, as Turner knew.' However, Gilbert was troubled by what had been lost through reclamation and enclosure, comparing an idealised past with that existing in the present:

> In those days the Fens were beautiful, not only on account of the wild life which abounded, but because of the diversity of the untrammelled landscape. Everything now is bent to a utilitarian end; the soil is so rich that no patch is left uncultivated, and trees – as robbers of plant food – have been practically exterminated ... and the successors of the fen-men are the factory workers of Barkston, who line the banks of the Gulland at the week-ends.[26]

In *Tyler of Barnet* Gilbert also puts into context the function of the district market town, 'with its surrounding area of villages' and its role as 'a political unit'. Here, the 'reciprocal knowledge cannot be that of the village, where everyone knows about everything about everybody, but it comes as near as is necessary'.[27] Gilbert would give full and sole treatment to Bly district's market town, also called Bly, in volume six of the 'Old England' series.[28] In *Tyler* Gilbert also set out the aim of his developing multi-volume set of works:

> My object is to place the reader in the position of an inhabitant of my district, and although his cognition must be extended to embrace the several thousand characters and the about one hundred and fifty square miles of churches, chapels, inns, dwellings, roads, fields, rivers, woods, wold, heath, fen, and marsh, he will have been provided with the material for such an extension.[29]

Moreover, although fictionalised, his literary creation was grounded in personal and direct observation:

---

25 *Ibid.*, p. xvii.

26 B. Gilbert, *Tyler of Barnet: a novel* (London, 1922), pp. 1–2.

27 *Ibid.*, p. xii.

28 B. Gilbert, *Bly market: moving pictures of a market day* (London, 1924). The preceding volume four is comprised of a collection of poetry, and volume five of short stories: B. Gilbert, *The rural scene* (London, 1924); B. Gilbert, *Cross lights: the tales* (London, 1923). Both relate to various places and their inhabitants across the district, in a similar manner to the body of plays in *King Lear*.

29 Gilbert, *Tyler of Barnet*, p. x.

> For thirty years I have lived in such a district ... I knew all the parishes well, and several of them very intimately, and there were few local inhabitants with whom I was unacquainted. I spent innumerable hours in cottages and farm-house kitchens, in cobblers' and barbers' shops, and inns ... and attending ... all those gatherings that form so large a part of country life.[30]

By 1926, the closing pages of the eighth volume of the Old England series could include an extract of a review from *The New Statesman*, which stated that Gilbert was 'an artist engaged in an experiment almost unique in literature'.[31] However, a year later, a contemporary would write upon Gilbert's death:

> The work he had projected was immense ... That microcosm was to contain everything, and there humanity had been stable and unchanging for nearly a thousand years. His method was to go back to the same scenes, the same situations, in novels, stories, plays and poems, cutting deeper, from new angles, the bas relief with which he had started.[32]

Conclusion

Unfortunately, Gilbert's grand scheme did not fully materialise. The Lincolnshire-derived Bly did not secure a place in literature in the same way that other now well-known literary landscapes have done. Gilbert, and his pre-First-World-War imaginary rural world, disappeared into obscurity.

Regional fiction writers, in common with local historians, oral historians and others, such as geographers and sociologists, have shared a fascination with place and associated themes, such as the passing of time, the character and condition of peoples and communities, and forms and processes playing out over geographical areas. The rural has also been a special attraction, with the same categories of authors expressing and evaluating continuity and change, progress and loss, and the stereotypical and unique. Dymond's and Gilbert's writings both understand the position and power of place, in both fact and in the imagination. Place is, in part, something physically determined and is itself a physical expression; it is also a creation of human forces and relationships, internal and external; and, in addition, it is a construction within the minds and mentalities of peoples. Also present are some of the challenges of approaching place, such as balancing the general and the particular, giving due accord to both the rural and the urban, and weighing up the forces of environmental determinism against the wit and will of people.

In local history and in regional literature are to be found what attracts authors to places; as Dymond expressed their essential associations over a number of decades of endeavour: 'scale', 'sense of place', 'place in space' and 'people in their place'.

---

30   *Ibid.*, pp. x–xiii.
31   B. Gilbert, *Letters to America* (Oxford, 1926).
32   K. Rodker, 'Bernard Gilbert', *Poetry*, 30/5 (1927), pp. 274–5.

Bibliography of David Dymond's writings

Compiled by Nicholas R. Amor with help from David Dymond,
Heather Falvey and David Sherlock

Books

Archaeology for the historian (London, 1967)

ed., *The county of Suffolk, surveyed by Joseph Hodskinson, 1783*, Suffolk Record Society 15 (Ipswich, 1972)

Archaeology and history: a plea for reconciliation (London, 1974)

Writing a church guide (London, 1977; rev. edn, London, 1986)

The parish churches of Stanton, Suffolk: a history and guide (Stowmarket, 1977)

Lavenham: a walk around Lavenham (Lavenham, 1977; rev. edn, 1985)

Writing local history: a practical guide (London, 1981; rev. edn, London, 1988)

with A. Betterton, *Lavenham: 700 years of textile making*; revised edition published as *Lavenham industrial town* (Woodbridge, 1982; rev. edn, Lavenham, 1989)

Along Melford (Sudbury, 1983; rev. edn, 1991)

The Norfolk landscape (London, 1985; rev. edn, Bury St Edmunds, 1990)

with P. Northeast, *A history of Suffolk* (Chichester, 1985; rev. edn, 1995)

with G. Johnstone, *A map of the manor of Melford Hall, Suffolk 1580. The property of Sir William Cordell, drawn by Israel Amyce* (Long Melford, 1987)

with E. Martin, eds, *An historical atlas of Suffolk* (Ipswich, 1988; rev. edn, 1989 and 1999)

with J. Jones, *Mendlesham and the Armada crisis of 1588* (Mendlesham, 1988)

with C. Paine, *The spoil of Melford church: the Reformation in a Suffolk parish* (Ipswich, 1989)

ed., *Register of Thetford priory, part 1: 1482–1517*, Norfolk Records Society 59 (Oxford, 1994), *part 2: 1518–1540*, Norfolk Records Society 60 (Oxford, 1995)

Researching and writing history: a guide to local historians (Lancaster, 1999; rev. edn, 2009, 2016)

ed., *The churchwardens' book of Bassingbourn, Cambridgeshire 1496–c.1540*, Cambridgeshire Record Society 17 (Cambridge, 2004)

ed., *Parson and people in a Suffolk village: Richard Cobbold's Wortham 1824–77* (Wortham, 2007)

ed., *The charters of Stanton, Suffolk, c.1215–1678*, Suffolk Records Society (Woodbridge, 2009)

with C. Paine, *Five centuries of an English parish church: 'The state of Melford church', Suffolk* (Cambridge, 2012)

The Suffolk cloth industry: 700 years of textile making, Suffolk Preservation Society (Lavenham, 2015)

The business of the Suffolk parish 1558–1625, Suffolk Institute of Archaeology and History (Needham Market, 2018)

Articles

with I. Stead, 'Grimthorpe: a hillfort on the Yorkshire Wolds', *Antiquity*, xxxiii (1959), pp. 208–13

'Easedike, nr. Tadcaster', *Yorkshire Archaeological Journal*, 161/1 (1962), p. 24

'The "henge" monument at Nunwick, near Ripon. 1961 Excavation', *Yorkshire Archaeological Journal*, 161/1 (1962), pp. 98–107

'Four prehistoric implements from the Vale of York', *Yorkshire Archaeological Journal*, 161/2 (1963), pp. 178–82

'Roman bridges on Dere Street, County Durham. With a general appendix on the evidence for bridges in Roman Britain', *Archaeological Journal*, 118 (1963), pp. 136–64

'Suffolk in the 1840s: the employment of women and children in agriculture', *Suffolk Review*, 3/2 (1965), pp. 16–20

'Suffolk and the Compton census of 1676', *Suffolk Review*, 3/4 (1966), pp. 103–18

'Ritual monuments at Rudston, E. Yorks, England', *Proceedings of the Prehistoric Society*, xxxii (1966), pp. 86–95

'The Suffolk landscape', in L.M. Munby (ed.), *East Anglian Studies* (Cambridge, 1968), pp. 17–47

'The writing of a church guide', *The Local Historian*, 10/7 (1973), pp. 344–54

'The excavation of a prehistoric site at Upper Chamberlain's Farm, Eriswell', *PSIA*, 33 (1973), pp. 1–15

'The parish of Walsham-le-Willows: two Elizabethan surveys and their medieval background', *PSIA*, 33 (1974), pp. 195–211

'Town and village feuds', *Suffolk Review*, 4/3 (1974), pp. 107–10

'Archaeologists and historians', in A. Rogers and T. Rowley (eds), *Landscape and documents* (London, 1974), pp. 5–14

'The Chilton bulge – the early mapping of Suffolk hundreds', *PSIA*, 33 (1975), pp. 318–21

'The landscape setting', in J. Corke, J. Blatchly, J. Fitch and N. Scarfe (eds), *Suffolk churches* (Lavenham, 1976; rev. edn, 1977), pp. 4–7

'A fifteenth-century building contract from Suffolk', *Vernacular Architecture*, 9 (1978), pp. 10–11

'Opposition to enclosure in a Suffolk village', *Suffolk Review*, 5/1 (1980), pp. 13–22

'The famine of 1527 in Essex', *Local Population Studies*, 26 (1981), pp. 29–40

with R. Virgoe, 'The reduced population and wealth of early-fifteenth-century Suffolk', *PSIA*, 36 (1986), pp. 72–100

'Churches and churchyards', in *An historical atlas of Suffolk*, pp. 54–5

'Vicarages and appropriated church livings', in *An historical atlas of Suffolk*, pp. 72–3

with H. Todd, 'Population densities, 1327 and 1524', in *An historical atlas of Suffolk*, pp. 80–3

'Mobility and surnames', in *An historical atlas of Suffolk*, pp. 84–5

'Enclosure and reclamation', in *An historical atlas of Suffolk*, pp. 104–5

'Parish and hundred workhouses before 1834', in *An historical atlas of Suffolk*, pp. 120–1

'Agriculture in 1854', in *An historical atlas of Suffolk*, pp. 136–7

'The woollen cloth industry', in *An historical atlas of Suffolk*, pp. 140–1

'Camping closes', in *An historical atlas of Suffolk*, pp. 154–5

with K. Wade, 'Smaller medieval towns', in *An historical atlas of Suffolk*, pp. 162–3

'The landscape', in C. Jennings (ed.), *Suffolk for ever* (Bury St Edmunds, 1989), pp. 18–35

'A lost social institution: the camping close', *Rural History*, 1/2 (1990), pp. 165–92

'Three entertainers from Tudor Suffolk', *Records of Early English Drama*, 16/1 (1991), pp. 2–5

'Mapping nonconformity in Suffolk', in E.S. Leedham-Green (ed.), *Religious dissent in East Anglia* (Cambridge, 1991), pp. 113–24

'An example of Tudor quantity surveying', *The Local Historian*, 22/1 (1992), pp. 41–2
'Place-names as evidence for recreation', *Jour. English Place-Name Society*, 25 (1992–3), pp. 12–18
'Vicarages and appropriated livings', in P. Wade-Martins and J. Everett (eds), *An historical atlas of Norfolk* (Norwich, 1993), pp. 62–3
'Medieval and later markets', in *An historical atlas of Norfolk*, pp. 76–7
'Suffolk', in C. Currie and C. Lewis (eds), *English county histories: a guide* (Stroud, 1994), pp. 366–74
'Chapels-of-ease and the case of Botesdale', in A. Longcroft and R. Joby (eds), *East Anglian studies: essays presented to J.C. Barringer on his retirement* (Norwich, 1995), pp. 58–65
'Sitting apart in church', in C. Rawcliffe, R. Virgoe and R.G. Wilson (eds), *Counties and communities: essays in East Anglian history: presented to Hassell Smith* (Norwich, 1996), pp. 213–24
'Churchwardens' accounts (Short Guide 25)', in K.M. Thompson (ed.), *Short guides to records; second series: guides 25–48* (London, 1997), pp. 11–15
'Swarming the church', *Folklore*, 109 (1998), pp. 110–11
'Five building contracts from fifteenth-century Suffolk', *Antiquaries Journal*, 78 (1998), pp. 269–87
'A misplaced Domesday vill: Otringhithe and Bromehill', *Norfolk Archaeology*, 43 (1998), pp. 161–8
'God's disputed acre', *Journal of Ecclesiastical History*, 50/3 (1999), pp. 1–34
'The parson's glebe: stable, expanding or shrinking?', in C. Harper-Bill, C. Rawcliffe and R.G. Wilson (eds), *East Anglia's history: studies in honour of Norman Scarfe* (Woodbridge, 2002), pp. 73–92
'The chapel-of-ease: symbol of local identity and ambition', in L. Visser-Fuchs (ed.), *Tant d'emprises – so many undertakings: essays in honour of Anne F. Sutton*, *The Ricardian*, 13 (2003), pp. 203–16
'Michael Cowan: administrator and general secretary of BALH, 1990–2003', *The Local Historian*, 33/3 (2003), pp. 130–2
'Book of sports', in F. Bremer and T. Webster (eds), *Puritans and puritanism in Europe and America: a comprehensive encyclopedia*, vol. 2 (Santa Barbara, Denver and Oxford, 2006), pp. 328–9
'Burial practices', in Francis J. Bremer and Tom Webster (eds), *Puritans and puritanism in Europe and America: a comprehensive encyclopedia*, vol. 2 (Santa Barbara, 2006), pp. 334–6
with K. Tiller, 'Local history at the crossroads', *The Local Historian*, 37/4 (2007), pp. 250–7
'Socio-religious gilds of the Middle Ages', in L. Visser-Fuchs (ed.), *Richard III and East Anglia: magnates, gilds and learned men* (London, 2010), pp. 91–104
'Does local history have a split personality?', in C. Dyer, A.J. Hopper, E. Lord and N. Tringham (eds), *New directions in local history since Hoskins* (Hatfield, 2011), pp. 13–28
'Fair and foul in historical evidence', *Archives*, 123/124 (2011), pp. 14–15
'Terriers, tithes and farming', *PSIA*, 42 (2012), pp. 434–54
'Surviving the Reformation in a Suffolk parish', *The Local Historian*, 45/3 (2015), pp. 178–94
'The local historian's progress (with apologies to John Bunyan)', *The Local Historian*, 47/2 (2017), pp. 92–5

In addition, David Dymond served as general editor of the Suffolk Record Society between 1992 and 2007 and, as such, oversaw the publication of sixteen volumes in the Society's series. He was editor of *The Local Historian* between 1976 and 1982. He is also author of innumerable book reviews.

Index

(Historic counties given)